Iron Age, Roman and Anglo-Saxon Settlement along the Empingham to Hannington Pipeline in Northamptonshire and Rutland

Simon Carlyle, Jason Clarke and Andy Chapman

Archaeopress Archaeology

ARCHAEOPRESS PUBLISHING LTD
Gordon House
276 Banbury Road
Oxford OX2 7ED

www.archaeopress.com

ISBN 978 1 78491 534 6
ISBN 978 1 78491 535 3 (e-Pdf)

© Archaeopress and the individual authors 2017

Cover: Glaston, the decorated urn, Burial B16

All rights reserved. No part of this book may be reproduced, in any form or
by any means, electronic, mechanical, photocopying or otherwise,
without the prior written permission of the copyright owners.

Printed in England by Holywell Press, Oxford
This book is available direct from Archaeopress or from our website www.archaeopress.com

Contents

Contributors xi
Acknowledgements xii

1. Introduction 1
   Background 1
   Topography and geology 1
   Excavation strategy 3
   Structure of the report 3
   Archive 6

2. Neolithic and Early Bronze Age (*c*.4000-1450BC) 7
   Neolithic and early Bronze Age activity 7
   Worked flint 7

3. Middle Bronze Age to Early Iron Age (*c*.1450-400BC) 9
   A late Bronze Age/early Iron Age pit alignment near Seaton 9
   Middle Bronze Age to early Iron Age activity at Glaston 9

4. Middle to Late Iron Age (400 BC - 43 AD) 15
   Middle to late Iron Age settlement near Seaton 15
      Possible ditches 75 and 84 15
      Gully 51 15
      Gullies 14, 18 and 37 15
      Pit group (pits 47, 54, 72, 82 and 88) 15
      Pits 40, 49, 62, 66 and 69 15
      Pits 77 and 80 17
      Pits 5, 7, 25 and 30 18
   Iron Age ditches and a cremation burial near Thorpe by Water 18
   Middle to late Iron Age settlement near Caldecott 20
      Ditches 73 and 38 20
      Features to the south of ditch 73 20
      Pit 44 and posthole 63 20
      Pits and postholes to the north of ditch 73 20
      Ditches to the north of ditch 73 23
      Cobbled surface, 78 23
   Middle to late Iron Age settlement at Swinawe Barn, Corby 24
      The enclosure (ditches 22, 46 and 92) 24
      The roundhouses 26
      Other features 28
   Late Iron Age ditches near Thorpe Malsor 29
      Ditch 18 29
      Ditch 52 31
   Middle to late Iron Age settlement at Willows Nursery 31
      The enclosure ditches, 15 and 39 33
      Other linear ditches 33
      Other features 33
   Finds and environment evidence from the Iron Age settlements: 33
   The Iron Age pottery 33
      Seaton 33
      Caldecott 36
      Swinawe Barn, Corby 36
         Fabrics 36
         Forms and decoration 37
         Pottery distribution 37
         The assemblage from Roundhouse B 38
         Chronology 38

- Illustrated Iron Age pottery from Swinawe Barn (Fig 4.20) 39
- Thorpe Malsor 39
- Willows Nursery 40
- Fired clay 41
  - Seaton 41
  - Swinawe Barn 41
- Faunal and environmental remains from the Iron Age settlements: 41
- Human bone 41
- The animal bone 42
  - Methodology 42
  - Swinawe Barn, Corby 43
    - Carcass representation and butchery 43
    - Species representation and diet 43
    - Animal husbandry 44
    - Discussion 44
- Charred plant remains 44
  - Swinawe Barn 45
- Radiocarbon dating 48

5. Roman Settlement (AD43 - AD450) 49
- Late Roman settlement at Glaston 49
  - Roman settlement 49
  - Ditch 34 49
- Roman activity near Seaton 49
- A Roman enclosure and cremation burials near Gretton 49
  - The Roman enclosure 49
  - Roman cremation burials 51
- A Roman pit at Swinawe Barn, Corby 52
- Roman enclosures at Rushton 52
  - The enclosure: ditches 12 and 21 52
  - The droveway: gullies 5 and 7 53
  - Gullies 9 and 17 54
- A Roman ditch system at Violet Lane 54
- Roman settlement near Thorpe Malsor 54
  - Earlier features, ditches 61, 63 and 128 and pit 67 55
  - The major ditch systems 55
  - Pebbled surface 131 58
  - The pit group 58
  - Other pits/postholes 74, 105 and 121 60
- Roman settlement at White Hill Lodge 60
  - A ditched enclosure system 61
  - Droveway: ditches 35 and 41 63
- Roman settlement near Great Cransley 64
  - Ditch 25 64
  - Enclosure 1 64
  - Enclosure 2: ditches 13 and 17 64
  - Enclosure 3: ditch 11 66
  - The trackway: ditches 40 and 31/36 67
  - Enclosure 4: ditch 44 67
  - Colluvium 58 67
- Finds from the Roman settlement: 67
- Roman pottery 67
  - Methodology 67
  - The Roman pottery from Thorpe Malsor (Figs 5.21-5.22) 69
    - Selected assemblages: 70
    - Ditch 39 (part of ditch system with ditches 12 and 94, see below) 70
    - Ditch 94 (part of ditch system with ditches 12, see above, and 39) 70
    - Ditch 112 (part of ditch system with ditches 72, 139, 117 and 145) 70

  Ditch 117 (part of ditch system with ditches 72, 112, 139 and 145) 71
  Ditch 139 (part of ditch system with ditches 72, 112, 117 and 145) 71
  Ditch 145 (part of ditch system with ditches 72, 112, 139 and 117) 71
  Ditch 150 (north end of site, aligned west-east) 72
  Pit 4 72
  Illustrated vessels (Figs 5.21 and 5.22) 73
  Cross-feature joins 75
  Samian ware 76
The Roman pottery from Great Cransley (Fig 5.23) 76
  Selected assemblages: 76
  Ditch 11, Enclosure 3, southern arm (same as ditch 23) 76
  Ditch 17 (Enclosure 2, southern arm) 77
  Ditch 23 (Enclosure 3, southern arm, same as ditch 7) 77
  Ditch 52 (late boundary, cutting trackway ditches, eastern side) 77
  Pit 29, Enclosure 2 78
  Illustrated vessels (Fig 5.23) 78
  Samian ware 78
 Other sites 78
Roman fired clay and ceramic building material 80
 Seaton 80
 Gretton Road 80
 Rushton 80
 Thorpe Malsor 80
 White Hill Lodge 80
 Great Cransley 81
Roman querns 81
 Thorpe Malsor 81
 Great Cransley 82
Other Roman finds 82
 Glaston 82
 Gretton Road 82
 Thorpe Malsor 82
  Coins 82
  Copper alloy objects 83
  Copper casting debris 83
  Iron 83
  Lead 83
  Worked bone 83
  Glass 83
 White Hill Lodge 84
 Great Cransley 84
Faunal and environmental remains from the Roman settlements: 84
Human bone 84
 Cremation burials from Gretton Road 84
 Infant burial from Thorpe Malsor 85
 The burial of infants during the Roman period in Britain 85
Animal bone 85
 Thorpe Malsor 86
  Carcass representation and butchery 86
  Species representation and diet 86
  Animal husbandry 86
 White Hill Lodge 87
 Great Cransley 87
 Discussion 88
Charred plant remains 88
 Thorpe Malsor 88
  Pit 4 88
 Conclusions 92

6. Anglo-Saxon burial and settlement (AD450-650) 93
An Anglo-Saxon cremation cemetery at Glaston 93
Anglo-Saxon activity at Rushton 96
Finds from the Anglo-Saxon cemetery and other sites: 96
Anglo-Saxon pottery 96
Fabric 97
Chronology and decorative symbolism 97
The undecorated urns and other vessels: 98
Burial B4 (SF3) 98
Burial B5 (SF4) 98
Burial B6 (SF7) 98
Burial B8 (SF6) 98
Burial B12 (SF11) 98
Burial B14 (SF16) 98
Burial B18 99
Burial B20 (SF13) 99
Pit 40 99
Pit 48 (SF 17) 99
Topsoil (1) 100
Field 15:07 (5), SFB 100
Pit 30 100
Pit 32 100
Catalogue of illustrated Anglo-Saxon pottery 100
The decorated urns: 100
Burial B7 (SF5) (Figs 6.11, 2 & 6.13) 100
Burial B9 (SF8) (Fig 6.12, 10) 103
Burial B11 (SF10) (Fig 6.12, 7-9 & 6.14 a, b & c) 104
Burial B16 (SF 15) (Figs 6.2; 6.11, 1; 6.15 & 6.16) 104
Other Anglo-Saxon pottery 106
Subsoil (2) 106
Ditch 10 (Fig 6.9, 6) 106
Discussion 106
Anglo-Saxon pottery from a watching brief, Field 15:07/4 107
Other Anglo-Saxon finds 107
Glaston 107
Burial B6 (adult, sex unknown) 107
Burial B7 (juvenile, 4-5 years, sex unknown) 108
Burial B9 (juvenile, greater than 10 years old, sex unknown) 108
Burial B11 (adult and juvenile, sex unknown) 108
Burial B12 (adult, 15-18 years, sex unknown) 108
Burial B13 (adult, sex unknown) 108
Burial B14 (adult, sex unknown) 108
Burial B16 (adult, probably female) 109
The beads 109
Rushton 109
Human bone from the Anglo-Saxon cemetery 110
Fragmentation, completeness and elemental representation 110
Pyre conditions 111
Demography 111
Sex 112
Pathology 112
Discussion 113
Radiocarbon dating 114

7. Medieval and post-medieval field systems 115
    A field boundary wall and furrows at Normanton Road 115
    A boundary ditch and furrows at Seaton 115
    A ditch and furrows near Thorpe by Water 115
    A stone drain and furrows at Caldecott 115
    Boundary ditches and furrows at Swinawe Barn, Corby 115
    Furrows at other sites 116
    Finds of medieval and post-medieval date: 116
    Medieval and post-medieval finds 116
        Glaston 116
        Cransley 116
        Caldecott 117
        Swinawe Barn, Corby 117
    Post-medieval floor tiles 117

8. Discussion 119
    Project objectives 119
    The late Bronze Age/early Iron Age pit alignment near Seaton 119
    The Iron Age landscape 120
    The Roman rural landscape 123
    The early Anglo-Saxon cremation cemetery at Glaston 125
    Medieval and post-medieval field systems 126

Bibliography 127
    Maps 131

List of Figures

Fig 1.1: Project location 2
Fig 1.2: Land relief and site locations 4
Fig 1.3: Geology and site locations 5

Fig 3.1: Seaton, the pit alignment in excavation and geophysical survey 10
Fig 3.2: Seaton, the excavated pit alignment 11
Fig 3.3: Seaton, the pit alignment, looking north-east 12
Fig 3.4: Seaton, pit 13 in the pit alignment, looking north-west (Scale 1m) 12
Fig 3.5: Glaston, Bronze Age jar from Anglo-Saxon cremation burial B13 (Scale 20mm) 13

Fig 4.1: Seaton, Iron Age settlement 16
Fig 4.2: Seaton, sections of Iron Age pits 17
Fig 4.3: Seaton, ditch 84, and pits 82 and 80, looking east (Scale 2m) 18
Fig 4.4: Thorpe by Water, Iron Age and later features 19
Fig 4.5: Caldecott, plan of Iron Age settlement (south) 21
Fig 4.6: Caldecott, plan of Iron Age settlement (north) 22
Fig 4.7: Caldecott, Sections of ditches and pit 44 23
Fig 4.8: Caldecott, Iron Age settlement, looking north-east 24
Fig 4.9: Swinawe Barn, Iron Age enclosure and roundhouses 25
Fig 4.10: Swinawe Barn, Sections of enclosure ditch 26
Fig 4.11: Swinawe Barn, Roundhouse A, looking east 27
Fig 4.12: Swinawe Barn, Sections of ring ditches and pits 28
Fig 4.13: Swinawe Barn, pit 83 with animal bone deposit, looking west (Scale 1m) 29
Fig 4.14: Thorpe Malsor, Iron Age settlement 30
Fig 4.15: Thorpe Malsor, Sections of enclosure ditch 31
Fig 4.16: Willows Nursery, Iron Age settlement 32
Fig 4.17: Willows Nursery, Sections of enclosure ditches 34
Fig 4.18: Willows Nursery, ditch 19 and gully 24, looking south-west (Scale 1m) 34
Fig 4.19: Caldecott, rim and base of scored ware jar from gully 36 (Scale 20mm) 36
Fig 4.20: Swinawe Barn, Iron Age pottery (1-7) (Scale 200mm) 40
Fig 4.21: Willows Nursery, rim of a large storage jar from pit 24 41

Fig 5.1: Glaston, plan of Roman ditch system 50
Fig 5.2: Seaton, plan of Roman features 51
Fig 5.3: Gretton Road, plan of Roman features 52
Fig 5.4: Rushton, plan of Roman ditch system 53
Fig 5.5: Rushton, Section of ditch 21 53
Fig 5.6: Violet Lane, plan of Roman ditch system 54
Fig 5.7: Violet Lane, Roman ditches 15 and 19, looking east (Scale 1m) 55
Fig 5.8: Thorpe Malsor, plan of Roman settlement 56
Fig 5.9: Thorpe Malsor, general view of the site, looking south 57
Fig 5.10: Thorpe Malsor, northern terminal of ditch 12, looking south (Scale 2m) 58

Fig 5.11: Thorpe Malsor, Sections of ditches 117/119 and 79..59

Fig 5.12: Thorpe Malsor, ditch and pit sections..60

Fig 5.13: White Hill Lodge, general view of Roman ditches, looking south 61

Fig 5.14: White Hill Lodge, plan of Roman settlement 62

Fig 5.15: White Hill Lodge, ditch sections..63

Fig 5.16: White Hill Lodge, Roman ditch 44, looking south-west (Scale 2m)...64

Fig 5.17: Great Cransley, plan of Roman ditch system..65

Fig 5.18: Great Cransley, Sections of enclosure ditches...66

Fig 5.19: Great Cransley, plan of Roman well 56 68

Fig 5.20: Great Cransley, Roman well 56, looking south (Scale 1m) 68

Fig 5.21: Thorpe Malsor Roman pottery (1-16) 74

Fig 5.22: Thorpe Malsor Roman pottery (17-27) 75

Fig 5.23: Great Cransley Roman pottery (28-37) 79

Fig 5.24: Great Cransley, circular copper alloy plate brooch (SF1) (Scale 10mm)..84

Fig 6.1: Glaston, plan of Anglo-Saxon cremation cemetery...94

Fig 6.2: Glaston, excavation of urn, Burial B16 95

Fig 6.3: Glaston, Burial B6, showing the concentration of large bone fragments (Scale 50mm)..............................95

Fig 6.4: Glaston, decorated urn and cremated bone, Burial B16 (Scale 50mm) 97

Fig 6.5: Glaston, heat distorted glass beads from Burial B6 (Scale 10mm) 97

Fig 6.6: Glaston, worked bone mount from Burial B7 (Scale 10mm)..97

Fig 6.7: Glaston, copper alloy quoit brooch, Burial B14, with heat distorted glass beads obscuring the pin (Scale 20mm)..........97

Fig 6.8: Glaston, plain-bodied urn (SF7), Burial B6 (Scale 20mm) 99

Fig 6.9: Glaston, accessory vessel from cemetery, pit 48 (Scale 10mm) 100

Fig 6.10: Field 15:07, miniature pot from sunken-featured building (Scale 10mm) 100

Fig 6.11: Glaston, Anglo-Saxon pottery (1-5)..101

Fig 6.12: Glaston, Anglo-Saxon pottery (6-10)..102

Fig 6.13: Glaston, urn (SF7), Burial B7, decorated with incised chevrons (Scale 20mm).......................................103

Fig 6.14: Glaston, Burial B11, sherds from decorated urn (SF10) showing stamp motifs: a) cruciform in round field, b) cruciform in cross-shaped field, and c) the S-shaped 'wyrm' (Scale 10mm) 105

Fig 6.15: Glaston, the decorated urn, Burial B16 (Scale 50mm)..105

Fig 6.16: Glaston, detail of decoration on urn, Burial B16...106

Fig 7.1: Swinawe Barn, medieval/post-medieval ditch 104, looking north (Scale 2m)...116

List of Tables

Table 4.1: Seaton, quantification of Iron Age pottery	35
Table 4.2: Swinawe Barn, rim form quantification	36
Table 4.3: Swinawe Barn, quantification of Iron Age pottery	38
Table 4.4: Swinawe Barn, Pottery distribution in Roundhouse B	39
Table 4.5: Swinawe Barn, quantification of fired clay	41
Table 4.6: Thorpe by Water, quantification of cremated bone	42
Table 4.7: Presence of major domesticates and ungulates for Iron Age sites	42
Table 4.8: Presence of minor domesticates and wild species for Iron Age sites	42
Table 4.9: Swinawe Barn, animal bone condition and taphonomy	43
Table 4.10: Swinawe Barn, number of identified bones fragments	43
Table 4.11: Swinawe Barn, representation of the main domesticates	44
Table 4.12: Swinawe Barn, animal bone species representation (NISP)	44
Table 4.13: Swinawe Barn, charred plant remains, Roundhouse A	45
Table 4.14: Swinawe Barn, charred plant remains, Roundhouse B	46
Table 4.15: Swinawe Barn, charred plant remains, Roundhouse C	47
Table 4.16: Swinawe Barn, charred plant remains from pits	47
Table 4.17: Swinawe Barn, charred plant remains from ditches	48
Table 4.18: Swinawe Barn, radiocarbon dating for Roundhouse B	48
Table 5.1: Thorpe Malsor, Roman pottery assemblage by principal fabrics	69
Table 5.2: Thorpe Malsor, quantification of selected Roman pottery assemblages	70
Table 5.3: Thorpe Malsor, ditch 39, percentages of principal fabrics	70
Table 5.4: Thorpe Malsor, ditch 94, percentages of principal fabrics	70
Table 5.5: Thorpe Malsor, ditch 112, percentages of principal fabrics	70
Table 5.6: Thorpe Malsor, ditch 117, percentages of principal fabrics	71
Table 5.7: Thorpe Malsor, ditch 139, percentages of principal fabrics	71
Table 5.8: Thorpe Malsor, ditch 145, percentages of principal fabrics	72
Table 5.9: Thorpe Malsor, ditch 150, percentages of principal fabrics	72
Table 5.10: Thorpe Malsor, pit 4, layer 21, percentages of principal fabrics	72
Table 5.11: Thorpe Malsor, pit 4, other layers, percentages of principal fabrics	73
Table 5.12: Great Cransley, Roman pottery assemblage by principal fabrics	76
Table 5.13: Great Cransley, quantification of selected Roman pottery assemblages	76
Table 5.14: Great Cransley, ditch 11, percentages of principal fabrics	77
Table 5.15: Great Cransley, ditch 17, percentages of principal fabrics	77
Table 5.16: Great Cransley, ditch 23, percentages of principal fabrics	77
Table 5.17: Great Cransley, ditch 52, percentages of principal fabrics	77
Table 5.18: Great Cransley, pit 29, percentages of principal fabrics	78
Table 5.19: Summary of Roman pottery from other sites	80
Table 5.20: Thorpe Malsor, quantification of querns	81
Table 5.21: Great Cransley, quantification of querns	82
Table 5.22: Thorpe Malsor, Roman glass	83
Table 5.23: Gretton Road, quantification of cremated bone	84

Table 5.24: Gretton Road, human infant long bone lengths and equivalent ages 85
Table 5.25: Roman animal bone assemblages by size (NISP) 85
Table 5.26: Animal bone condition by bone number 85
Table 5.27: Animal bone taphonomy by percentages 85
Table 5.28: Thorpe Malsor, number of identified animal bones 86
Table 5.29: Thorpe Malsor, representation of bone elements (epiphysis count) 86
Table 5.30: Thorpe Malsor, animal bone species (NISP) 87
Table 5.31: White Hill Lodge, number of identified animal bones 87
Table 5.32: White Hill Lodge, animal bone species (NISP) 87
Table 5.33: Great Cransley, number of identified animal bones 87
Table 5.34: Great Cransley animal bone species (NISP) 87
Table 5.35: Thorpe Malsor charred plant remains 89
Table 5.36: Thorpe Malsor, charred plant remains, pit 4 (1) 90
Table 5.36: Thorpe Malsor, charred plant remains, pit 4 (2) 91

Table 6.1: Glaston, catalogue of burials and grave goods 96
Table 6.2: Glaston, catalogue of Anglo-Saxon glass beads 109
Table 6.3: Glaston, weight of cremated bone deposits by bone size 110
Table 6.4: Glaston, summary of cremated bone deposits 111
Table 6.5: Glaston, quantification of human bone by element 112
Table 6.6: Glaston, age estimations from the epiphyses, dentition and other sources 113
Table 6.7: Glaston, relative number of people per age group for contemporary sites 113
Table 6.8: Glaston, radiocarbon date for Burial B16 114

Contributors

Paul Blinkhorn BTech
Freelance pottery specialist

Simon Carlyle BSc MSc MI EnvSc MCIfA
Former Senior Project Officer, Northamptonshire Archaeology

Andy Chapman BSc MCIfA FSA
Senior Project Manager, MOLA (Museum of London Archaeology)

Pat Chapman BA CMS AIfA
Project Supervisor (post-excavation), MOLA (Museum of London Archaeology)

Jason Clarke BSc, MA, MCIfA
Former Project Supervisor, Northamptonshire Archaeology

Val Fryer BA MCIfA
Freelance environmental specialist

Matilda Holmes BSc MSc PhD
Consultant archaeozoologist, University of Leicester

Tora Hylton
Finds Manager, MOLA (Museum of London Archaeology)

Sarah Inskip PhD
Osteoarchaeologist, Leiden University, formerly Southampton University

J M Mills
Freelance pottery specialist

Rob Perrin BA MCIfA MLitt PGCE FSA
Freelance pottery specialist

Yvonne Wolframm-Murray BA PhD
Supervisor, MOLA (Museum of London Archaeology)

Acknowledgements

The geophysical surveys, trial trenching, excavation, analysis, reporting and publication has been funded by Anglian Water Services. Mott MacDonald commissioned Northamptonshire Archaeology to carry out all aspects of fieldwork and reporting. The final preparation of the report for publication was carried out following Northamptonshire Archaeology becoming part of MOLA (Museum of London Archaeology).

Geophysical surveys along the route were managed by Andrew Mudd and Adrian Butler, and were carried out by Dan Cherry, Paul Clements, Ian Fisher, Paul Kajewski, Stephen Morris, Emma Rae and John Walford.

The fieldwork was managed by Andrew Mudd. Fieldwork supervisors for the trial trenching and the excavations were Jim Burke, Adrian Burrow, Jason Clarke, Karen Deighton, Leon Field, Nathan Flavell, Anne Foard, Paul Kajewski, Mark Patenall, Carol Simmonds and Yvonne Wolframm-Murray.

Project assistants for the fieldwork were Adrian Adams, Amir Bassir, James Brown, Rosie Chapman, Paul Clements, Jonathan Elston, Heather Griggs, Liz Hawksley, David Haynes, Peter Haynes, Tomasz Kolosek, Adam Kostrzon, James Ladocha, Laszlo Lichtenstein, Fanny Martin, Bryan Murray, Daniel Nagy, Stephen Porter, Jonathan Rampling, Paul Squires, Josh Seaman, Rob Smith, Thomas Stewart, Kerryn Stoppel and Luke Yates. The urned cremations were excavated *ex situ* by Pat Chapman.

The post-excavation was managed by Simon Carlyle and the client report was drafted by Simon Carlyle and Jason Clarke with subsequent copyediting and revision by Andy Chapman (Carlyle *et al* 2011). The specialist reports were prepared by Paul Blinkhorn, Andy Chapman, Pat Chapman, Val Fryer, Matilda Holmes, Tora Hylton, Sarah Inskip, J M Mills, Rob Perrin and Yvonne Wolframm-Murray. The client report is available online through the Archaeology Data Service (ADS), Library of Unpublished Fieldwork Reports. The published report is an edited and slightly reduced version of the client report prepared by Andy Chapman and Pat Chapman. As the client report was prepared in 2011, the opportunity has been taken to update the discussion section incorporating references to relevant sites published more recently.

1. Introduction

Background

Anglian Water Services constructed a new pipeline, approximately 41km in length, between Empingham, Rutland and Hannington, Northamptonshire as part of a major infrastructure project to increase the supply of water to homes and businesses in the south-east Midlands region (NGR: SK947081 to SP826712; Fig 1.1). The pipeline links the abstraction site at Rutland Water, where a new pumping station has been built at Empingham, with Wing Water Treatment Works, which has been upgraded. From Wing, the pipeline extends southwards, to the west of Corby and Kettering, and terminates at the reservoir complex at Hannington.

In line with national and European legislation concerning the impact of capital schemes on the environment, Mott MacDonald, in their role as environmental consultants on the project, prepared an Environmental Statement (ES) to assess the environmental impact of the scheme (Lunt 2006). A material consideration of the assessment was the impact of the development on buried and upstanding archaeological remains along the route of the pipeline, so a cultural heritage assessment, commissioned from Northamptonshire Archaeology, was included in the ES.

The cultural heritage assessment noted that the potential impact of the pipeline on archaeological sites along the route was, at that time, largely unknown due to a lack of archaeological prospection. To gather further information, Northamptonshire Archaeology was commissioned by Mott MacDonald to carry out a programme of archaeological evaluation. The first stage was a desk-based assessment (Westgarth 2006a and b), presenting the archaeological and historical background of a defined study area along the route of the proposed pipeline corridor. This was followed by fieldwork, comprising geophysical survey (Butler and Mudd 2006; Butler 2007; Butler et al 2008), trial trench evaluation (Clarke 2007a; Upson-Smith 2007) and test pit evaluation (Clarke 2007b).

The fieldwork evaluation identified a number of sites of archaeological significance along the route of the pipeline. It was also proposed that a watching brief should be carried out during the removal of topsoil along the pipeline easement and the cutting of the pipe trench. Following evaluation nineteen sites were investigated as part of the mitigation measures; two of these were identified during the watching brief (Fig 1.2). The general, scheme-wide aim of the archaeological investigations, as stated in the Environmental Statement (Lunt 2006), had been to investigate all deposits of archaeological significance within the easement of the pipeline and to preserve them either *in situ* or by record.

The major sites comprised a late Bronze Age/early Iron Age pit alignment, five middle to late Iron Age rural settlements, five Roman settlements, including one associated with a villa, and an Anglo-Saxon cremation cemetery. This report presents the principal results of these works carried out by Northamptonshire Archaeology between January 2008 and July 2009. Two minor sites included in the assessment report, those of Hockley Lodge and Great Cransley South, have not been included in the client report or the published report as they only contained modern field boundaries or furrows of former field systems.

On completion of the fieldwork, an assessment report and updated project design (UPD) was prepared (Clarke and Carlyle 2010). This presented a summary and assessment of the investigated sites, a programme of further work and revised research objectives, with reference to the regional research agenda for the East Midlands (Cooper 2006), to bring the project to publication.

The client report (Carlyle, Clarke and Chapman 2010) was prepared in accordance with Appendix 7 of the English Heritage procedural document *Management of Archaeological Projects 2* (EH 1991), relevant sections of *Management of Research Projects in the Historic Environment* (EH 2006), and appropriate national standards and guidelines, as recommended by the Institute for Archaeologists (IfA).

The client report was issued in 2010 and can be found on ADS under OASIS number 161012 (http://archaeologydataservice.ac.uk/archives/view/greylit/). The report on the geophysical survey and metal detecting, Butler, A, and Walford, J, 2006, *Empingham to Hannington pipeline route: Archaeological Geophysical and Metal Detecting Surveys Phase 1*, Northamptonshire Archaeology report 06/189, is also available on ADS, OASIS number 30001. The published report is an edited version of the client report.

Topography and geology

The route of the pipeline extends from Empingham, Rutland to Hannington, Northamptonshire, a distance of approximately 41km (Fig 1.1). From the pumping station in the valley of the River Gwash at Empingham, it heads south-westwards, crosses the valley of the River Chater near Lyndon and then ascends the southern slope of the river valley to reach the water treatment works at Wing, a total distance of *c*.8km. From Wing the pipeline heads south-south-west, crosses the valley of the River Welland near Caldecott and skirts the western edge of Corby. From Corby it continues on its course, crosses the River Ise at Rushton, passes to the west of

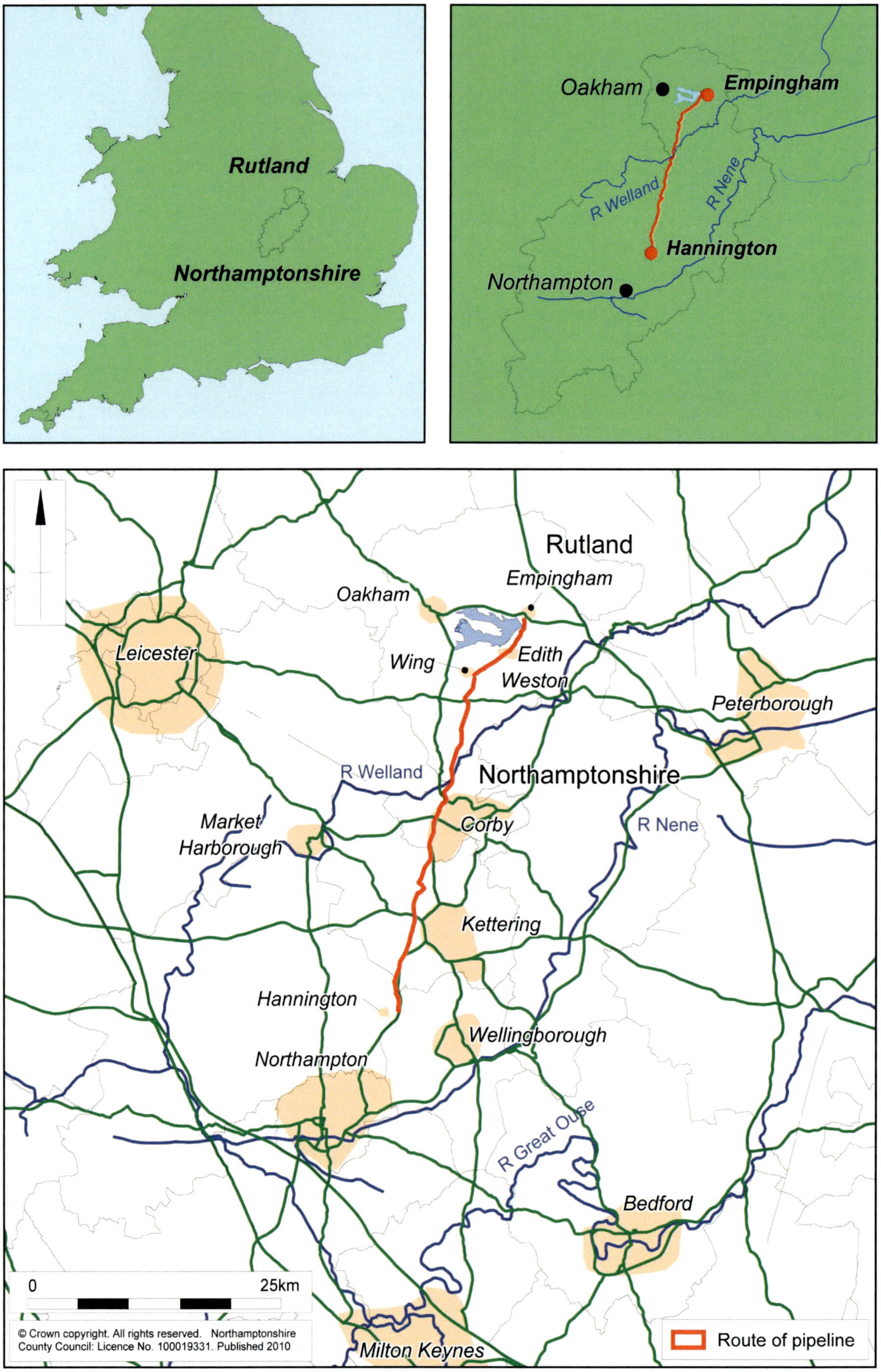

Excavations along the Empingham to Hannington pipeline 2008-2009

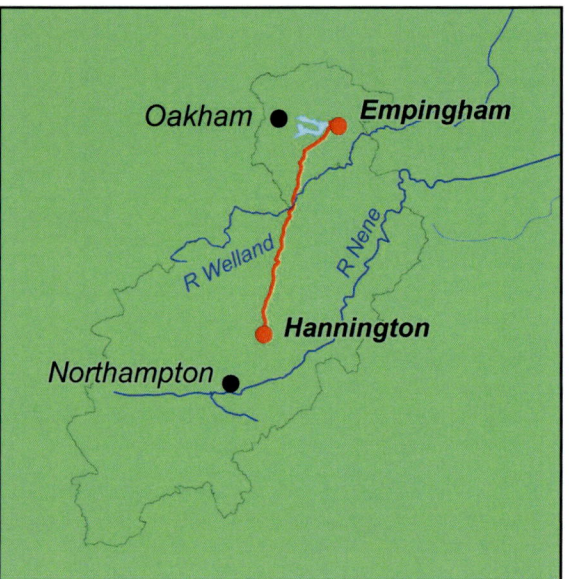

Fig 1.1: Project location

Kettering and terminates at the Hannington reservoir complex, a distance of *c*.33km from Wing. The terrain varies from undulating ground or plateaux on the hilltops between the river and tributary valleys, to steeply sloping ground on the valley sides and level ground on the floodplains of the major rivers. The height above sea-level ranged between 40m and 120m above Ordnance Datum (Fig 1.2).

The pipeline crosses a landscape composed entirely of Jurassic rocks, occasionally overlain by Quaternary drift and alluvial deposits (Fig 1.3). The main rocks and drift deposits encountered on the hill tops were Northamptonshire Sands and Ironstone, Lower Lincolnshire Limestone and Boulder Clay, and in the river valleys Upper, Middle and Lower Lias clays and alluvium (BGS 1976; 1978). Details of the geology encountered at each excavation site are provided in the site narratives.

Excavation strategy

The sites were marked out by NA using Leica System 1200 GPS surveying equipment, using data supplied by Mott MacDonald. The areas were stripped under archaeological supervision using 360° tracked mechanical excavators fitted with toothless ditching buckets. The topsoil and subsoil were removed in separate operations and stored in temporary bunds at the edges of the sites.

Once each individual area had been opened and the archaeological surface cleaned sufficiently to enhance the features, a grid was established and a digital base plan was produced using GPS, with the grid and site datum related to the Ordnance Survey National Grid and Datum. The general site plan was hand drawn at a scale of 1:50 or 1:100.

Discrete features were half-sectioned, and only fully excavated if features were part of recognisable structures, contained deposits or artefacts of particular value or were likely to hold significant artefact or environmental assemblages. Intersections were investigated to establish stratigraphic relationships. Representative sections of linear and curvilinear features were excavated away from intersections with other features or deposits, to obtain unmixed samples of material. Sections were drawn at a scale of 1:10 or 1:20, as appropriate. Recording followed the procedures outlined in the Northamptonshire Archaeology's *Fieldwork Manual* (NA 2006).

Artefacts and ecofacts were collected by hand and retained, receiving appropriate care prior to removal from site (Watkinson and Neal 1998). The stripped areas and spoil heaps were scanned with a metal detector to ensure maximum finds retrieval. All finds have been catalogued and boxed by material type.

Soil samples of up to 40 litres, dependant on deposit size, were taken for flotation from dateable contexts with the potential for the recovery of charcoal and charred plant remains. The sampling strategy followed the guidelines set out in the English Heritage document *Environmental Archaeology: A Guide to Theory and Practice for Methods, from sampling to post-excavation* (EH 2002).

A photographic record of the project was maintained using 35mm black and white negative and colour transparency film, supplemented with digital images. All records were compiled during fieldwork into a comprehensive and fully cross-referenced site archive.

All works were conducted in accordance with the method statement prepared by NA (2008) and the then Institute for Archaeologists (IfA) *Standard and Guidance for Archaeological Excavation* (2008a), *Standard and Guidance for Archaeological Watching Briefs* (2008b) and *Code of Conduct* (2008c). Health and Safety considerations complied with the Health and Safety Policy of Northamptonshire County Council.

Structure of the report

The report provides a single, chronologically and geographically structured presentation of the archaeological sites investigated along the route of the pipeline by period, and within each period by their position on the pipeline. The sites start from the northern end in Rutland at Empingham, followed by Normanton Road, Glaston (and Bisbrooke), Seaton, Thorpe by Water and Caldecott. These follow in Northamptonshire with Gretton Road, Swinawe Barn, Rushton, Violet Lane, Thorpe Malsor, White Hill Lodge, Great Cransley and finishes with Willows Nursery (Fig 1.3).

Finds and environmental reports have also been grouped by period, which has facilitated reporting by increasing the cumulative value of the assemblages. Reflecting the age range of the archaeological sites and artefacts, the periods have been presented in this report as follows:

Neolithic and early Bronze Age (*c*.4000-1450 BC)
Middle Bronze Age to early Iron Age (*c*.1450-400 BC)
Middle to late Iron Age (*c*.400 BC-43 AD)
Roman (43 AD-450 AD)
Early Anglo-Saxon (*c*.450-650 AD)
Medieval and post-medieval

Archaeological investigations along pipeline routes are often constrained by the narrow confines of the pipeline easement. As a result only thin strips through the individual sites, often no more than 20m wide, could be examined by excavation. Although geophysical survey and cropmark evidence have assisted in establishing the

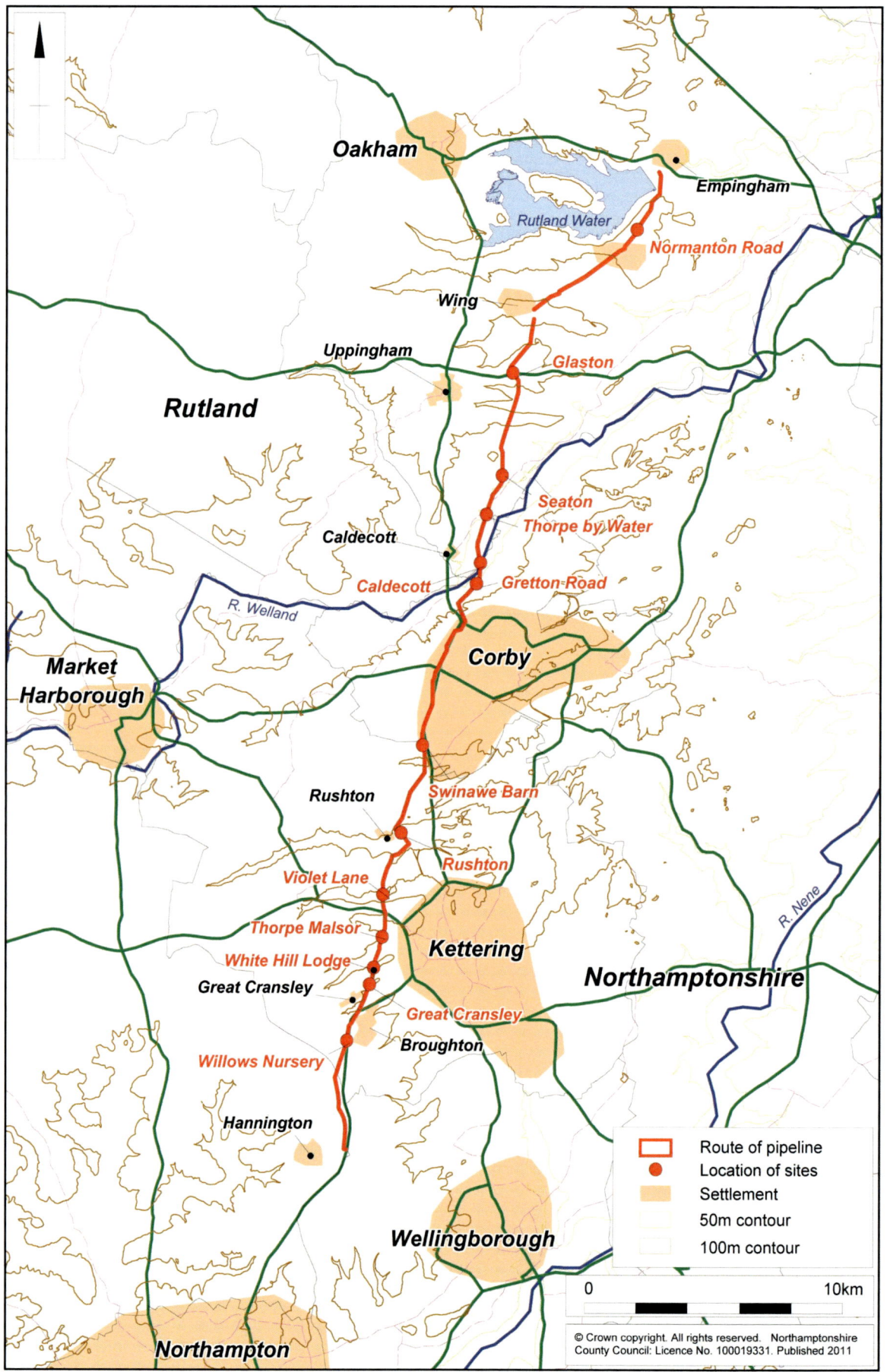

Fig 1.2: Land relief and site locations

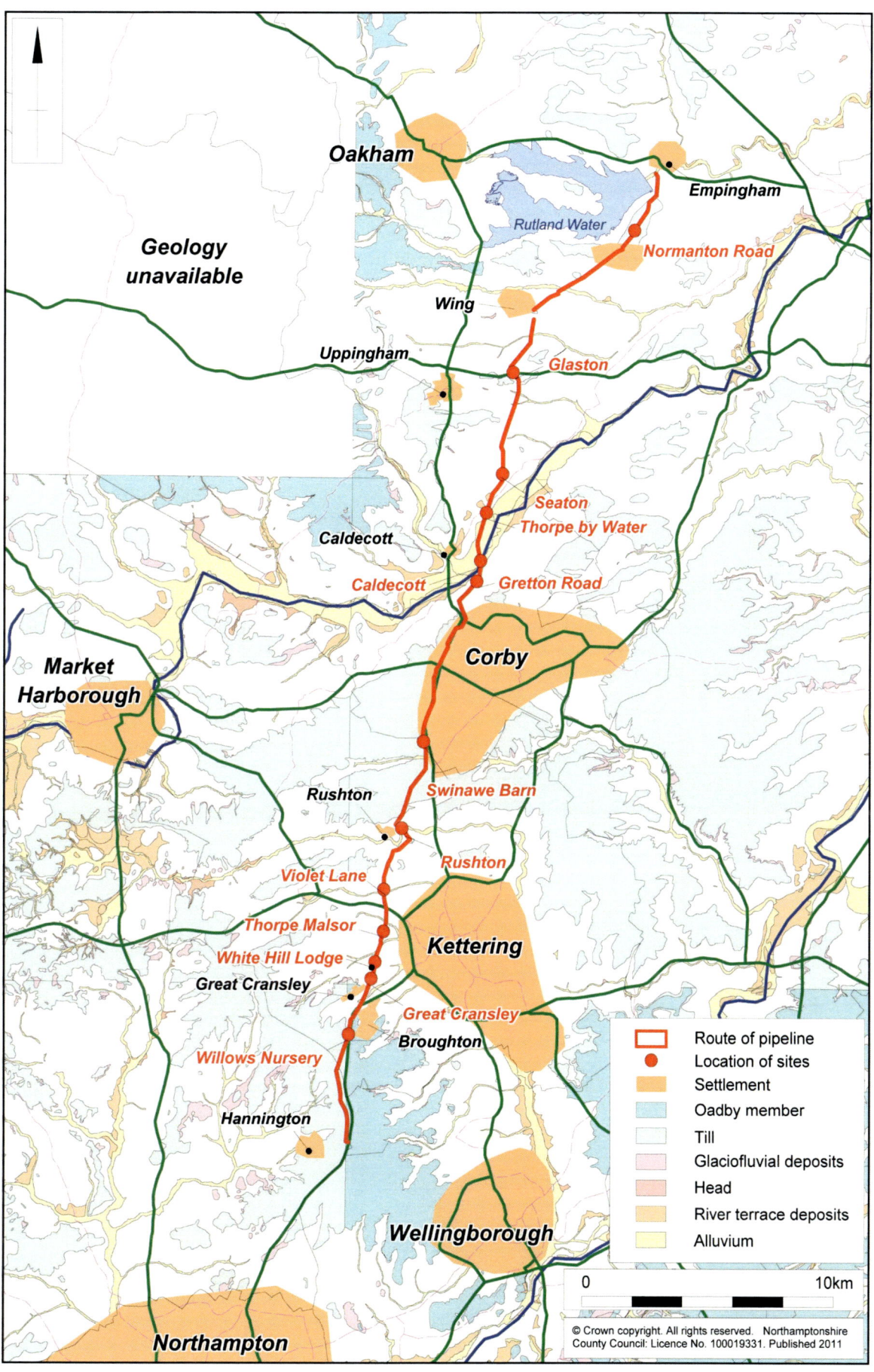

Fig 1.3: Geology and site locations

possible extent and general layout of the settlements, it has not been possible to gain a clear understanding of the development and use of the settlements. Individual discussions on each site would therefore be somewhat limited, so a more thematic approach has been adopted for the discussion, whereby the sites dating to each period have been grouped together and considered in relation to each other and the wider archaeological landscape. The individual discussion sections are as follows:

The late Bronze Age/early Iron Age pit alignment near Seaton
The Iron Age landscape
The Roman rural landscape
The Anglo-Saxon cremation cemetery at Glaston
Medieval and post-medieval remains

Archive

The physical archive for the Rutland sites including both finds and paperwork will be fully catalogued and deposited with Rutland County Museum under Accession Number OAKRM.2009.14. The archive for the Northamptonshire sites will be housed by Northamptonshire County Council until a dedicated county archive store becomes available.

2. Neolithic and Early Bronze Age (*c.*4000-1450BC)

Neolithic and early Bronze Age activity

No features dating to this period were encountered along the route of the pipeline, although a small assemblage of worked flint was recovered from the topsoil and subsoil, or as residual finds in later features. The quantity and concentration of worked flint from the individual sites was low and the assemblage can only be regarded as background material resulting from the casual loss of flint tools or the discard of flint waste associated with the transient activities of peoples living in the general area in the Neolithic and early Bronze Age.

Worked flint
by Yvonne Wolframm-Murray

Fifty-three pieces of worked flint, broadly dating from the Neolithic period to the early Bronze Age, were recovered during the watching brief and from excavations along the route of the pipeline. The assemblage comprises 34 flakes, 12 blades, two flake cores, four scrapers and one miscellaneous retouched flint.

They were recovered from the topsoil and subsoil or as residual finds in Iron Age, Roman and medieval features. The condition of the flints is generally good, showing little post-depositional edge damage; 11 pieces show slight to heavy patination. One flint is burnt and one flint is frost damaged.

The raw material is similar across all sites, mostly a vitreous flint of mid to dark greyish-brown colour, with some a light greyish-brown, mid grey or a mid brown colour. Also, there are two pieces of an opaque light and mid grey coloured flint. The cortex present on the dorsal surfaces of 19 of the flints is a white or a light to dark brown colour. The raw material is probably local gravel flint.

3. Middle Bronze Age to Early Iron Age (*c.*1450-400BC)

A late Bronze Age/early Iron Age pit alignment near Seaton

A prehistoric pit alignment was located to the north and south of Seaton Road, approximately 1.3km to the north-west of Seaton village, Rutland (Seaton 1, NGR: SP89049895; Fig 3.1). The geophysical survey recorded a length of 190m, but at either end it reached the limit of the pipeline easement and was still continuing (Butler 2007, fig 36).

The geophysical survey results show that the pit alignment followed a linear course but with abrupt, if slight, changes of angle at intervals of perhaps 50-60m. The direction of angle change alternates within the survey area, so that the overall course is approximately linear. Such abrupt but slight changes in alignment have been seen at other pit alignments in the region, as at Gayhurst Quarry, Buckinghamshire (Chapman 2007, 180-190).

Within the excavated site to the north of Seaton Road, the pit alignment was situated on a relatively steep, north-facing slope overlooking a small stream, and was aligned north-east to south-west (Fig 3.2). The ground level descends from *c.*110m aOD at the southern end of the site by the road to *c.*102m aOD at the lower end of the site to the north. The pits were cut into the underlying ironstone of the Upper Lias Clay formation (BGS 1978).

Within the excavated area there were twenty-one circular or sub-angular pits, spaced *c.*1.5m apart (Figs 3.2 and 3.3). Of these, eighteen were excavated, one was almost entirely truncated by a furrow and the remaining two were only partly exposed within the excavation area. One of the slight changes in angle lay within the excavated area, and this point was marked by a pit offset 1.0m to the west of its neighbours (Fig 3.2, pit 21).

The pits were all circular in plan, but varied from 0.6-1.6m in diameter, with shallow, U-shaped profiles, 0.35-0.55m deep (Fig 3.4). They had fills of orange-brown silty clay with occasional to moderate ironstone pebbles and appear to have silted due to natural weathering, with no evidence of deliberate infilling or recutting. One pit, 19, contained several ironstone cobbles, which may have been used as post-packing, although there was no other evidence for a post in this or any of the other pits. It is possible that the vagaries of natural silting have broadened the range of diameters, and that the pits may have shown greater uniformity when originally excavated.

As already noted, pit 21 was noticeably offset to the west of the other pits, and lay at a possible change in the alignment of the pit alignment. It may also indicate a division between the works of separate gangs during the construction of the monument.

Unfortunately, not enough of the pit alignment was exposed within the pipeline easement to explore these patterns of layout any further, although to the north, there was an extra pit, 42, set to the immediate west of the alignment, perhaps marking a further point of change.

No dateable artefacts were recovered, and there was no animal bone or charcoal to provide a radiocarbon date. The pit alignment can therefore be only broadly placed within the late Bronze Age/early Iron Age context that has been demonstrated elsewhere in the region through radiocarbon dating.

Middle Bronze Age to early Iron Age activity at Glaston
by Andy Chapman

Sherds from the rim and upper body of a hand-built vessel that probably dates to somewhere between the early/middle Bronze Age and the late Bronze Age/early Iron Age were recovered from the area of an Anglo-Saxon cremation cemetery at Glaston, Rutland. The sherds were found in close association with a spread of cremated human bone (cremation burial B13) and fragments of an Anglo-Saxon bone comb, in a localised spread of mid orange-brown silty clay, 31. The group comprises two joining sherds that make up part of the rim and body and a further 12 smaller non-joining sherds from the rim and body of the same vessel, which together represent perhaps 10% of the whole vessel.

The soft fabric contains voids, possibly from the leaching of sparse large shell inclusions, and it has a dark grey core and inner surface and a light orange-brown external surface. The vessel is a near cylindrical jar, *c.*150mm in diameter, with a simple rounded rim. At 20-30mm below the rim there is a single row of deep fingertip impressions, some showing a fingernail impression in the base (Fig 3.5).

The style of decoration is similar to that on rusticated Beakers of the latter part of the early Bronze Age, the early 2nd millennium BC, although fingertip impressions are a common form of decoration through to the late Bronze Age/early Iron Age, in the mid 1st millennium BC.

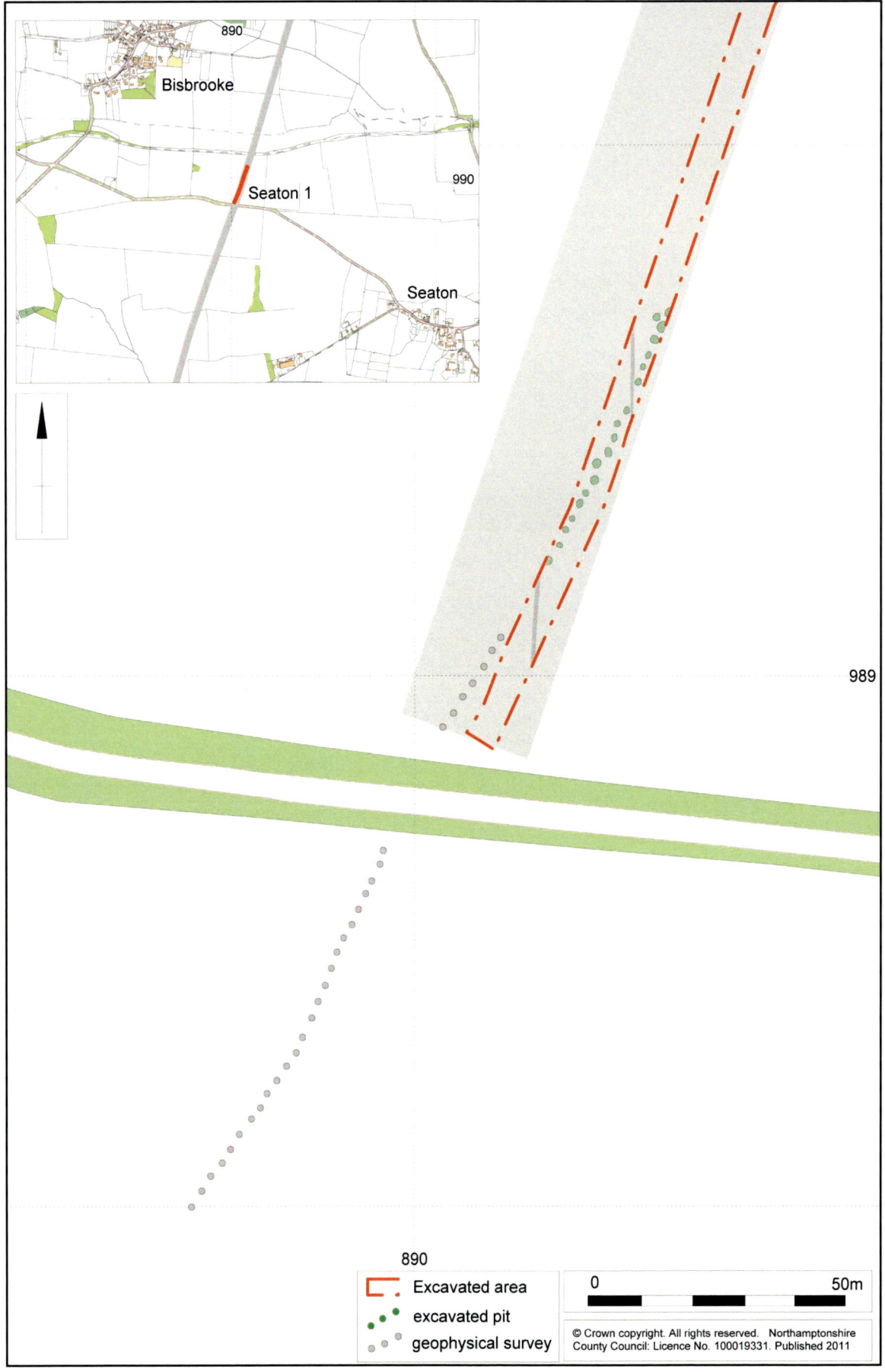

Fig 3.1: Seaton, the pit alignment in excavation and geophysical survey

3. Middle Bronze Age to Early Iron Age (c.1450-400BC)

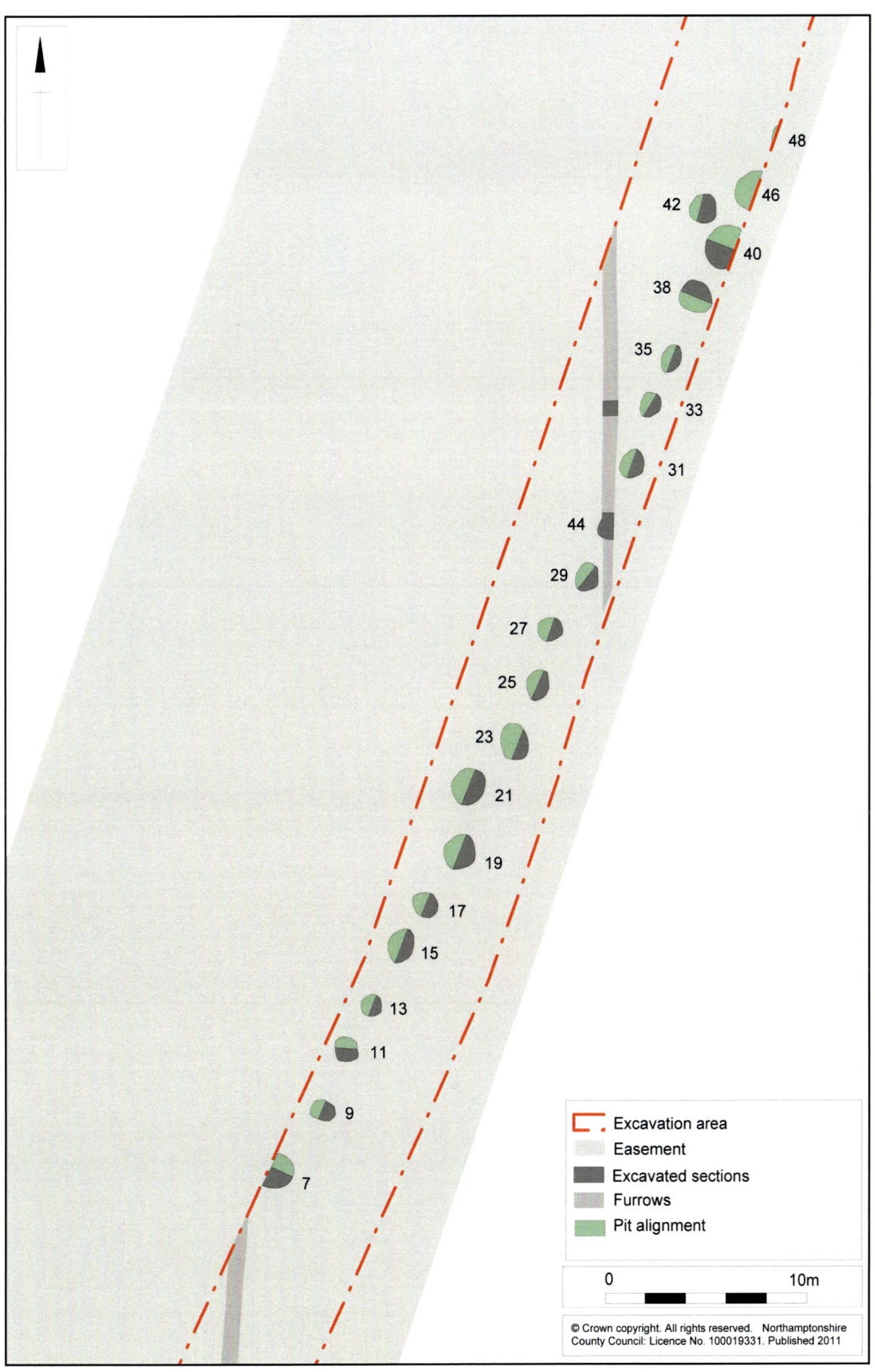

FIG 3.2: SEATON, THE EXCAVATED PIT ALIGNMENT

Fig 3.3: Seaton, the pit alignment, looking north-east

Fig 3.4: Seaton, pit 13 in the pit alignment, looking north-west (Scale 1m)

3. Middle Bronze Age to Early Iron Age (c.1450-400BC)

There are no contemporary features or other prehistoric pottery from this site, but it seems unlikely that the presence of this vessel was fortuitous, especially given the large size of the sherds. Its presence may suggest that a nearby Bronze Age burial or at least a pit deposit, had been disturbed and the pottery collected and later reinterred with an Anglo-Saxon burial.

This might suggest that the Glaston cremation cemetery had been located on and around a Bronze Age round barrow; a practice recognised at many sites in the region. A barrow mound might, therefore, lie unrecognised, closely adjacent to the excavated area. The presence of round barrows in the vicinity has been shown by cropmark evidence for a ring ditch, possibly a Bronze Age barrow, in a field to the south of Uppingham Road, c.200m to the south of the cremation cemetery.

FIG 3.5: GLASTON, BRONZE AGE JAR FROM ANGLO-SAXON CREMATION BURIAL B13 (SCALE 20MM)

4. Middle to Late Iron Age (400 BC - 43 AD)

Six sites produced significant settlement remains dating to the middle Iron Age: Seaton, Thorpe by Water and Caldecott in Rutland and Swinawe Barn, Thorpe Malsor and Willows Nursery in Northamptonshire.

Middle to late Iron Age settlement near Seaton

The site was situated near the top of a south-facing slope, at a height of *c*.105m aOD, overlooking a small tributary valley on the north side of the Welland Valley (centred at NGR: SP 8884 9841; Fig 4.1). The underlying geology is Upper Lias Clay (BGS 1978). The site largely comprised a cluster of intercutting pits, which were probably associated with a nearly settlement, although the geophysical survey and aerial photographs provide no indication as to where the focus of the settlement may lie.

The main concentration of features extended along the easement for *c.*15m and comprised at least ten large pits, measuring up to 3.2m across and 0.6m deep, and a gully terminal. It is possible that two small ditches terminated within the pit group, but geophysical survey and excavation within the narrow confines of the easement was inconclusive in determining their exact nature and extent.

Many of the pits contained pottery, mainly undiagnostic body sherds, but combed decoration and a footring base suggests that they date to the late 1st century BC into the early decades of the 1st century AD.

Possible ditches 75 and 84

These were the possible western terminals of two ditches which could not be traced on the surface as they were both cut by later disturbance and masked by a soil layer, 73. Features 75 and 84 were close to the eastern edge of the geophysical survey area, so it was not possible to determine if they were ditches extending further to the east, or were merely elongated pits.

Ditch/pit 84, 0.8m wide by 0.22m deep, was aligned north-west to south-east, and appeared to have a narrow pointed terminal (Fig 4.3). Ditch/pit 75, 1.5m wide by 0.25m deep, was aligned east to west and appeared to have a slightly squared terminal. The relationship between the two features could not be determined due to truncation by a later pit, 77. Both features were filled with mid brown silty clay containing late Iron Age pottery, animal bone, burnt cobbles and charcoal.

Gully 51

Gully 51 lay immediately to the south of the pit cluster (Fig 4.1). It was 0.4m wide by 0.09m deep and aligned north-east to south-west for 5m from its north-eastern terminal to where it passed beyond the limits of the easement. The fill of orange-brown silty clay (50) contained occasional charcoal flecks.

Gullies 14, 18 and 37

A curvilinear gully, 14, lay 70m to the north of the pit cluster (Fig 4.1). It was 0.4m wide by 0.12m deep, with a fill of light grey-brown sandy clay with charcoal flecks (13). A contemporary gully, 18, with a similar fill (17), branched off to the west from gully 14, to beyond the easement. The north-east terminal of gully 37, 0.6m wide by 0.22m deep, lay 9m to the south of the terminal of gully 18. No artefacts were recovered to provide dating evidence, but they probably formed part of a system of gullies associated with the Iron Age settlement.

Pit group (pits 47, 54, 72, 82 and 88)

Amongst the earliest features in the pit group were pits 47, 54, 72, 82 and 88. Pit 47, was roughly oval, 1.8m long by over 1.0m wide and 0.66m deep, with a fill of mid to dark brown silty clay (46) (Fig 4.2, Section 13). Pit 54, 0.45m to the east, was similar in size but shallower, at 0.38m deep. This pit had a primary fill of mid orange-brown sandy clay (53) derived from weathering, overlain by mid to dark grey-brown silty clay (52). Pottery from a single vessel, dated to *c* 0-20AD, was recovered from both pits, suggesting that they were contemporary features.

Pit 72 was a large circular pit with a flat base, *c.*2.5m in diameter and 0.79m deep, 3m to the north of pits 47 and 54. The primary fill was mid orange-brown sandy clay (71), overlain by orange-brown silty clay containing pottery, animal bone and quantities of charcoal (Fig 4.2, Section 16).

Pit 82 was largely truncated, with only part of its base remaining, 0.5m wide and 0.23m deep (Fig 4.3). Iron Age pottery and animal bone were recovered from the mid orange-brown sandy clay fill (81).

Pit 88 was not excavated, but was roughly circular in plan, 1.0m diameter, with a fill of mid grey-brown silty clay (87). Part of its western half was truncated by pit 80.

Pits 40, 49, 62, 66 and 69

Pits 62, 66 and 69 had cut pit 72 (Fig 4.2, Section 16). Pit 62 cut the east side and was 1.2m in diameter and 0.41m deep. Against the steep southern slope of the pit and overlying the primary fill (58) of weathered material, there was a tip deposit of brown-orange sandy clay (59). This was succeeded by a layer of grey, orange-mottled

Excavations along the Empingham to Hannington pipeline 2008-2009

Fig 4.1: Seaton, Iron Age settlement

4. Middle to Late Iron Age (400 BC - 43 AD)

sandy clay (60) and an upper layer of mid to dark grey-brown sandy clay (61).

To the north pit 66 was roughly oval, 2.2m long by 1.5m wide by 0.82m deep, with very steep sides and a narrow, concave base (Fig 4.2, Section 16). The fills comprised orange-brown silty/sandy clays, with the upper deposits, (63) and (64), containing animal bone and fired clay.

Pit 69, which cut the south-west side of pit 72, was oval, 2.0m long by 1.1m wide and 0.51m deep, with a slightly tapered western side, and a steep, near vertical slope and a flat base (Fig 4.2, Section 16). The fills comprised orange-brown silty clays, although the upper fill (67) was slightly darker and contained more charcoal.

Pit 49, which cut the northern side of pit 47, was sub-rectangular, 1.0m long by 0.9m wide by 0.42m dee,p with steeply sloping sides and a flat base (Fig 4.2, Section 13). The fill of mid to dark brown silty clay (48) contained charcoal and animal bone.

Lying close to the northern edge of the pit group, pit 40 was oval, 1.9m long by 1.2m wide and 0.31m deep. The fills comprised orange-brown clayey silts, with the upper deposit (38) slightly darker. Late Iron Age pottery and animal bone was recovered from both fills.

Pits 77 and 80

These were the latest two features in the pit cluster. Pit 77 was 1.2m in diameter and 0.33m deep, with a

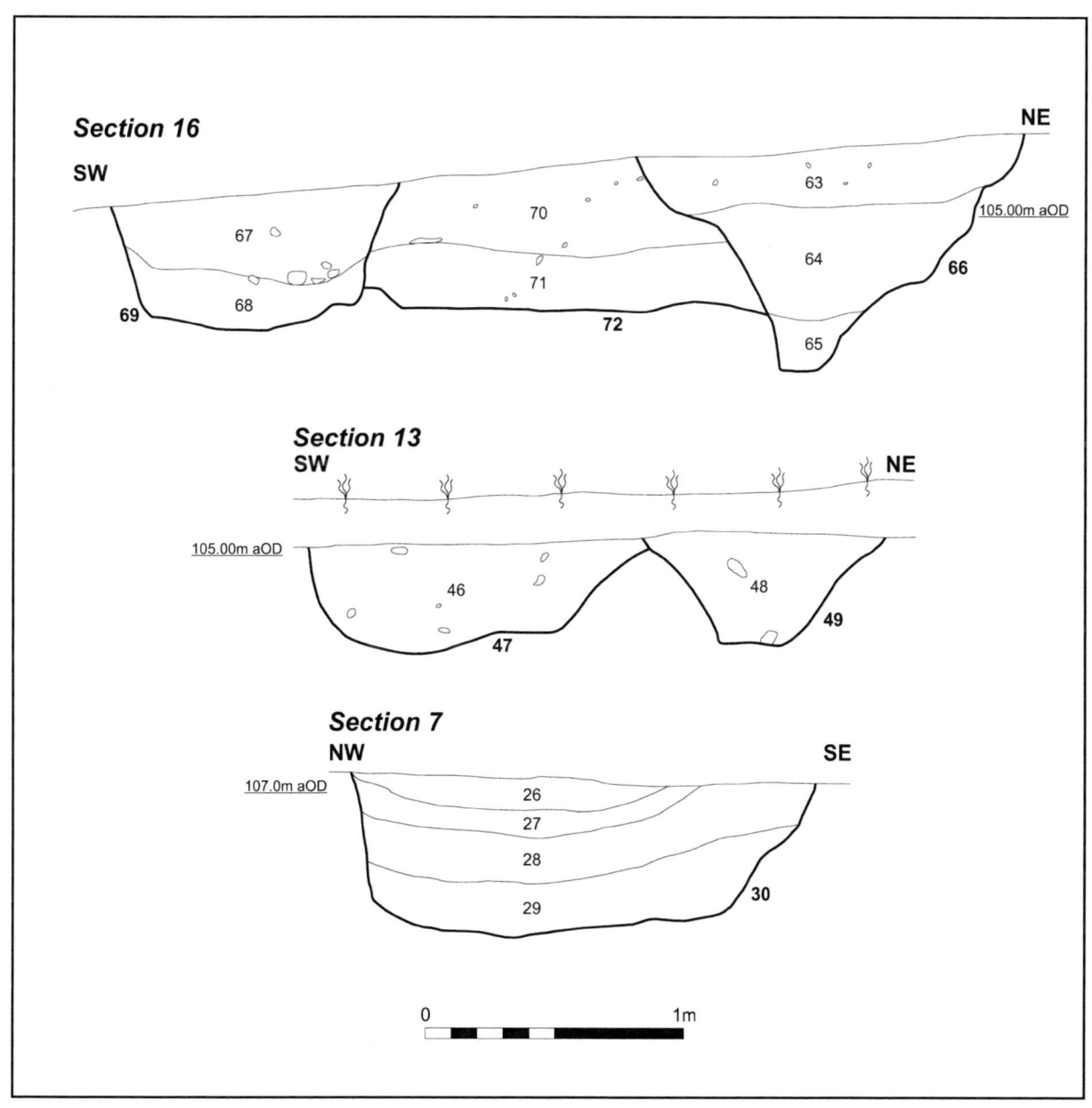

FIG 4.2: SEATON, SECTIONS OF IRON AGE PITS

Fig 4.3: Seaton, ditch 84, and pits 82 and 80, looking east (Scale 2m)

fill of charcoal-flecked brown silty clay (76). Pit 80, immediately to the south, was the largest pit in the group, 3.2m long by 2.2m wide and 0.43m deep. The fill of mid orange-brown sandy clay (79) contained late Iron Age pottery, iron working slag and animal bone.

Pits 5, 7, 25 and 30

Four isolated pits lay to the north of the pit group (Fig 4.1). The northernmost pit, 30, was some 60m to the north of the main concentration of features and cut into a large periglacial feature. It was roughly oval, 1.8m long by 1.1m wide by 0.60m deep (Fig 4.2, Section 7). The primary fill was mid grey silty clay (29), overlain by mid orange-brown sandy clay (28), mid grey silty clay (27) and mid yellow-brown silty clay (26).

Pit 5, was a small truncated feature, 0.66m in diameter and 0.08m deep, which lay 7m to the south of pit 30. The fill of charcoal-flecked mid brown-blue clay (4), may have been the remnant of a clay lining, several burnt, rounded cobbles were embedded in the clay.

Pit 25, partly exposed at the western edge of the easement, was 0.9m wide and 0.49m deep. The primary fill (24) of orange-brown silty clay was overlain by a similar but slightly darker deposit (23), containing charcoal, late Iron Age pottery and animal bone. Pit 7, 2.5m to the north-west, was smaller than the other pits in the group, 0.5m in diameter and 0.16m deep, with a fill of dark grey-brown silty clay (6).

Iron Age ditches and a cremation burial near Thorpe by Water

The site was north of Thorpe Road, about 0.6km to the west of Thorpe by Water, Rutland, on a south-east-facing slope, at *c*.64m aOD, overlooking the River Welland (NGR: SP 8866 9659; Fig 4.4). The underlying geology is Middle Lias silt and silty clay.

The excavation was targeted upon the junction between two ditches identified from the geophysical survey as part of a more extensive ditch system (Butler 2007, fig 42). The geophysical survey shows a ditch, 90m long, aligned north-south with an abrupt turn westward to the south of the excavated area. This ditch, 9, 1.2m wide by 0.39m deep, had a mixed fill of mid yellowish-brown and grey silty clay (8), suggesting that it may have been deliberately backfilled, and a sherd of Iron Age pottery.

The later ditch, 11, aligned near east-west, was wider but shallower, 1.8m wide by 0.26m deep, with a fill of mottled mid brown silty clay (10). An abraded sherd of Roman grey ware came from the surface of the ditch, but its worn condition suggests that it may be intrusive, so the date of the ditch is uncertain.

Nearby, the remains of a cremation burial were unearthed by a mechanical digger during construction works to the south of Thorpe Road, in Field 33:01. The context of the burial was destroyed by the machine, but it was clear that the burial was sealed by a layer of alluvium up to 1.0m thick. Cremated bone, probably that of an adult, was

4. MIDDLE TO LATE IRON AGE (400 BC - 43 AD)

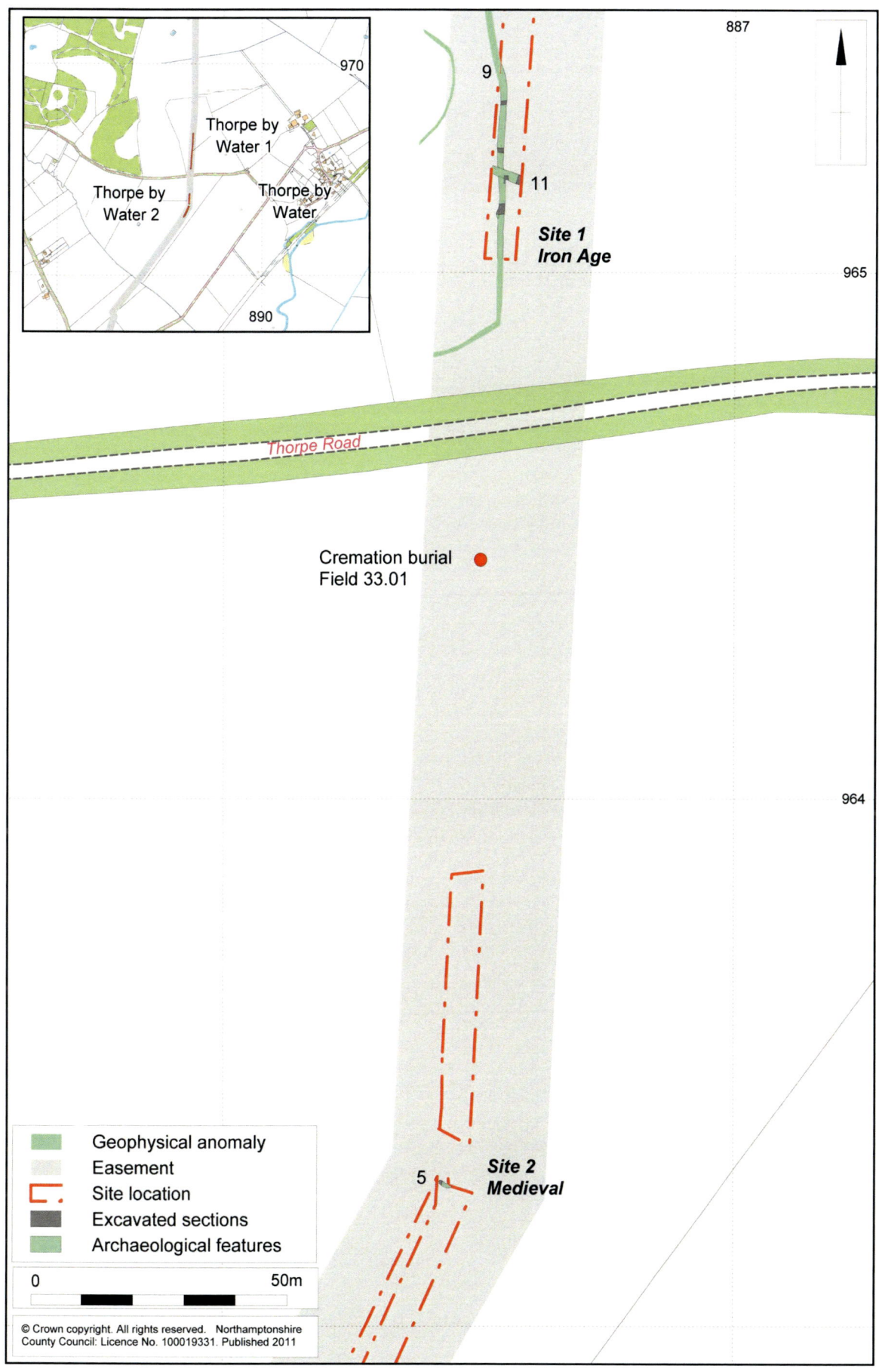

FIG 4.4: THORPE BY WATER, IRON AGE AND LATER FEATURES

spread over an area of approximately 1.0m² and there were traces of associated scorched soils, but no charcoal. No artefacts were recovered with the remains, but it is probably either prehistoric or Roman in date.

Middle to late Iron Age settlement near Caldecott

The site was situated close to the northern edge of the River Welland floodplain, at the northern end of Lyddington Road, about 2km to the north-east of Caldecott (NGR: SP 8805 9512; Figs 4.5 and 4.6). The ground, which sloped imperceptibly to the south-east, lies at c.45m aOD. The underlying geology is Lower Lias Clay (BGS 1976).

The excavation was targeted on a substantial enclosure identified by the geophysical survey (Butler 2007, fig 44). The north-western corner of this sub-rectangular enclosure measured over 50m north to south and over 30m east to west. There was a probable entrance in the western arm which, if central, would suggest that the enclosure was at least 60m long, and more than 0.25ha in extent. To minimise the impact of the pipeline on the archaeological remains, the pipe trench was positioned along the western edge of the easement to avoid the enclosure, but excavation was required to investigate other remains in this area associated with the settlement (Fig 4.5).

Ditches 73 and 38

Ditch 73 ran south-westwards from the north-west corner of the enclosure, perhaps forming an annexe lying to the west of the main enclosure. The southern boundary may have been a much slighter ditch, 38, lying 40m to the south (Fig 4.5).

Ditch 73 had a V-shaped profile, 6.0m wide by 0.86m deep, with steep sides and a narrow, 'ankle-breaker'-type base (Fig 4.7, Section 24). The primary fills were dark brown-grey silty clay (72) with blue-grey mottles, overlain by mid blue-grey silty clay (70) with orange-brown mottles; the mottling indicative of seasonal waterlogging. The ditch had almost entirely silted before it was recut to a little over half of its original depth, 0.53m, ditch 80. The fill of the recut was, mid grey-brown silty clay (69) with charcoal-flecks. A small sherd of Roman pottery was recovered from the top of this deposit, but it is likely that both the ditch and recut are late Iron Age in date.

Ditch 38 to the south was much less substantial, 0.45m wide by 0.06m deep, with a fill of mid grey-brown sandy clay (37).

Features to the south of ditch 73

Ditch 50 was 0.43m deep with a primary fill of mid brown-grey clay (49) under a thin layer of mid brown-orange silty clay (48). The full extent of this ditch to the south-west was not determined.

Two curvilinear gullies, 9 to the north and 47/57 to the south, may have formed the western side of a small enclosure at least 7m wide, with a north-western entrance and perhaps abutting the enclosure ditch to the east. Gully 9 was 0.7m wide by up to 0.42m deep, with a narrow, slightly pointed western terminal. The fill of mid grey silty sandy clay (8) with orange-brown mottles, and to the east an upper fill of mid grey sandy silt (58) contained burnt pebbles and charcoal.

Gullies 47 and 57 were probably successive cuts, but due to the similarity of the fills it was not possible to determine the sequence. Gully 47 had a steep-sided, U-shaped profile, 0.4m wide by up to 0.34m deep, while gully, 57, was 0.5m wide by 0.16m deep (Fig 4.7, Section 20). The fills were mid orange-brown silty clay, with the fill (56) of gully 57 containing more stones. Late Iron Age pottery was recovered from gully 47.

Gully 36 to the west, 0.8m wide by 0.04m deep, with a rounded northern terminal, had a fill of mid grey-brown silty clay (35) containing middle to late Iron Age scored ware pottery. The ditch was 4.5m long, and to the south it turned westward, perhaps forming the eastern arm of a small enclosure.

Pit 44 and posthole 63

Pit 44 was oval, up to 1.2m in diameter and 0.35m deep, with a fill of orange-grey sandy clay (43) (Fig 4.7, Section 17).

Posthole 63, which lay immediately to the south of gully 9, was 0.3m in diameter and 0.42m deep. The fill was grey-black sandy silt (62) containing charcoal and burnt pebbles, with an upper fill of black, charcoal-rich silt (61). Pebbles and small cobbles around the edge of the cut may have been used for post-packing.

Pits and postholes to the north of ditch 73

Four features interpreted as pits, and one posthole, lay to the north of ditch 73. Three of the pit-like features were cut by the ditches in this area, perhaps suggesting that the pits were the truncated bases of post-pits forming timber fences that predated the ditches.

Pit 5, c.0.7m wide by 0.11m deep, was cut by ditch 7. Pits 17 and 32, which were of a similar size, were cut by ditch 15 (Fig 4.7, Section 12). All three had fills of orange-brown, stony sandy silt.

Posthole 22, 0.5m in diameter and 0.22m deep, lay 0.9m to the south of the dog-leg of ditch 26. It had a primary fill of orange-grey sandy clay (21), overlain by mid to dark blue-grey sandy clay (20).

4. Middle to Late Iron Age (400 BC - 43 AD)

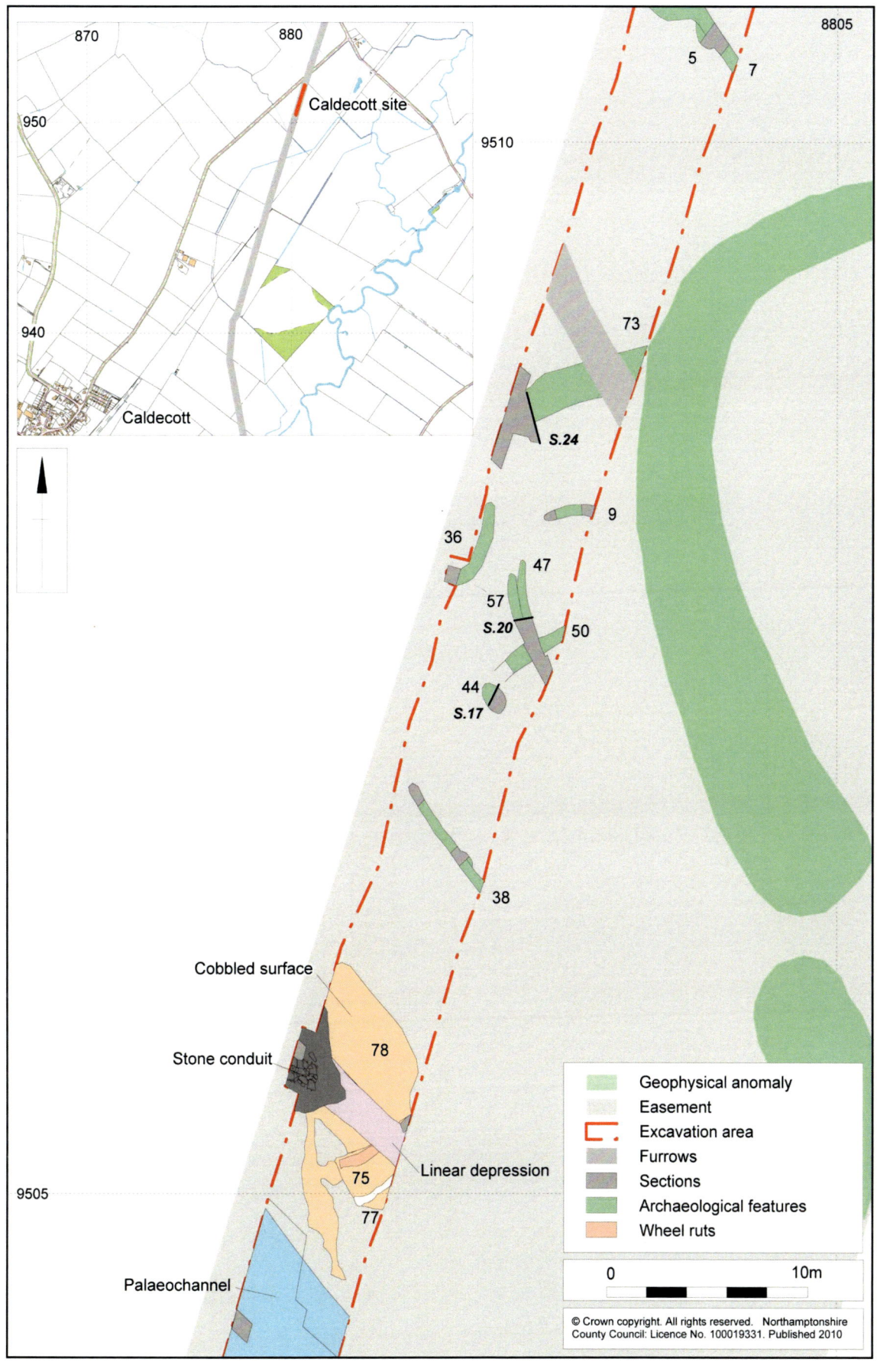

Fig 4.5: Caldecott, plan of Iron Age settlement (south)

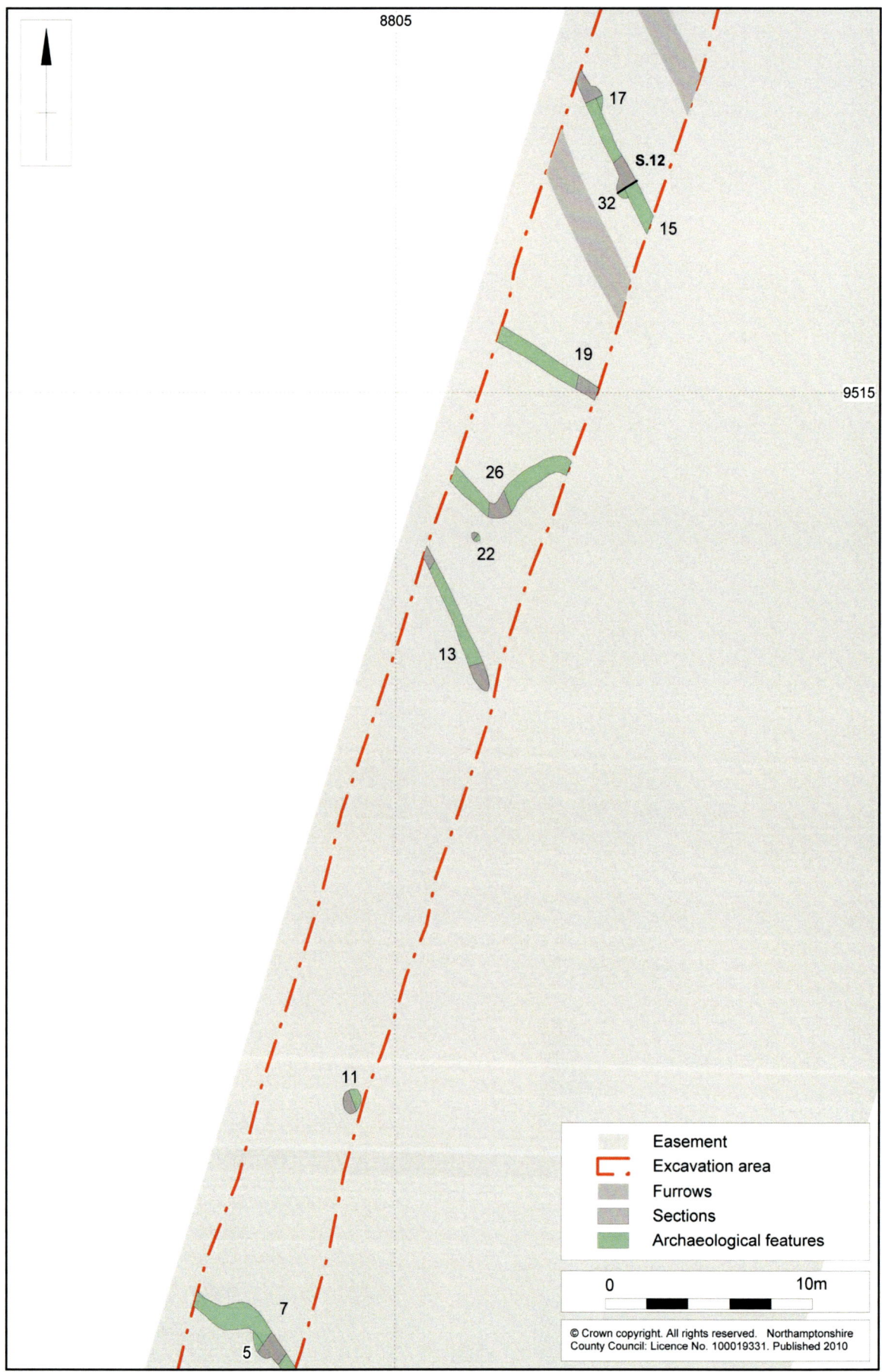

FIG 4.6: CALDECOTT, PLAN OF IRON AGE SETTLEMENT (NORTH)

4. Middle to Late Iron Age (400 BC - 43 AD)

Pit 11 was an isolated feature *c*.13m to the north of ditch 7. It was oval, 1.3m long by 0.9m wide and 0.19m deep, with a fill of orange-brown sandy silt (10).

Ditches to the north of ditch 73

A ditch, 7, lay less than 10m to the north of the enclosure, while four ditches, all on similar north-west to south-east alignments, lay a further 30-60m to the north (Fig 4.6).

Ditch 7 was aligned north-west to south-east, with an abrupt dog-leg where it cut pit 5. It was up to 1.1m wide and 0.1m deep, with a fill of mid orange-brown sandy silt (6).

To the north, ditches 13 and 15 were 18m apart on similar alignments. They were up to 0.8m wide by 0.34m deep, and ditch 13 had a rounded south-eastern terminal. Ditch 13 had a fill of dark grey sandy silt (12), whereas ditch 15 had a paler fill of mid orange-brown sandy silt (14) (Fig 4.7, Section 12).

Ditch 19 was 0.7m wide by 0.31m deep. Ditch 26 was on a similar alignment to ditch 19 to the west, but to the east it dog-legged sharply to the north. Both features had fills of brown-grey sandy clay.

Cobbled surface, 78

Towards the southern end of the site, beneath a layer of alluvium (64), a cobbled surface, 78, lay to the north of an old stream bed, a palaeochannel, which skirted the southern edge of the settlement (Fig 4.5 and 4.8). The surface, formed from river pebbles and cobbles embedded in the underlying natural clay, covered an area of over 60m². It may have been associated with the access to the western entrance of the unexcavated enclosure, which lay immediately to the north-east. Impressed into the surface, and spaced *c*.1.3m apart, were linear wheel ruts, 75 and 77. A small sherd of Roman grog-tempered ware was recovered from the surface of the cobbled area.

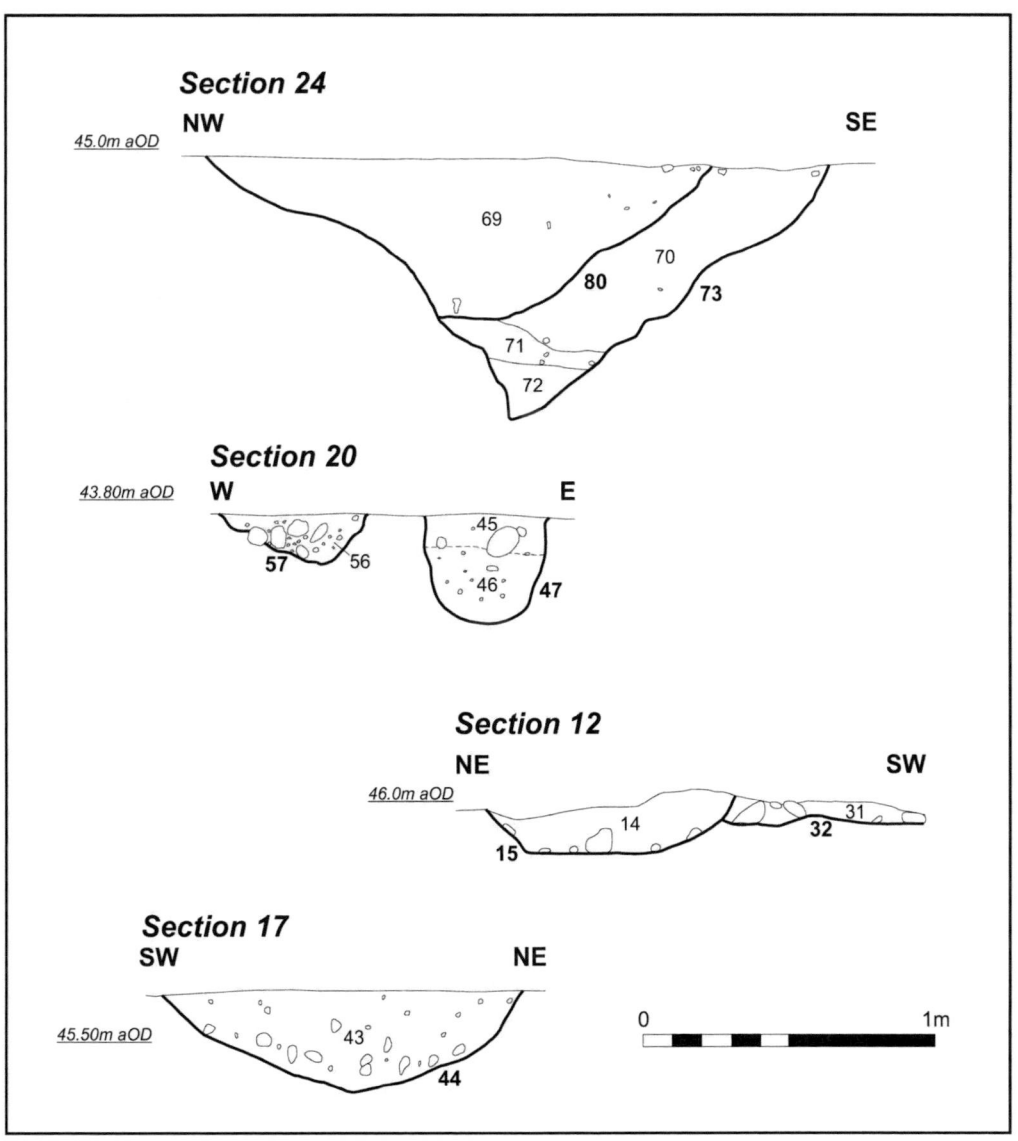

Fig 4.7: Caldecott, Sections of ditches and pit 44

Middle to late Iron Age settlement at Swinawe Barn, Corby

During the watching brief a significant number of Iron Age features were identified during topsoil stripping immediately to the west of the A6003, Corby. Due to the extent of the remains, an excavation area was established, 100m long by 20m wide. The site was located on a gentle, north-east facing slope, at 117m aOD, approximately 0.7km to the north-east of Swinawe Wood (NGR: SP 8559 8638; Fig 4.9). The underlying geology is Boulder Clay (BGS 1976).

The Iron Age features first identified in the watching brief formed part of a small enclosed farming settlement. Within the excavation area this comprised substantial enclosure ditches to the north and south, the remains of three roundhouses and a number of pits and postholes. The settlement was probably occupied from the 1st century BC into the early decades of the 1st century AD.

The enclosure (ditches 22, 46 and 92)

The enclosure was 68m long north to south, but the distance east to west was not established. If square, it would have enclosed some 0.46ha, and probably formed a small family farmstead.

The southern enclosure ditch, 22, aligned east to west, had a V-shaped profile, 1.6m to 2.3m wide and up to 1.0m deep (Fig 4.10, Section 6). It terminated to the west, where there may have been an entrance. The primary and secondary fills were light grey-brown clay (21), overlain by a similar, though slightly browner upper fill (20). Iron Age pottery and animal bone were recovered from both deposits. The slope of the ditch sides indicated that they had eroded as the ditch slowly silted, with little differentiation in the naturally accumulating silts.

Within the probable entrance there was a separate length of ditch, 46, 8m long with a rounded terminal to the south turning sharply to the south-east as if forming a funnel-shaped entrance passage. The northern terminal was truncated by a post-medieval/modern ditch. Ditch 46 was 1.8m wide by 0.5m deep. The fill of orange-mottled mid to dark grey silty clay (45), was overlain by a more extensive deposit of dark grey silty clay (44), which merged with the upper fill of ditch 22. Iron Age pottery and animal bone were recovered from both deposits.

Fig 4.8: Caldecott, Iron Age settlement, looking north-east

4. Middle to Late Iron Age (400 BC - 43 AD)

FIG 4.9: SWINAWE BARN, IRON AGE ENCLOSURE AND ROUNDHOUSES

The northern enclosure ditch, 92, was similar to the southern ditch, but slightly deeper, 2.0m wide by 1.2m deep (Fig 4.10, Section 28). The steeper sides suggest that this ditch had silted more rapidly, confirmed by the more complex sequence of fills that included the deposition of a range of domestic debris. The initial silting comprised light brown-yellow silty clay (91), largely derived from weathering, but this was overlain by an accumulation of light brown silty clay (97), mid brown clay (89) and mid grey-brown clay (88), which contained Iron Age pottery and animal bone, including a horse skull.

The cutting of a new ditch, 95, along the northern edge of ditch 92, may have been necessitated by the rapid filling of the ditch. The new ditch also had a V-shaped profile but was shallower, 1.3m wide by 0.53m deep, with fills of light brown-grey clay (94), overlain by mid grey-brown clay (93), containing Iron Age pottery and animal bone.

The roundhouses

Within the enclosure there were three ring ditches that all probably enclosed roundhouses. Two were in excess of 10m in internal diameter, Roundhouse A to the south and Roundhouse B to the north. Roundhouse B produced a wide range of finds, animal bone, charred plant remains and charcoal, and can be interpreted as the principal house, while to its immediate south there was a small ancillary building, Roundhouse C.

Roundhouse A was defined by a ring ditch enclosing an area with a diameter of 11m; the eastern half, including the probable entrance, had been truncated by a late medieval or post-medieval ditch. The ring ditch was 0.45-0.88m wide and up to 0.88m deep, with a variable profile (Figs 4.11 and 4.12, Sections 15 and 24). The fill of the ditch was generally mid brown or brown-grey silty clay with charcoal-flecks, although on the western side, where the ditch was at its widest and deepest, there was an upper deposit of dark grey silty clay with charcoal-flecks (76) (Fig 4.12, Section 24). The fills contained pottery and animal bone.

To the south-west, the ring ditch cut a small pit, 60, which was 0.9m in diameter by 0.21m deep, with steep, near vertical sides and a slightly concave base. The fill

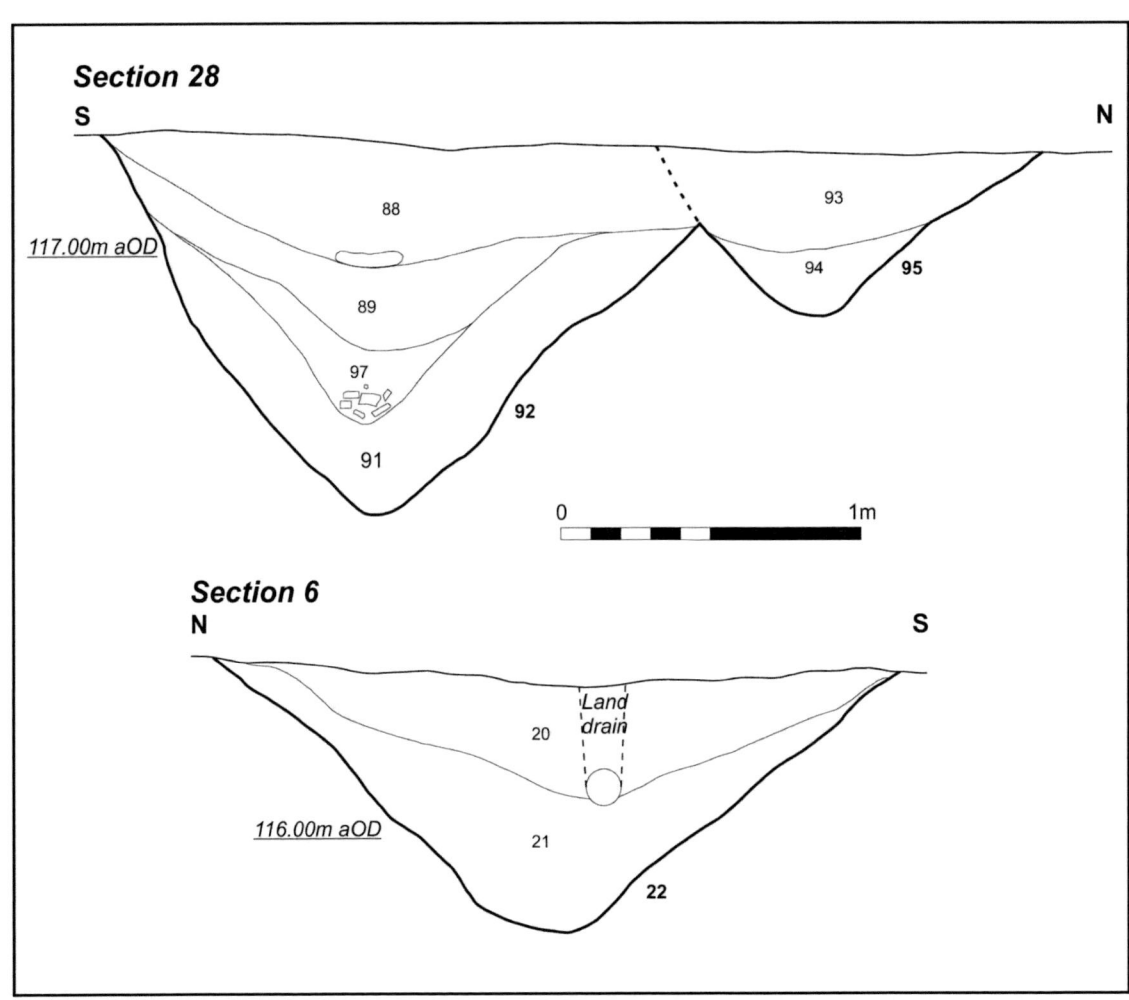

FIG 4.10: SWINAWE BARN, SECTIONS OF ENCLOSURE DITCH

4. Middle to Late Iron Age (400 BC - 43 AD)

was mid to dark brown-grey silty clay with charcoal flecks (59), containing numerous burnt, rounded cobbles (Fig 4.12, Section 15).

Roundhouse B was defined by a ring ditch enclosing an area with a diameter of 12m; the eastern part, including the probable entrance, had been removed by a medieval/post-medieval ditch. The original ring ditch, 7, had a steep-sided, V-shaped profile, c.0.8m wide by up to 0.55m deep (Fig 4.12, Section 29). The fill was generally of mid grey-brown clay (11), overlain by mid to dark grey silty clay (6), but there was a more complex sequence of deposits to the north, where ditch segment 120 contained a primary fill of mottled mid brown silty clay (116), overlain by deposits of darker mid brown silty clay: lower fill (117) which contained large quantities of charcoal and (118) (Fig 4.12, Section 39). Further west there was an additional upper fill of relatively 'clean' mid to dark brown silty clay, which may have been deliberate backfilling into the ditch when the adjacent recut was dug.

The recut ditch, 5, lay just beyond the original ditch around the western half of the ring ditch circuit. It had a similar V-shaped profile, 0.7m wide by up to 0.43m deep, but was shallower on the northern side. To the north, ditch 119 contained a primary fill of mid to light brown silty clay (115), largely eroded from the ditch sides, overlain by mottled mid to dark grey silty clay with charcoal flecks (114) containing middle Iron Age pottery and animal bone, and an upper deposit of charcoal-flecked dark grey silty clay (113) (Fig 4.12, Section 39).

Approximately 70% of the pottery from the site came from this building, along with animal bone and the only occurrences of charred cereal grains.

Animal bone from the ditch fill provided a date of 40 Cal BC-80 Cal AD (95% confidence, 1980+/-30 BP, Beta-293241), suggesting that the roundhouse may still have been in use into the 1st century AD, although the pottery assemblage indicates that the main usage was no later than the 1st century BC.

Two circular pits, 83 and 85, and a smaller, sub-rectangular pit/posthole, 106, lay within Roundhouse B. Pit 83 had near vertical sides and a flat base, 1.2m in diameter by 0.39m deep (Fig 4.12, Section 30). An initial mixed fill of orange and grey-brown silty clay (100), was overlain by successive dumped layers of grey-brown silty clay (99), dark brown-black silty clay (98) and mottled dark grey-brown silty clay (82), containing burnt pebbles, small cobbles and charcoal flecks, along with Iron Age pottery and a deposit of animal bone (Fig 4.13). Pit 85 lay 0.7m to the north-west of pit 83, and was 0.9m in diameter and 0.16m deep, with a fill of mottled grey-brown silty clay (84), containing Iron Age pottery and bone. An elongated

Fig 4.11: Swinawe Barn, Roundhouse A, looking east

pit/posthole, 106, 0.81m long by 0.23m wide and 0.14m deep, had a fill of mid grey-brown silty grey fill (105).

Roundhouse C, with an internal diameter of 6.0m, was defined by an arc of ditch to the north, 141, while any ditch to the south may have been truncated by a modern farm track. Ditch 141 was up to 0.70m wide by 0.16-0.30m deep, with fills of orange-mottled mid brown silty clay (140), containing Iron Age pottery and animal bone, overlain by mid brown-grey silty clay (139) (Fig 4.12, Section 40). To the east the ditch terminal probably defined the original entrance, and a steep-sided posthole, 149, in the base of the ditch at the terminal, was 0.33m in diameter by 0.27m deep, with a fill of light brown clay (148) overlain by grey-brown silty clay (147). It may have held a gatepost.

Other features

Slot 52, which lay 6m to the south-east of Roundhouse B, was 2.0m long with a steep-sided, U-shaped profile, 0.5m wide by 0.40m deep. The fill of dark grey-brown silty clay (51) contained Iron Age pottery, animal bone and large fragments of charcoal.

Pit 40, lying 3m south of slot 52, was 0.8m in diameter and 0.36m deep, steep-sided with a flat base and had a primary fill of mid grey-brown silty clay (39), overlain by dark grey to black silty clay (38), both deposits with charcoal flecks, animal bone, some of which were burnt, and Iron Age pottery.

A further 3m south a small circular pit, 16, was almost identical in shape. A layer of burnt, rounded cobbles lay on the base of the pit, overlain by dark grey to black silty clay (15), which contained animal bone, some of which were burnt, and Iron Age pottery.

To the north-east of Roundhouse B there was a row of three closely set pits/postholes. Postholes 160 and 162 were very similar, 0.35m in diameter and 0.17m deep, with fills of mid brown-grey clay. Pit 165, was oval, 1.1m long by 0.5m wide and 0.36m deep, with a fill of clean light grey silty clay (164), overlain by charcoal-

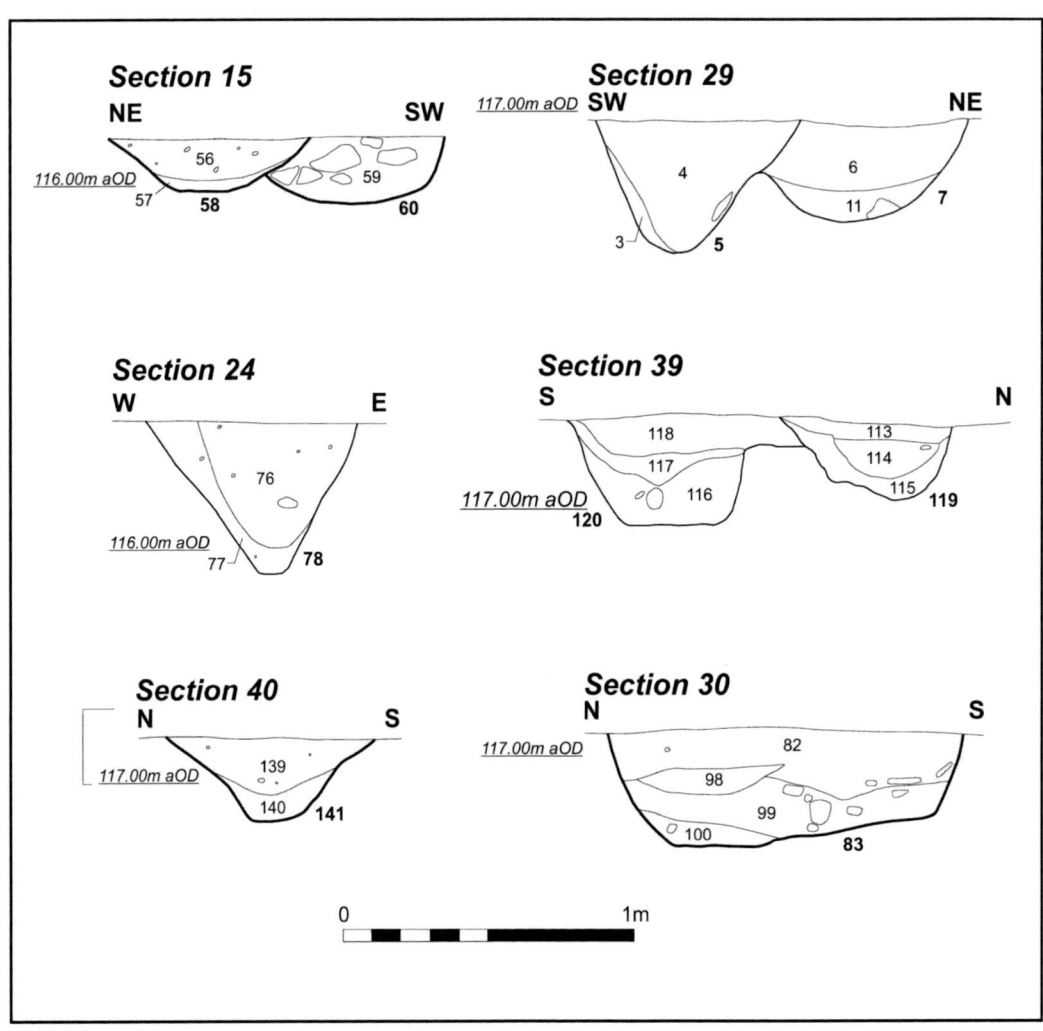

FIG 4.12: SWINAWE BARN, SECTIONS OF RING DITCHES AND PITS

4. Middle to Late Iron Age (400 BC - 43 AD)

Fig 4.13: Swinawe Barn, pit 83 with animal bone deposit, looking west (Scale 1m)

flecked mid brown-grey clay (163), containing Iron Age pottery and animal bone.

Late Iron Age ditches near Thorpe Malsor

The site lay 0.6km to the north-east of the village of Thorpe Malsor, situated on a spur of high ground between two small streams that flow to the north and south of the village, reaching their confluence near Brooklands Farm to the east (NGR: SP 8407 7924; Fig 4.14). The Iron Age ditches lay on a relatively steep, north-east facing slope, 99.5-97.5m aOD, which descended into the valley of the northern stream. A Roman settlement was located at the top of the slope, c.50m to the south. The underlying geology is Northampton Sand and Ironstone of the Inferior Oolite Series (BGS 1976).

The two ditches, 18 and 52, may have formed the north-western corner of a large rectangular enclosure, as located by geophysical survey (Butler 2007, fig 78). However, as the junction of the ditches lay at the margin of the survey area it is also possible that the ditches were two elements of a boundary system meeting at a near right angle.

Ditch 18

The ditch at the squared southern terminal was 4.5m wide by 1.8m deep, with steep sides and a broad base (Fig 4.15, Section 4).

Primary silts (87, 88, 86 and 85) of relatively stone-free sandy silts, derived from weathering, were overlain by a more extensive deposit (84) containing ironstone pebbles and cobbles. This had accumulated against the eastern side of the ditch, perhaps suggesting that the material had slumped from an adjacent bank. This episode was followed by a period of gradual natural silting of mid grey-brown (82) and mid orange-brown (81) sandy silt. A layer of mid orange-brown sandy silt (80) with charcoal flecks, containing late Iron Age pottery and animal bone, had been deposited from the east, the potential interior of the enclosure. It was the only deposit containing a quantity of domestic debris, although an upper fill, 16, also deposited from the east produced a few sherds of pottery including a sherd possibly from an unused triangular crucible of the type used in copper alloy casting.

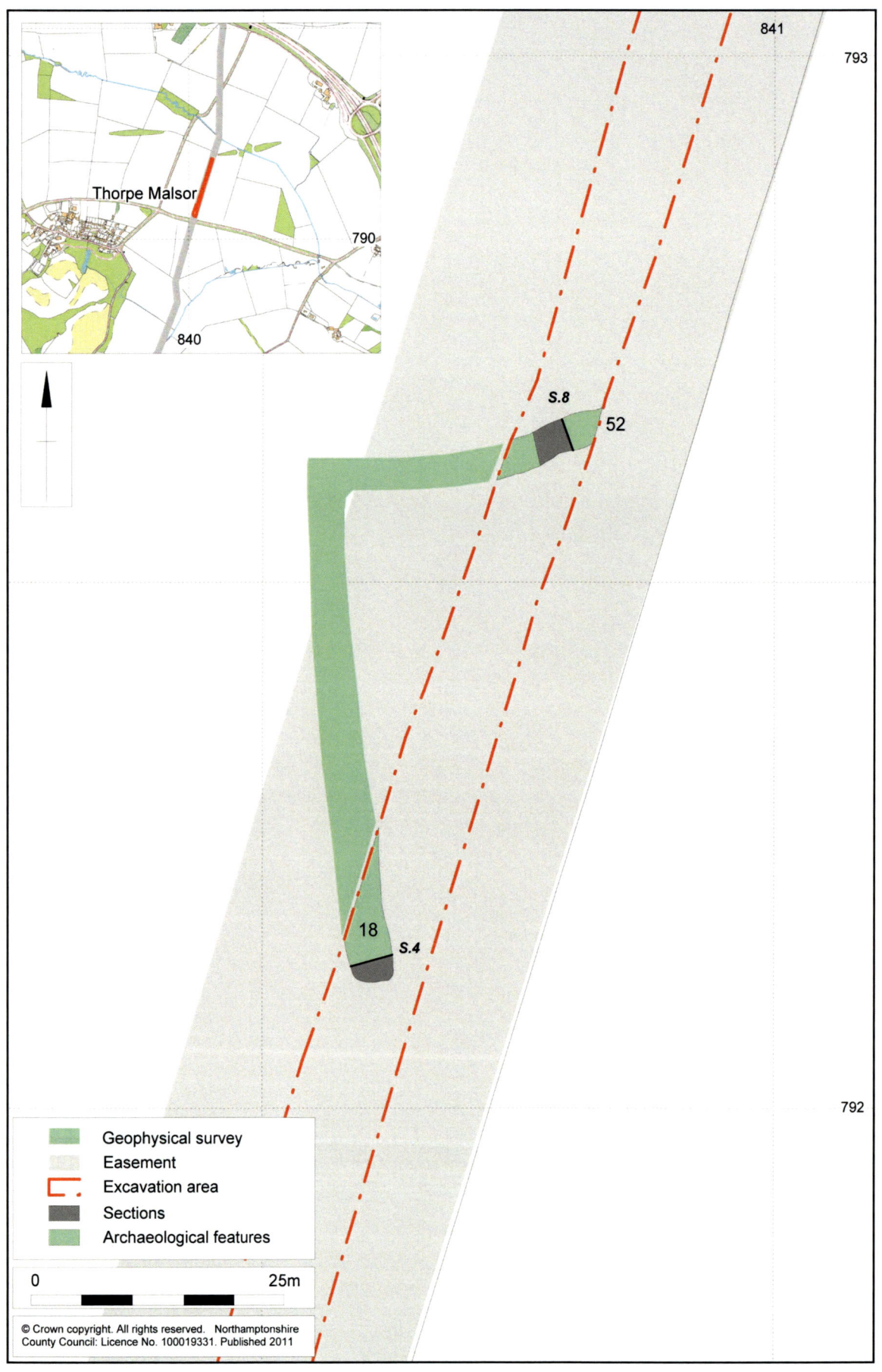

Fig 4.14: Thorpe Malsor, Iron Age settlement

4. MIDDLE TO LATE IRON AGE (400 BC - 43 AD)

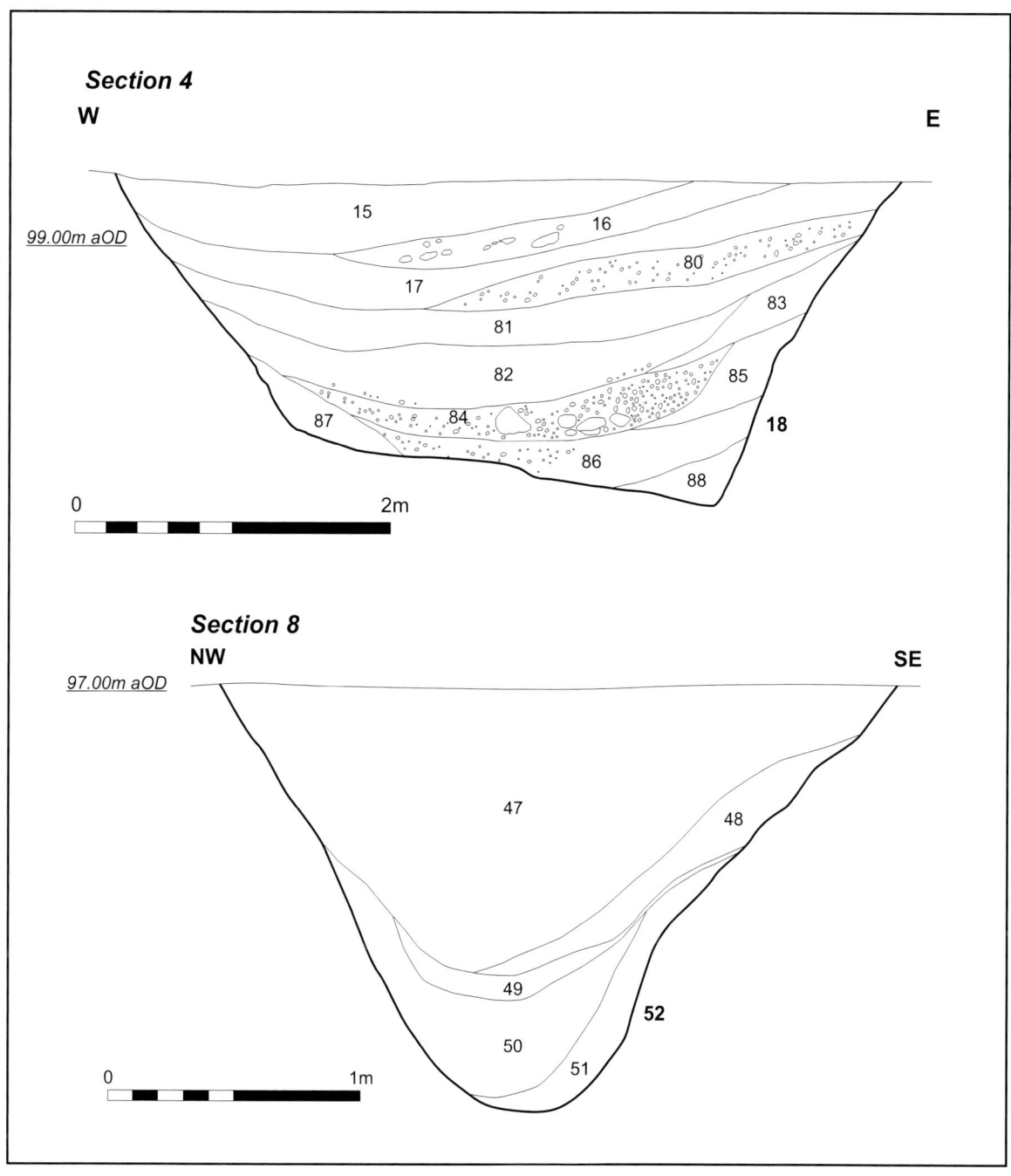

FIG 4.15: THORPE MALSOR, SECTIONS OF ENCLOSURE DITCH

Ditch 52

The northern ditch, 52, was 2.7m wide by 1.65m deep, with a steep-sided, V-shaped profile and a narrow concave base (Figs 4.14 and 4.15, 21, Section 8). The primary fills had accumulated rapidly and comprised light brown silty clay (51), mid brown silty clay (50) and mid to dark brown silty clay containing some small stones (49). A layer of light brown silty clay (48), had come in from the southern side. The upper fills showed little differentiation, comprising mid to dark brown silty sandy clay (47), with a few sherds of late Iron Age pottery.

Middle to late Iron Age settlement at Willows Nursery

Willows Nursery, which lay approximately 1km to the south-west of Broughton, to the west of the A43, was situated on a low-relief spur at 129m aOD (NGR: SP 8267 7524; Fig 4.16). The underlying geology is Boulder Clay.

The excavation, an area 80m long by 20m wide, was targeted on a sub-rectangular enclosure identified by geophysical survey (Butler 2007, fig 88). To minimise the impact of the pipeline on the archaeological remains, the pipe trench was positioned towards the western edge

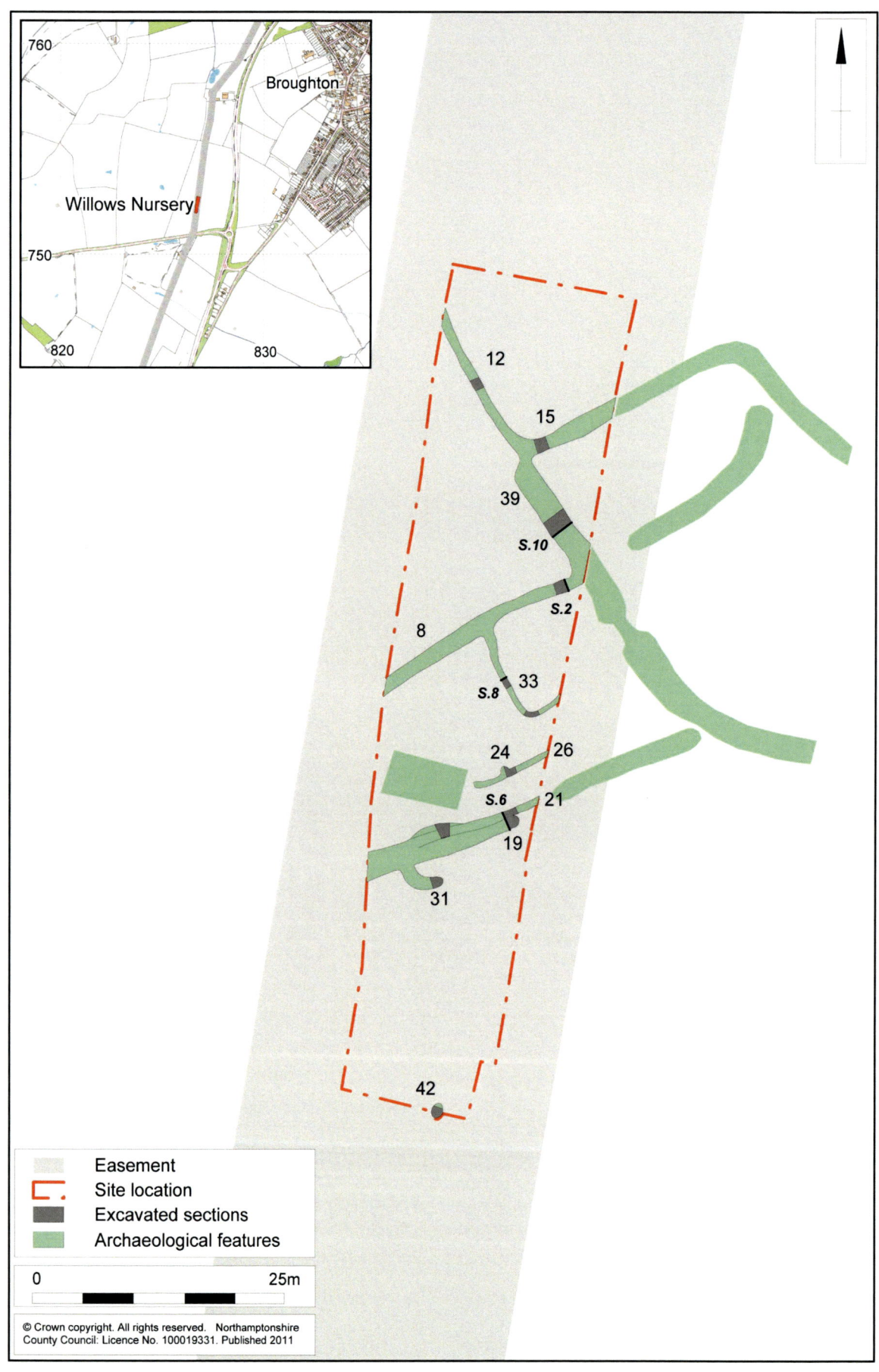

FIG 4.16: WILLOWS NURSERY, IRON AGE SETTLEMENT

of the easement to avoid the majority of the enclosure, but excavation was required to investigate its north-western corner and other associated remains (Fig 4.16).

The eastern corner of the enclosure lay beyond the surveyed area, but it measured at least 40m long by 27m wide, perhaps enclosing an area of some 0.1ha. The geophysical survey shows an abrupt narrowing at the centre of the western arm which is likely to be an entrance, perhaps incorporating a timber gateway set between the ditch terminals.

The enclosure ditches, 15 and 39

Ditch 39, the western arm of the enclosure, had a broad U-shaped profile, 2.0m wide by 0.8m deep (Fig 4.17, Section 10). The fill of dark brown-grey silty clay (36) contained some late Iron Age pottery, and had a higher stone content, of chalk pebbles and occasional small cobbles, (38), against the western edge of the ditch. This ditch appeared to have a rounded terminal to the north at its junction with ditch 15.

Ditch 15, the northern arm of the enclosure, had a similar profile but was less substantial, at 1.5m wide by 0.38m deep. On the northern side of the ditch there was a shallow step, 0.4m wide, near the top of the slope, with an overlying fill of mid brown sandy clay (14). Overlying this and filling the main body of the ditch was dark grey-brown silty clay (13).

Other linear ditches

A series of linear ditches, sharing the same alignments as the enclosure, appeared to define a series of rectangular plots or paddocks lying to the west of the enclosure.

Ditch 12 continued the line of the western arm of the enclosure northwards. It was a narrow, U-shaped ditch, 0.9m wide by 0.32m deep, the fill of mid grey-brown silty clay (11), contained late Iron Age pottery.

Ditches 8 and 19, spaced 15m apart, ran westwards from the enclosure defining an elongated plot with the enclosure entrance at the eastern end.

Ditch 8 had a steep, V-shaped profile, 1.25m wide by 0.65m deep (Fig 4.17, Section 2). The primary silting, from erosion of the sides, was mid bluish-grey silty clay (7). The secondary fill of charcoal-flecked brown-grey silty clay (6), contained several burnt cobbles, middle to late Iron Age pottery and animal bone. Several of the sherds came from the same vessel as sherds from pit 24, some 18m to the south. The upper layer (5) was similar, though less clayey and did not contain any finds.

A short, curving length of ditch, 31, was cut by the boundary ditch, 19, indicating that the boundary was a later addition.

Ditch 19 had steep sides and a broad, flat base, 1.2m wide by 0.47m deep, with a sequence of fills similar to ditch 8 (Fig 4.17, Section 6; Fig 4.18). Ditch 19 terminated to the east, suggesting that there may have been an entrance that was later removed when the boundary was recut. The recut, ditch 21, was shallower, 0.18m deep, with a fill of mid brown-grey silty clay (20), which contained Iron Age pottery and animal bone (Fig 4.17, Section 6).

Other features

An L-shaped gully, 33, formed a small rectangular sub-enclosure, 11m long by 9m wide, in the angle between ditch 8 and the main enclosure ditch. The gully was V-shaped, 0.5m wide by 0.36m deep (Fig 4.17, Section 8). The fill of dark grey, almost black silty clay (32), was considerably darker than the fills of the other ditches, and contained small amounts of middle to late Iron Age pottery, charcoal, animal bone and burnt stones, suggesting occupation within and around the sub-enclosure.

To the south, a length of gully, 26, may have flanked the original entrance through the southern boundary, ditch 19. A pit, 24, cut into the edge of gully 26, was steep-sided with an almost flat base, 0.8m in diameter and 0.37m deep. The primary fill of mid brown-grey silty clay, (23), was overlain by darker brown, charcoal-flecked silty clay, (22), containing small burnt cobbles, Iron Age pottery and animal bone, again indicative of nearby occupation.

Pit 42, which lay at the southern end of the site, was oval with a bowl-shaped profile, 1.4m long by 1.1m wide and 0.24m deep. The primary fill of mid grey-brown silty clay (41) was overlain by a deposit of dark grey, almost black silty clay (40), containing flecks of charcoal, fragments of fired clay and small sherds of degraded pottery, which disintegrated when lifted. The debris within the pit may have come from a clay-domed oven or kiln.

Finds and environment evidence from the Iron Age settlements:

The Iron Age pottery
by Andy Chapman

Seaton

A total of 204 sherds, weighing 756g, of hand-built pottery was recovered (Table 4.1). The majority of the context groups comprise less than 10 sherds, and the degree of fragmentation is indicated by the average sherd weight of only 3.7g. Only two context groups exceed 100g in weight.

Shelly fabrics are dominant, at 63%, although in many cases the shell has been lost to leaching. Sandy fabrics,

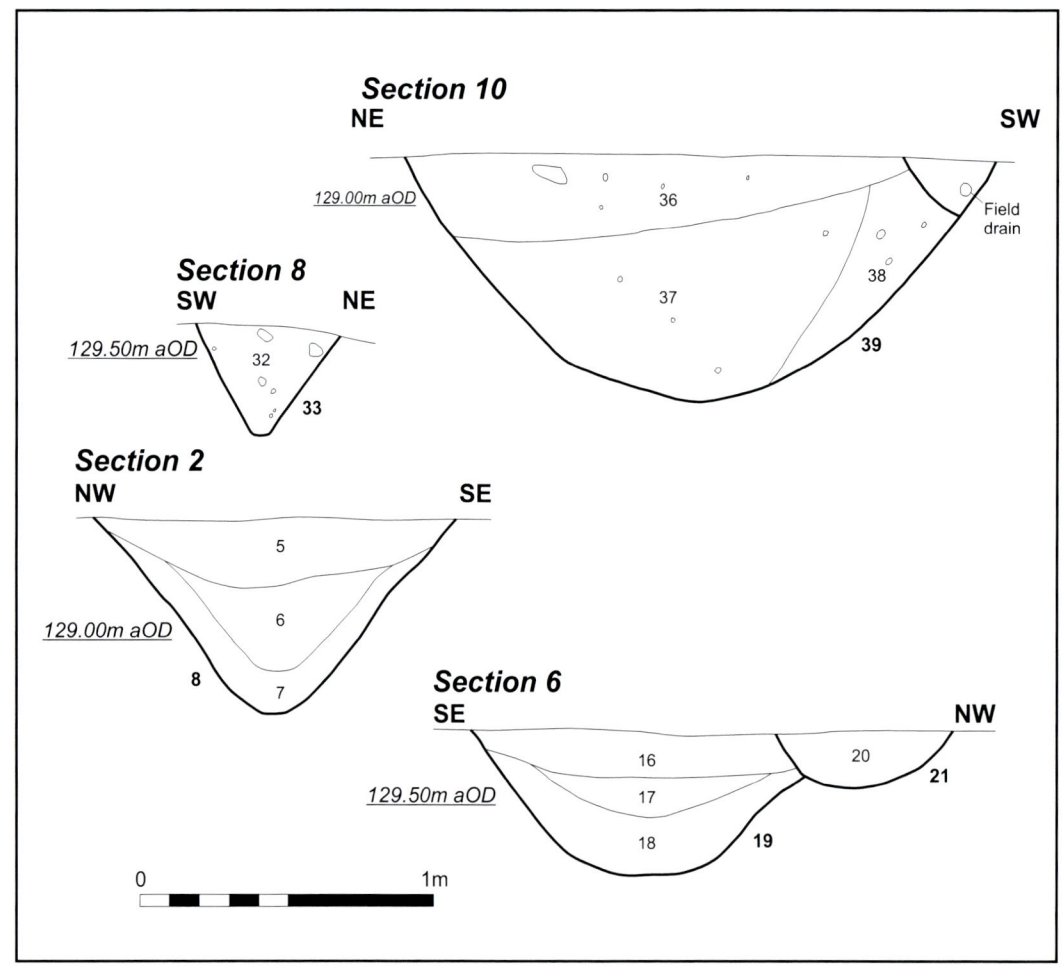

FIG 4.17: WILLOWS NURSERY, SECTIONS OF ENCLOSURE DITCHES

FIG 4.18: WILLOWS NURSERY, DITCH 19 AND GULLY 24, LOOKING SOUTH-WEST (SCALE 1M)

4. Middle to Late Iron Age (400 BC - 43 AD)

Context/feature	Sherd No	Weight (g)	Sherd families	Sherds/fabric	Comments
2	42	170	2	42 sandy	Thick flat base Fine rounded rim
6/7	6	23	1	6 shelly	Plain body
13/14	6	30	3	2 grog 4 shelly	Plain body
23/25	8	8	1	8 shelly	Fragments
27/30	5	15	2	1 sandy 4 shelly	Lightly scored
29/30	17	81	4	1 grog 16 shelly	Plain body
38/40	1	2	1	--	Fragment
39/40	1	3	1	1 shelly	Fragment
41/45	10	18	2	10 shelly	Plain body
46/47	26	56	6	4 grog 22 shelly	Comb decorated (1st century AD)
52/54	5	10	1	5 shelly	Comb decorated (1st century AD)
55/57	2	17	2	2 grog	Base and body
63/66	6	19	2	6 grog	Body and flat rim
64/66	1	5	1	1 grog	Body
70/72	10	30	3	2 grog 8 shelly	Body
73/75	26	133	5	8 sandy 8 shelly	Body
74/75	1	3	1	--	Small fragment
78/80	2	18	1	2 sandy	Small bowl, fine everted rim
79/80	14	69	1	1 grog 13 shelly	Thickened rounded Rim
85/86	15	46	4	2 grog 1 sandy 12 shelly	Footring base (1st century AD)
Totals	**204**	**756**	**44**	**127 shelly 54 sandy 21 grog**	**(63%) (27%) (10%)**

TABLE 4.1: SEATON, QUANTIFICATION OF IRON AGE POTTERY

typically with very fine and sparse rounded quartz inclusions, make up 27% of the assemblage, and fabrics containing small rounded pellets of grog form 10% of the group. The vessels typically have grey-black cores and inner surfaces. The outer surfaces vary from orange-brown to grey, but with the oxidised colours slightly dominating. The surfaces of the shelly sherds are pitted with voids, where the shell has been lost, but the sandy and grog tempered wares are typically hard with smoothed surfaces.

The majority of the sherds are undiagnostic plain body sherds. The few rim sherds are mainly from small, thin-walled vessels, and include simple flat and rounded rims. A single vessel, from the fill (79) of pit 80, has a thickened rounded rim, although too thick and poorly executed to be called a bead rim. A single small sherd from the fill (27) of pit 30 has lightly scored decoration, typical of middle to late Iron Age assemblages. Sherds from the fill (46) of pit 47 and the fill (52) of pit 54 are probably from the same vessel, which is thin-walled and decorated with fine, shallow comb impressions. This would date no earlier than the early decades of the 1st century AD. Many contexts also contain sherds from small, thin-walled vessels, which are characteristically in a shelly fabric that is dark grey throughout. This material includes a footring base, 70mm diameter, from a small, thin-walled vessel in a shelly fabric from the fill (85) of pit 86, which would also date no earlier than the early decades of the 1st century AD.

While an origin in the middle Iron Age cannot be ruled out, it would seem most likely that this assemblage dates to the late Iron Age, perhaps spanning the 1st century BC to the early decades of the 1st century AD.

Caldecott

Three contexts produced 54 sherds, weighing 667g (average sherd weight 12.4g), of hand-built pottery dated to the middle to late Iron Age.

The entire assemblage is in a fabric with a slightly soapy texture that contains frequent small rounded pellets of red-brown grog, typically *c* 1-2mm in diameter but with sparser pieces of up to 3-4mm diameter.

The fill (16) of pit 17 and the fill (45) of gully 47 both contained small assemblages of body sherds lacking diagnostic features. The fill (35) of gully 36, contained a large group of diagnostic material comprising large sherds, some joining, from either one or two scored ware storage jars, with walls 8-9mm thick. The flat base of one jar is 110mm in diameter, with sharply defined scored decoration running to the base of the vessel, while the scored sherds from the upper body have been eroded, so that the scoring has been partly lost (Fig 4.19). This may suggest that they derive from a single vessel that had been partially buried in the floor of a roundhouse, resulting in differential wear between the exposed upper body and the protected base. The upper part of the vessel is rounded, and has a simple upright rounded rim, 250mm in diameter, above a short slightly concave neck (Fig 4.19).

Scored ware is characteristic of middle Iron Age assemblages in Northamptonshire and the adjacent areas of the surrounding counties, but grog tends to occur only in later Iron Age assemblages. It is therefore suggested that the assemblage, which is all grog tempered, dates to the late middle to late Iron Age, perhaps the 2nd into 1st centuries BC.

Swinawe Barn, Corby

This site produced a large and well-preserved assemblage of 1,809 sherds, weighing 13.9kg, of hand-built pottery of the middle Iron Age. Pottery was recovered from 56 contexts, but only 16 of these produced totals in excess of 100g, and just six contexts produced more than 500g of pottery. The average sherd weight is 8g. This is above average for Northamptonshire sites, where the assemblages usually contain a substantial proportion of shelly ware, which often loses much of the shell to leaching and tends to fragment and laminate. In this assemblage the higher than average sherd size reflects the presence of many larger sherds that provide clear indications of vessel form, although no full profiles could be reconstructed.

Fig 4.19: Caldecott, rim and base of scored ware jar from gully 36 (Scale 20mm)

Rim form	Number	Percentage
Rounded	17	45%
Flat-topped	11	29%
Fingertip/fingernail decoration	7	18%
Expanded and grooved	3	8%
Totals	38	

Table 4.2: Swinawe Barn, rim form quantification

Fabrics

Four fabric groups have been identified by simple visual inspection:

1. Coarse shelly: containing dense coarse shell, often 5mm of more across. A soft fabric, often with abraded surfaces and a corky texture due to leaching of the shell. 1392 sherds, 77%
2. Fine shelly: a hard fabric containing finely crushed shell (*c* 1mm), typically used in smaller thinner-walled vessels with smoothed surfaces. 162 sherds, 9%
3. Sandy: a hard fabric containing fine sand giving a coarse surface texture, but without quartz inclusions larger than 1mm. 219 sherds, 12%
4. Grog and fine shell: a hard fabric containing dense small pellets (1-2mm) of rounded red-brown grog together with sparse finely crushed shell (1-2mm). 36 sherds, 2%

4. Middle to Late Iron Age (400 BC - 43 AD)

The predominant fabric, which makes up three-quarters of the assemblage, contains quantities of large crushed shell, with these vessels often larger, thick-walled (8-12mm thick) storage jars, both plain and scored.

There is a smaller quantity containing sparse finely crushed shell, and these sherds are almost exclusively from smaller, thin-walled vessels (5-7mm), often well-made with smoothed/burnished surfaces. Many of these have grey-black cores and surfaces, but finer vessels with orange-red surfaces are also present.

Sherds in a fine sandy fabric occur occasionally, but the proportion of the assemblage is perhaps exaggerated by the presence of multiple small sherds from single vessels in Roundhouse B (45 sherds from ditch 112) and the northern boundary ditch (102 sherds from ditch 90).

The smallest group is a distinctive fabric containing quantities of grog and some finely crushed shell. This is a hard fabric, and the majority of the sherds come from two ditch sections in Roundhouse B, indicating that the sherds are from only a couple of vessels, both large, thick-walled (10mm) plain jars, with flat bases.

Forms and decoration

From the surviving base, body and rim sherds, it is clear that the assemblage comprises a mixture of bowls and jars, with the jars ranging from medium-sized vessels (Fig 4.20, 1, 3 & 4) up to larger thick-walled storage jars perhaps around 500mm high (not illustrated); all with simple flat bases.

The majority of the body sherds come from plain vessels, but scored ware comprises 10% of the assemblage by sherd count; a higher than usual proportion. The site mean is boosted by the large proportion of scored ware, 17%, in the assemblage from Roundhouse B.

The rims (Table 4.2) are usually simple upright and rounded (17, 45%) or flat-topped (11, 29%). In addition, seven rims (18%) are decorated with fingertip indentations along the top of the rim or oblique fingernail impressions either on the top or the outer edge of the rim (Fig 4.20, 1).

Of particular interest are three squared rims with a shallow groove along the upper surface. In one instance there are grooves along both the upper surface and the outer edge of an exceptionally thick rim from a vessel 310mm in diameter (Fig 4.20, 2). At the base of the surviving sherd the sides are steep, indicating that the flaring rim stood above steep to near vertical sides. This vessel also has horizontal scoring on both the external and internal surfaces.

Examples of similar flared rims, also squared and grooved, have been seen from sites at Great Houghton, Northampton (Chapman 2001, 23, fig 13, 15), Tattenhoe, Milton Keynes (Chapman 2010a, fig 28, 8) and Coton Park, Rugby, Warwickshire (Chapman forthcoming). It appears that this rim form is associated with a particular vessel type, a large diameter bowl with steep sides and a flaring squared rim with at least a grooved upper surface. While these vessels are present at a number of Midland sites, they only occur in small quantities, usually no more than one vessel per assemblage. It may be tentatively suggested that this vessel form is associated with dairying, perhaps similar to the open and even larger diameter bowls, or pancheons, of the medieval and post-medieval periods.

The profiles of the jars range from slack-shouldered examples (Fig 4.20, 1 & 3) where there is little distinction between the body and the neck, to jars with pronounced shoulders and a well-defined neck (Fig 4.20, 4).

The majority of the scored ware comprises thick-walled sherds that are probably from large storage jars, but there is also at least one small bowl with scored decoration, and this example was particularly poorly made, with a very uneven surface and rim (Fig 4.20, 5).

A rare occurrence are sherds from a small bowl with a flat rim, a concave neck, smoothed/burnished surfaces and a footring base (Fig 4.20, 6) The body has impressed curvilinear decoration but, unfortunately, too little survives to reconstruct the full decorative pattern. There is a shallow groove at the base of the neck, and there may have been a chain of ovals running around the body.

There are also sherds from a small, shallow bowl, 90mm diameter and perhaps 40mm deep (Fig 4.20, 7). This is perhaps better described as a ladle, as a remnant of a 'handle', 15mm in diameter, is attached immediately below the rim, although a non-joining fragment of handle is curved, suggesting this may have been a thin lug also attached to the lost lower body.

Pottery distribution

A majority of the larger pottery groups, totalling 70% of the site assemblage, came from Roundhouse B, and some of these groups comprise multiple sherds from single vessels, but with few joins. This material was concentrated in the ditches towards the east, nearest the presumed entrance, but the actual ditch terminals, where pottery tends to occur in the greatest quantity had been lost beneath a later ditch. A further 13% of site assemblage came from the pits, particularly pit 83, lying within this ring ditch (Table 4.3).

In contrast, Roundhouse A, which was similar in size to Roundhouse B, produced only 335g of pottery (2% of the assemblage), and Roundhouse C, a small ancillary building, produced only 10 small sherds.

Feature Groups	Sherds	% total	Weight (g)	% total	Scored ware (sherds)	% total	% of group
Roundhouse A	85	5%	335	2%	4	2%	5%
Roundhouse B	966	53%	9657	70%	166	89%	17%
Roundhouse B internal pits 85 & 83	316	17%	1787	13%	12	6%	4%
Roundhouse C	10	1%	41	0.3%	0	0	0
Northern enclosure ditch 92 & 95	143	8%	483	3%	0	0	0
Southern enclosure ditches 46 & 22/48	38	2%	120	1%	4	2%	11%
Slot 52	125	7%	544	4%	0	0	0
Other features	126	7%	917	7%	1	1%	1%
Totals	1809		13884		187	10%	

TABLE 4.3: SWINAWE BARN, QUANTIFICATION OF IRON AGE POTTERY

The rest of the assemblage comprised small groups of pottery from the boundary/enclosure ditches at the northern and southern ends of the site and from the scatter of pits and other features.

The assemblage from Roundhouse B

The fill near the southern ditch terminal, 9, produced 2.6kg of pottery, which comprises the partial remains of at least 15 vessels (Table 4.4). A large part of the assemblage is thick-walled shelly body sherds from both plain and scored ware jars. However, there were small numbers of sherds from several smaller bowls or jars. The ten rim sherds include six rounded, three flat-topped and one decorated with closely spaced fingertip impressions. Of particular interest are the sherds from a small bowl with impressed curvilinear decoration (Fig 4.20, 6). The group also includes several sherds from flat bases. The largest of these is 150mm diameter, while the base from a particularly thick-walled jar containing dense large shell is 110mm diameter.

From the southern arm of the ditch, 43, there is another substantial group, weighing 1.8kg. While this contains sherds from perhaps ten vessels, the majority of the sherds are from only two vessels. There is the entire flat base, 130mm diameter with a domed internal surface, 10-15mm thick, and the lower body of a thick-walled plain jar in a fabric containing dense large shell. In contrast, there is 80% of the rim and upper body of a small jar, 110mm diameter (Fig 4.20, 5). The rim is very uneven and irregular, varying from flat to rounded. The body is similarly rough and uneven and has lost part of the original surface, which was scored. The assemblage also includes small numbers of sherds from other vessels, including part of a large lug, and a rim with fingertip impressions.

The later cut west of the northern terminal, 112, produced 3kg of pottery comprising a wide range of vessels. Of the nine rims five have a range of finger-impressed decoration, and all of these are vessels with deep concave necks. The distinctive open bowl with a broad, grooved rim (Fig 4.20, 2) also came from this deposit. There are also numerous sherds from scored ware vessels. The fabrics are typically shelly, but there are also coarse sandy fabrics and a hard fabric contained grog and fine shell.

The fills of pit 83 within Roundhouse B produced nearly 2kg of pottery. The lower fill contained sherds from one or two large thick-walled, flat-based scored ware jars, although many of the sherds were heavily abraded leaving little or no trace of the scoring. There were also sherds from a small, shallow vessel with a remnant of either a handle or a lug, with may have been a ladle or spoon (Fig 4.20, 7). Nearly 1kg of pottery in the upper fill largely came from the body of a thick-walled, poorly preserved scored ware jar in a distinctive fabric containing shell and large rounded pellets of limestone, often 5-8mm in diameter.

Chronology

This group of pottery is a classic Midlands scored ware assemblage of the middle Iron Age, exhibiting all the characteristics of the type. Indeed, it is rare to see such a display of characteristics on the often poorly-preserved assemblages that come from so many Northamptonshire sites. The group includes a high proportion of rims with fingertip and fingernail decoration and a high proportion of shouldered jars with long concave necks. These characteristics are usually considered typical of earlier assemblages, 4th-3rd centuries BC (Jackson 2010, appendix 1, 147-150), but they also reappear in late assemblages. In this instance, the presence of a majority of darker coloured vessels, many without distinct necks, as well as vessels with smoothed surfaces and a curvilinear bowl with a footring base, are characteristics suggestive of a date between the 1st century BC and the early 1st century AD. This date is also consistent with the radiocarbon date obtained from Roundhouse B, which spans the late Iron Age to early Roman periods (Table 4.19). The combined evidence therefore indicates a period of occupation from the late 1st century BC into the early decades of the 1st century AD.

4. Middle to Late Iron Age (400 BC - 43 AD)

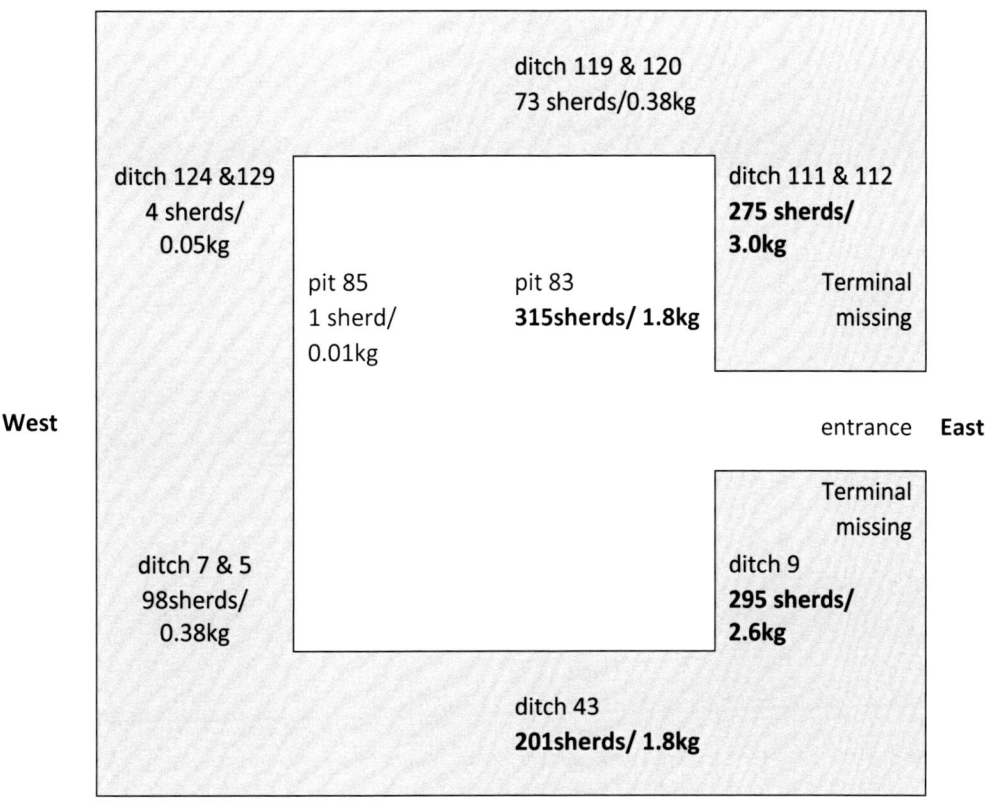

TABLE 4.4: SWINAWE BARN, POTTERY DISTRIBUTION IN ROUNDHOUSE B

Illustrated Iron Age pottery from Swinawe Barn (Fig 4.20)

1. Jar; with upright flattened rim decorated with alternating fingernail and fingertip impressions. Fabric 4, dark grey core and mottled grey and brown surfaces. Fill (121) of ditch 112, Roundhouse B
2. Open bowl; steep-walled flared rim is thickened and grooved; decorated below the rim with horizontal scoring on both surfaces. Fabric 2, grey-black with grey-black surfaces. Fill (121) of ditch 112, Roundhouse B
3. Rounded bowl, Fabric 1, grey core and brown to grey-brown surfaces. Fill (6) of ditch 7, Roundhouse B
4. Shouldered jar, rounded rim, Fabric 1, dark grey core and mottled grey-brown surfaces. Fill (121) of ditch 112, Roundhouse B
5. Scored ware bowl, Fabric 1, grey core with orange-brown surfaces. Fill (42) of ditch 43, Roundhouse B
6. Bowl with flattened rim, footring base, smoothed/burnished surface and curvilinear decoration. Fabric 2, dark grey core, grey to grey-brown surfaces. Fill (8) of ditch 9, Roundhouse B
7. Bowl with handle/lug, rounded rim. Fabric 2, grey core and orange-brown surfaces. Fill (99) of pit 83 within Roundhouse B

Thorpe Malsor

Two of the upper fills of a large ditch [18] produced small quantities of hand-built pottery, a total of only 18 sherds and some crumbs, weighing 42g.

Fill (80) contained 14 sherds and a mass of small crumbs, weighing 30g, from a single vessel. The sherds are thin walled, 4-5mm thick, with a light grey core and mottled grey to brown surfaces. The fabric had contained quantities of crushed shell, but this had been lost to leaching, leaving the sherds friable and crumbling. The majority of the sherds are plain body sherds, but a single angled sherd may be from a thickened inturned rim of unusual form.

From fill (16) there are four sherds and some crumbs, weighing 12g. Three of the sherds and the crumbs are very similar to the material from fill (80), but from a thicker-walled vessel, 7-8mm thick.

In addition, there is a single small sherd that is uniformly dark grey and containing only sparse small voids from the loss of fine shell inclusions. The uniform fabric,

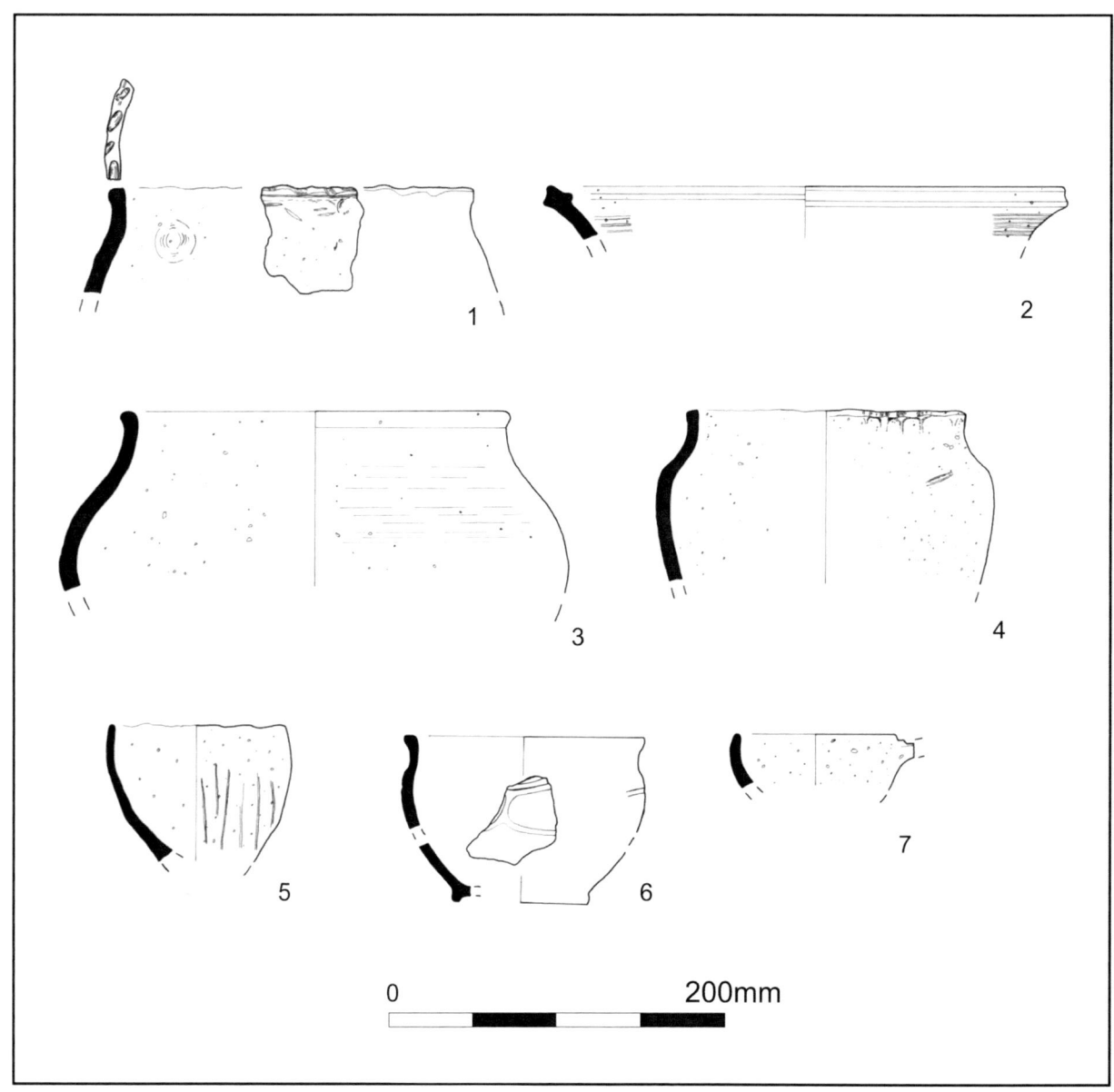

FIG 4.20: SWINAWE BARN, IRON AGE POTTERY (1-7) (SCALE 200MM)

the small diameter of the internal surface and a distinct vertical angle on the external surface suggest that this sherd is from a crucible, probably of the characteristic triangular form used in the Iron Age for copper alloy casting. If so, the state of the fabric suggests that it had fashioned as a crucible but had not been used.

This very small group offers few diagnostic features, but the general characteristics are broadly appropriate for the early-middle and middle to late Iron Age, anywhere between 400BC and the early decades of the 1st century AD.

Willows Nursery

There is a small assemblage of 39 sherds, weighing 221g, with an average sherd weight of 5.7g, which can be broadly dated to the middle/late Iron Age.

Most context groups comprise only two or three small sherds of hand-built pottery in shelly fabrics, with no diagnostic features. However, a small group of eight sherds from the fill (6) of ditch 8, included a simple rounded rim, while the fill (22) of pit 24, contained joining sherds from a plain jar with no defined neck and a flat-topped rim weighing 100g (nearly half of the total assemblage) (Fig 4.21). The vessel has a rim diameter of c 300mm, indicating that it was a large storage jar, with walls 10mm thick. The fabric is devoid of mineral inclusions, and is dark grey with an oxidised, brown, external surface. The form is typical of the later middle Iron Age. Two joining sherds from the fill (30) of gully 31 come from the concave neck of a thinner-walled and better finished, perhaps wheel-finished jar, in a fabric containing angular flint inclusions, with orange, oxidised surfaces.

4. MIDDLE TO LATE IRON AGE (400 BC - 43 AD)

FIG 4.21: WILLOWS NURSERY, RIM OF A LARGE STORAGE JAR FROM PIT 24

The assemblage may date to the late middle Iron Age (2nd to 1st centuries BC), with a possible continuation into the 1st century AD, but a definitive conclusion is hindered by the small size of the group.

Fired clay
by Pat Chapman

Seaton

Just five fragments of fired clay, weighing 33g, were recovered from four late Iron Age contexts at Seaton 2. They are irregular, composed of fine silty clay with occasional calcareous inclusions, ranging from soft pink to hard grey.

Swinawe Barn

An assemblage of 92 fragments of fired clay, weighing 964g, came from nine contexts, predominantly the Roundhouse B ring ditch (Table 4.5). The fabrics are typically sandy orange or reddish clay or fine orange clay, with flint and other calcareous inclusions, either very hard or slightly soft.

Two hard irregular black fragments, from Roundhouse B and pit 154, each have a wattle impression, 20mm and 13mm in diameter. A heavy curved wrinkled lump exposed to high temperatures, was also from Roundhouse B. Some fragments have quite smooth, though slightly uneven, surfaces on one side, perhaps from the surface of a superstructure.

These small fragments are scattered debris derived from various activities and structures, such as open hearths or closed oven, with a particular concentration in the ditch of Roundhouse B.

Faunal and environmental remains from the Iron Age settlements:

Human bone
by Sarah Inskip

An undated cremation burial was discovered during the watching brief in Field 33:01, to the south of Thorpe Road. The recovered bone weighs 102g (Table 4.6). Complete adult cremations weigh 1-3kg and juveniles around 0.5kg (Trotter and Hixon 1974), but as a proportion of the bone was most probably lost during machining the recovered quantity does not reflect the original deposition.

The bone consists entirely of white fragments, which indicates a pyre temperature exceeding 600°C (Brickley and McKinley 2004). Observable bones include skull and mandible in addition to phalanges, long bone fragments and the atlas. Fused phalanges indicate an individual over 14 years of age (Scheuer and Black 2000, 466), and some apophyseal facet remodelling and pronounced palmer flexor attachments on the phalanges, indicate a more mature adulthood. It is unlikely that more concise estimates can be found as the major indicators of age

Context/Feature	Feature group/type	No	Weight (g)	Comment
4/5	Roundhouse B	2	14	--
8/9	Roundhouse B	11	100	7 smooth brown flattish surfaces
73/75	Roundhouse A	11	21	--
76/78	Roundhouse A	1	4	--
114/119	Roundhouse B	3	140	1 c.70x60x20mm thick
121/112	Roundhouse B	36	370	80x40x30 rounded, heavy, smooth and wrinkled; wattle impression 20mm diameter
152/154	Pit	19	217	Wattle impression 13mm diam
152/154	Pit	8	70	--
153/154	Pit	1	28	--
Totals		92	964	

TABLE 4.5: SWINAWE BARN, QUANTIFICATION OF FIRED CLAY

Total	Weight by bone size				
weight	>10mm	>5mm	>2mm	>1mm	<1mm
102g	32g	31g	25g	8g	<1g

TABLE 4.6: THORPE BY WATER, QUANTIFICATION OF CREMATED BONE

(pubis, auricular surface and the occlusial surfaces of teeth) are not present. No information is observable for sex. There are no notable pathologies except for the minor apophyseal remodelling of bone.

The animal bone
by Matilda Holmes and Karen Deighton

Animal bone was recovered from several Iron Age settlements (Tables 4.7 and 4.8, after Deighton 2010), but only the assemblage from Swinawe Barn, Corby was sufficiently large to permit further analysis beyond the assessment stage. This assemblage has been fully recorded and analysed to provide an indication of the animal husbandry practices adopted at the settlement.

Methodology

The following methodology was followed in the analysis and recording of the animal bone assemblages of all periods recovered from settlements along the pipeline. Bones were identified using the author's reference collection. Due to anatomical similarities between sheep and goat, bones of this type were assigned to the category 'sheep/goat', unless a definite identification (Prummel and Frisch 1986; Payne 1985) could be made.

Bones that could not be identified to species were, where possible, categorised according to the relative size of the animal represented (small: rodent/rabbit size; medium: sheep/pig/dog size; or large: cattle/horse size). Ribs and skull fragments were not identified to species with the exception of the maxilla, zygomatic arch and occipital areas of the skull.

Tooth wear and eruption were recorded using guidelines from Grant (1982) and Silver (1969), as were bone fusion (Amorosi 1989; Silver 1969), metrical data (von den Driesch 1976), anatomy, side, zone (Serjeantson 1996) and any evidence of pathological changes, butchery (Lauwerier 1988) and working. The condition of bones was noted on a scale of 1-5, where 1 is perfectly preserved and 5 the bone is so badly degraded to be almost unrecognisable (Lyman 1994). Other taphonomic factors were also recorded, including the incidence of burning, gnawing, recent breakage and refitted fragments.

The animal bone recovered from bulk soil samples was also examined, but because of the highly fragmentary nature of such material a selective process was undertaken, whereby fragments were recorded only if they could be identified to species and/or element, or showed signs of taphonomic effects. All fragments were recorded, although articulated or associated fragments were entered as a count of 1, so they did not bias the relative frequency of species present. Details of such associated bone groups were recorded in a separate table. The bones of small species largely belonged to amphibians or rodents that have a tendency to burrow, so are probably intrusive.

Bones from all sites were in fair to good condition, although they were extremely fragmentary; nearly half of all assemblages consisted of fragments identifiable as 1 or fewer zones (Table 4.9). This is perhaps not surprising, given that a high proportion showed signs of fresh breakage from excavation from a stiff clay matrix, and a large number of fragments could be refitted, indicating that burial conditions rendered the bones friable, causing them to fragment.

Taphonomic factors affecting the bones were also similar from all sites. A high proportion showed signs of gnawing, mostly by dogs, but also rodents, which may explain the low numbers of butchery marks observed,

Site	Cattle (Bos)	Sheep/goat (Ovicaprid)	Pig (Sus)	Horse (Equus)	Small ungulate	Large ungulate
Seaton 2	18	33	1	1	7	3
Caldecott	2	1	-	-	-	1
Swinawe Barn	244	141	65	28	28	31
Thorpe Malsor	133	96	11	19	25	13
Total	397	271	77	48	60	48

TABLE 4.7: PRESENCE OF MAJOR DOMESTICATES AND UNGULATES FOR IRON AGE SITES

Site	Dog (Canis)	Domestic fowl	Bird	Small mammal	Amphibian	Water vole
Seaton 2	-	-	-	-	-	1
Thorpe Malsor	19	3	1	1	1	-
Total	21	3	3	1	3	1

TABLE 4.8: PRESENCE OF MINOR DOMESTICATES AND WILD SPECIES FOR IRON AGE SITES

given the obliteration of many of the ends of bones. Additionally, over five times as many loose teeth were recovered to those that remained within the mandibles, and this, coupled with the high number of gnawed bones indicates that many of the bones were not buried immediately after use. Instead, they were available for dogs to chew, and the mandible's connective tissue surrounding the teeth had enough time to decay, and the teeth to fall out of the jaw. Very few fragments showed signs of burning, indicating that they were not routinely exposed to fire, either through processing or as a means of disposal.

Swinawe Barn, Corby

The majority of animal bone was recorded from Roundhouse B, although numerous fragments also came from other ditch, pit, slot and posthole features (Table 4.10). All were dated to the period of the Iron Age settlement. Preservation was poor, but the identified assemblage was considerable and worth comparing with other sites in the region.

Carcass representation and butchery

All parts of the carcass were represented, although they were not present in proportions that would be expected if complete carcasses had been deposited. Statistically, the percentage similarity with a standard given for the likely recovery of elements from a complete carcass was very low, between 22% and 27% for cattle, sheep and pigs (Brain 1981). This implies that some redistribution of carcass parts occurred, and the elements deposited in the ring ditch of Roundhouse B were not the result of the processing and deposition of complete carcasses. When the proportions of parts of the carcass present are analysed (Table 4.11), it is evident that for all three of the major species, there are greater numbers of the higher meat bearing bones (skull and upper limbs for all species, and lower cattle limbs), and fewer of the lower meat bearing bones (lower limbs, vertebrae and feet).

As noted above, butchery marks were infrequent, the majority (81%) were made by a chopper-type implement to disarticulate, joint and fillet the carcass. The rest were knife marks often recorded around joints such as the hock (on astragali and calcanei) and shoulder (humerus) indicative of disarticulation, but also on metapodials, which is more consistent with removal of the skin. The majority were observed on cattle bones, but pig and sheep bones were also affected. Several vertebrae had been chopped bilaterally, ie one or both sides had been chopped through, leaving the body intact.

The evidence points to this being an assemblage of domestic origin, that is, one resulting from food preparation and mealtime refuse. Both in the nature of the bones present, coming from high meat bearing elements, and bearing butchery marks, as well as a relative absence of horn cores and sheep and pig lower limb bones, which are often removed from these species with the skin, which seems to have been taken elsewhere for processing.

Species representation and diet

Only a limited range of domestic species were recovered, which is surprising given the reasonable size of the assemblage, and suggests a real dearth of wild species from the diet of the inhabitants. Cattle were present in almost half the assemblage, then sheep and pigs. Horse and dog were also present, but in far smaller numbers (Table 4.12). Few samples were available, and again were devoid of wild species, with only two pig bones (phalange and maxilla fragment) recovered.

This site falls within the parameters recorded for the region by Hambleton in her review of Iron Age sites in Britain. The proportion of cattle is towards the higher end of those observed, but this is also consistent with the underlying boulder clay geology, which appears to have been related to the preferential keeping of cattle over sheep (Hambleton 1999, 46-48).

Condition	No of bones	Taphonomy	%
Excellent (1)	1	Butchery	9
Good (2)	122	Gnawing	23
Fair (3)	190	Fresh break	30
Poor (4)	35	Burning	3
Bad (5)	3	Refit	48 (184)
Total	351	loose teeth: mandibles*	55:13

* mandibles with 2 or more molars

TABLE 4.9: SWINAWE BARN, ANIMAL BONE CONDITION AND TAPHONOMY

Feature	No of bones
Ditch	91
Pit	74
Postholes	15
Ring Ditch A	19
Ring Ditch B	874
Ring Ditch C	1
Slot	32
Tree Hole	5
Total	1111

TABLE 4.10: SWINAWE BARN, NUMBER OF IDENTIFIED BONES FRAGMENTS

Element	Cattle	Sheep	Pig
Horn Core	6	1	--
Occipitale	3	3	1
Zygomaticus	2	--	2
Mandible	11	3	5
Scapula	14	3	6
Humerus P	3	--	--
Humerus D	6	3	2
Radius P	10	3	6
Radius D	7	--	--
Ulna	5	2	3
3rd Carpal	1	--	--
Pelvis	8	3	2
Femur P	6	2	1
Femur D	4	3	2
Tibia P	8	4	3
Tibia D	11	6	4
Calcaneum	6	1	2
Metatarsal D	3	1	--
Metacarpal D	6	--	1
Metacarpal P	8	2	1
Metatarsal P	9	--	1
1st phalange	2	1	1
2nd phalange	3	--	1
3rd Phalange	1	--	--
Atlas	2	--	--
Axis	2	2	1
Cervical	--	3	--
Thoracic	2	4	--
Lumber	--	7	--
Sacrum	1	1	2
Caudal	4	--	--
Total	154	58	47

TABLE 4.11: SWINAWE BARN, REPRESENTATION OF THE MAIN DOMESTICATES

Species	No	%
Cattle	404	49
Sheep/ Goat	207	26
Sheep	4	-
Goat	1	-
Pig	150	18
Horse	58	7
Dog	2	-
Total Identified	826	-
Unidentified Mammal	639	-
Large Mammal	704	-
Medium Mammal	528	-
Total	2697	

TABLE 4.12: SWINAWE BARN, ANIMAL BONE SPECIES REPRESENTATION (NISP)

the tooth wear data was slightly different to this, coming from animals at stages D, F and G, those at stages D and F were from juvenile animals presumably slaughtered for meat. This contrast between fusion and tooth wear data may be due to the small sample size, or poor preservation of more porous bones from younger animals, combined with the destruction of the ends of the bones by dogs. Pigs had generally not reached maturity, which is a common strategy for culling animals for meat which are of limited use for secondary products.

All horse bones were fused, indicating that they were important for transport or draught purposes.

Discussion

The animal economy of the Iron Age settlement at Swinawe Barn is consistent with findings of other sites in the region, one based on cattle husbandry, and the keeping of cattle, sheep and pigs for meat production, although a number of older cattle and sheep implied their use for breeding or small-scale secondary products such as traction and wool production. These patterns are consistent with a subsistence-based economy (Bogaard 2005, 187).

Charred plant remains
by Val Fryer

Excavations along the route of the pipeline investigated nineteen sites of all periods, from which 115 bulk soil samples were taken for the retrieval of plant macrofossils and other ecofacts. Of this number, 52 samples were taken from Iron Age contexts at five sites. The aim of the sampling strategy was to recover palaeo-environmental information that could be used to assist in the modelling

Animal husbandry

Most ageing data came from the fusion of long bones. The majority of cattle had been culled at prime meat age, before reaching 3 years of age. This was reflected by the tooth wear data, which came from mandibles at wear stages D/E, E and two at G (after Hambleton 1999). The remainder were probably kept alive for secondary production such as milk, traction or breeding. The fusion data indicate that a high proportion of the sheep/goat population were mature at death, however,

4. Middle to Late Iron Age (400 BC - 43 AD)

of past landscapes, so as to gain a better understanding of prehistoric land use and settlement activities. All of the bulk samples were processed by NA and the flots were collected in a 300 micron mesh sieve. The dried flots were scanned under a binocular microscope, at magnifications of up to x16, and those that contained plant macrofossils were sent for assessment.

The plant macrofossils and other remains from Swinawe Barn was the only Iron Age site to produce viable results. All plant remains were charred. Modern contaminants, including fibrous roots, chaff, seeds and arthropod remains, were present throughout. Nomenclature within the tables follows Stace (1997).

Swinawe Barn

Thirty-eight samples were taken from fills within three ring ditches, from pit and ditch fills and from a small number of other contexts.

The assemblages from Roundhouse A (Table 4.13) are all very small (ie considerably less than 0.1 litre in volume), with charcoal/charred wood fragments being the principal component throughout. Only three cereal grains are recorded along with a very low density of other remains.

In contrast, although still small, the assemblages from the fills within Roundhouse B (Table 4.14) contain cereals, seeds, nut shell/fruit stone fragments and high densities of charcoal/charred wood, particularly from the sections to the east, ditches [9] and [112]. The composition of these assemblages is consistent with their being derived from small quantities of domestic refuse. It was Roundhouse B that also produced other domestic debris, including quantities of pottery and the majority of the animal bone from the site.

Only four samples were taken from the much smaller structure, Roundhouse C (Table 4.15) and of these, only one (context 142) contains material of note, namely cereal grains/chaff, a moderate density of charcoal/charred wood and a high density of minute pellets of burnt or fired clay. The origin of this material is currently unclear, although the composition of the assemblage would be consistent with a small deposit of hearth waste.

Sample	7	10	11	12	13
Context	49	56	67	69	71
Feature	50	58	68	70	72
Cereals					
Triticum sp. (grains)	x	-	-	-	-
Cereal indet. (grains)	-	-	-	x	-
Other plant macrofossils					
Charcoal <2mm	xxx	xxx	xx	xxxx	xxx
Charcoal >10mm	-	-	-	x	-
Volume of flot (litres)	<0.1	<0.1	<0.1	<0.1	<0.1
% flot sorted	100%	100%	100%	100%	100%

Sample	14	15	16	17	20
Context	73	76	79	61	86
Feature	75	78	81	63	18
Cereals					
Cereal indet. (grains)	-	-	-	x	-
Other plant macrofossils					
Charcoal <2mm	xx	xx	xx	xx	xx
Charcoal >10mm	x	-	-	-	x
Volume of flot (litres)	<0.1	<0.1	<0.1	<0.1	<0.1
% flot sorted	100%	100%	100%	100%	100%

Key to Table
x = 1 – 10; xx = 11 – 50; xxx = 51 – 100 specimens and xxxx = 100+ specimens

TABLE 4.13: SWINAWE BARN, CHARRED PLANT REMAINS, ROUNDHOUSE A

Sample	1	19	23	24
Context	4	42	121	122
Feature	5	43	112	124
Cereals				
Hordeum sp. (grains)	-	-	xcf	-
Triticum sp. (grains)	-	-	x	-
Cereal indet. (grains)	x	x	xx	-
Herbs				
Bromus sp.	-	-	x	-
Small Poaceae indet.	-	x	x	-
Rumex sp.	-	-	x	-
Vicia/Lathyrus sp.	-	-	xcf	-
Wetland plants				
Carex sp.	x	-	-	-
Montia fontana L.	-	-	x	-
Tree/shrub macrofossils				
Corylus avellana L.			x	
Other plant macrofossils				
Charcoal <2mm	xxxx	xxxx	xxxx	xx
Charcoal >2mm	xxxx	xxx	xxx	xx
Charcoal >5mm	-	x	xx	xx
Charcoal >10mm	-	xx	xx	-
Charred root/stem	x	x	x	-
Indet.fruit stone/nut shell frag.	-	x	x	-
Indet.thorn (*Rosa* type)	-	x	-	-
Volume of flot (litres)	<0.1	<0.1	<0.1	<0.1
% flot sorted	100%	100%	100%	100%

Sample	25	26	35	
Context	126	114	08	
Feature	129	119	09	
Cereals				
Hordeum sp. (grains)	-	-	x	
Cereal indet. (grains)	-	x	x	
Herbs				
Polygonum aviculare L.	-	x	-	
Polygonaceae indet.	-	x	-	
Other plant macrofossils				
Charcoal <2mm	xxx	xxxx	xxxx	
Charcoal >10mm	x	xx	xx	
Volume of flot (litres)	<0.1	<0.1	<0.1	
% flot sorted	100%	100%	100%	

TABLE 4.14: SWINAWE BARN, CHARRED PLANT REMAINS, ROUNDHOUSE B

Of the four pit fill assemblages (Table 4.16), only that from pit 83 is of possible note as it contains a moderate density of cereal grains, weed seeds and charcoal/charred wood fragments. As with the above material from Roundhouse B, it would appear most likely that these remains are derived from a small, discrete deposit of domestic refuse. The other pit assemblages contain little, other than charcoal/charred wood fragments.

The six Iron Age ditch assemblages (Table 4.17) are extremely sparse although two, from ditches 19 and 31, do contain individual cereal grains/chaff elements. It would appear most likely that all the remains within the ditch assemblages are derived from scattered or wind-blown refuse, much of which was probably accidentally incorporated within the fills of the features.

The assemblages from four postholes and the fill of slot 52 are all small, and almost entirely composed of charcoal/charred wood fragments. It would appear most likely that these remains were accidentally included within the fills of these features, like the ditch assemblages.

4. MIDDLE TO LATE IRON AGE (400 BC - 43 AD)

Sample	28	29	30	31
Context	139	142	144	150
Feature	141	143	146	151
Cereals				
Triticum sp.(rachis internode)	-	x	-	-
Cereal indet. (grains)	-	x	-	-
Other plant macrofossils				
Charcoal <2mm	x	xx	x	x
Charcoal >2mm	x	xx	-	x
Charcoal >5mm	x	x	-	-
Volume of flot (litres)	<0.1	<0.1	<0.1	<0.1
% flot sorted	100%	100%	100%	100%

TABLE 4.15: SWINAWE BARN, CHARRED PLANT REMAINS, ROUNDHOUSE C

Sample	2	9	27	38
Context	15	65	99	163
Feature	16	66	83	165
Cereals				
Avena sp. (grains)	-	-	xcf	-
Hordeum sp. (grains)	-	-	xx	-
H. vulgare L.(grains)	-	-	x	-
Triticum sp. (grains)	x	-	-	-
(glume bases)	x	-	-	-
Cereal indet. (grains)	-	-	xx	-
Herbs				
Bromus sp.	-	-	x	-
Small Poaceae indet.	-	-	xx	-
Polygonaceae indet.	-	-	x	-
Ranunculus sp.	-	-	xcf	-
Rumex sp.	x	-	x	-
Wetland plants				
Carex sp.	-	-	xcf	-
Tree/shrub macrofossils				
Prunus domestica ssp. *insititia* (L.) Bonnier & Layens	-	-	x	-
Other plant macrofossils				
Charcoal <2mm	xxxx	x	xxxx	xxx
Charcoal >2mm	xxxx	-	xxxx	x
Charcoal >5mm	xx	-	xx	x
Charcoal >10mm	xx	-	xx	xx
Charred root/stem	-	-	xx	x
Indet.fruit stone/nut shell frag.	-	-	x	-
Indet.seeds	-	-	x	-
Volume of flot (litres)	<0.1	<0.1	0.1	<0.1
% flot sorted	100%	100%	100%	100%

TABLE 4.16: SWINAWE BARN, CHARRED PLANT REMAINS FROM PITS

Cereal grains/chaff, seeds of common weeds and wetland plants, and tree/shrub macrofossils were present, mostly at a low density, within fourteen of the assemblages studied. Preservation was variable; the grains/seeds within some assemblages were severely puffed and distorted, probably as a result of combustion at very high temperatures, whilst other remains were very well preserved.

Barley (*Hordeum* sp), wheat (*Triticum* sp) and oat (*Avena* sp) grains were recorded, with barley and wheat occurring most frequently. The wheat grains were mostly of an

Sample	3	4	21	22	32	33	34
Context	18	30	91	103	34	133	135
Feature	19	31	92	104	28	134	138
Cereals							
Triticum sp. (grains)	x	x	-	x	-	-	-
T. aestivum/compactum type (rachis node)	x	-	-	-	-	-	-
Cereal indet. (grains)	x		-	x	-	-	-
Other plant macrofossils							
Charcoal <2mm	x	xx	xx	x	x	x	xx
Charcoal >2mm	-	x	-	-	-	-	x
Charcoal >5mm	-	-	-	-	-	-	x
Indet.seeds	-	-	-	-	-	-	x
Volume of flot (litres)	<0.1	<0.1	<0.1	<0.1	<0.1	<0.1	<0.1
% flot sorted	100%	100%	100%	100%	100%	100%	100%

TABLE 4.17: SWINAWE BARN, CHARRED PLANT REMAINS FROM DITCHES

elongated 'drop' form typical of emmer (*T. dicoccum*) or spelt (*T. spelta*), although a small number of more rounded hexaploid type forms were also noted. Spelt chaff was predominant but bread wheat (*T. aestivum/compactum*) type rachis nodes were also recovered from ditch 19. Asymmetrical lateral grains of six-row barley (*H. vulgare*) were noted within a single sample from pit 83. Oat grains occurred infrequently and most were probably present as contaminants of the main barley/wheat crops.

Weed seeds were generally scarce, with most occurring as single specimens within an assemblage. Seeds of common segetal weeds were predominant, with taxa noted including broom (*Bromus* sp), grass (Poaceae), knotgrass (*Polygonum aviculare*), dock (*Rumex* sp) and vetch/vetchling (*Vicia/Lathyrus* sp). Nutlets/fruits of wetland plants, namely sedge (*Carex* sp) and water chickweed (*Montia fontana*) were also recorded along with occasional fragments of hazel (*Corylus avellana*) nutshell and damson/bullace (*Prunus domestica* ssp *insititia*) type fruit stones. Charcoal/charred wood fragments were present and were frequently the major component of the assemblage.

Shells of terrestrial and freshwater obligate molluscs were present with a number of the assemblages studied (not tabulated). However, as most retained delicate surface structures and excellent coloration, it was considered most likely that all were intrusive within the contexts from which the samples were taken.

Radiocarbon dating

A fragment of animal bone from the fill (8) of ring ditch segment 9 (Roundhouse B) at Swinawe Barn has returned a date in the late Iron Age/early Roman period (40 Cal BC-80 Cal AD, 95% confidence, 1980+/-30 BP, Beta-293241; Table 4.18).

Lab no. sample no.	Origin of sample	Sample details	13C/12C ratio	Conventional radiocarbon age BP	Cal BC/AD 68% confidence 95% confidence
Beta-293241 SWB08/8	Fill 8, gully 9	Animal bone	-21.6	1980+/- 30	*Cal BC 10-Cal AD 60* **Cal BC 40-Cal AD 80**

Radiocarbon dating laboratory: Beta Analytic, Florida, Miami, USA
Method of analysis: AMS-standard delivery
Material pre-treatment: Bone carbonate extraction (cremated human bone)
Calibration: INTCAL04 (*Radiocarbon*, 2004, **46/3**)

TABLE 4.18: SWINAWE BARN, RADIOCARBON DATING FOR ROUNDHOUSE B

5. Roman Settlement (AD43 - AD450)

Nine sites along the pipeline produced settlement activity dated to the Roman period, with some having origins in the late Iron Age.

Late Roman settlement at Glaston

To the west of Glaston, Rutland, excavation revealed parts of a Roman ditch system that was probably associated with a settlement lying to the south of the A47 Uppingham Road, near Wellesley Spinney, known from cropmarks on aerial photographs and from the geophysical survey (Butler 2007, figs 32-33) (NGR: SK 8929 0022; Fig 5.1). The small pottery assemblage includes Lower Nene Valley colour coat dated to the 4th century AD.

On the slope to the south of the A47 the underlying geology comprises beds of Northampton Sand, with fine sands and clays, with low-grade ironstone, of the Grantham Formation (Middle Jurassic) on the slope to the north of the road (BGS 1978), where there was an Anglo-Saxon cremation cemetery and a single Roman ditch.

Roman settlement

The Roman settlement probably comprised several large, at least partly conjoining, sub-rectangular enclosures, a ladder settlement perhaps, extending over an area of *c.*8 hectares, but the full plan has not been defined. It lies on a gentle, south-facing slope above a spring, located in Wellesley Spinney, which feeds a stream that flows to the south in a small tributary valley. The excavated ditches lay near the top of the slope at *c.*117m aOD (NGR: SK 8919 0028, Fig 5.1).

The most substantial of the excavated ditches was a broad, shallow ditch, 10, aligned east to west, 3.0m wide by 0.32m deep, with steep concave sides and a wide flat base. The primary fill was light brown silt (9) and the upper fill was mid red-brown silt (8). A small quantity of late Roman pottery and the additional presence of Anglo-Saxon pottery, suggests that the ditch was still open in the sub-Roman period (see Fig 6.9, 6). Ditch 5, to the immediate south of ditch 10, was 0.8m wide by 0.1m deep, but the fill of orange-brown silty clay (4), contained no dateable finds.

Approximately 40m to the north of ditch 10, there was the terminal of a small, shallow ditch, 7, 1.1m wide by 0.16m deep, from which sherds of Roman pottery were recovered.

Ditch 34

To the north of the Anglo-Saxon cemetery, in the grounds of Bisbrooke Hall, a ditch crossed the pipeline easement on level ground at *c.*128m aOD (NGR: SK 8903 0057; Fig 5.1). Ditch 34 was 0.75m wide by 0.19m deep. The fill of orange-brown silty clay (33) with frequent ironstone inclusions, contained Roman pottery dated to the late 4th century, animal bone and an iron nail.

Roman activity near Seaton

Situated near the foot of a south-facing slope, at *c.*72m aOD, overlooking a small tributary valley on the north side of the Welland Valley below an Iron Age site (Seaton, Chapter 4), there was an irregular shallow ditch and two pits (NGR: SP 8878 9823; Fig 5.2). The small pottery assemblage of eight sherds indicates an early date, the late 1st to 2nd centuries AD.

The ditch, 13, aligned east to west, was 1.3-2.1m wide and up to 0.44m deep. The primary fill of dark grey, charcoal-flecked silty clay (12), was overlain by a deposit of light grey-brown clayey silt (11) that contained several burnt cobbles. The upper fill was black silty clay (10), containing charcoal, burnt pebbles and pottery.

Approximately 5m to the north of the ditch were two shallow, poorly defined pits, 7 and 9. Pit 7 was 1.05m long by 0.74m wide and 0.20m deep; while pit 9 was 0.6m in diameter by 0.08m deep. Both pits were burnt around the edges and contained burnt pebbles and pottery.

A Roman enclosure and cremation burials near Gretton

This site was situated close to the edge of the floodplain on the south bank of the River Welland, to the south of Rockingham Road and 1.2km to the north-east of Rockingham (NGR: SP 8767 9250; Fig 5.3). The site lay at *c.*54m aOD and the underlying geology is Lower Lias Clay (BGS 1976).

Evaluation of the site (Clarke 2007b) had revealed an archaeological horizon containing medieval pottery, and geophysical survey and cropmarks suggested that there may be a deserted medieval village in this location, but no evidence for this was found within the easement.

The Roman enclosure

At the northern end of the site there was a silted-up stream bed, a palaeochannel, approximately 7m wide. The topography of the slope above the site suggests that it had been a small tributary stream of the River Welland and had probably been fed by a spring on the slope above. Old maps show that this stream had run northwards along a field boundary, since removed.

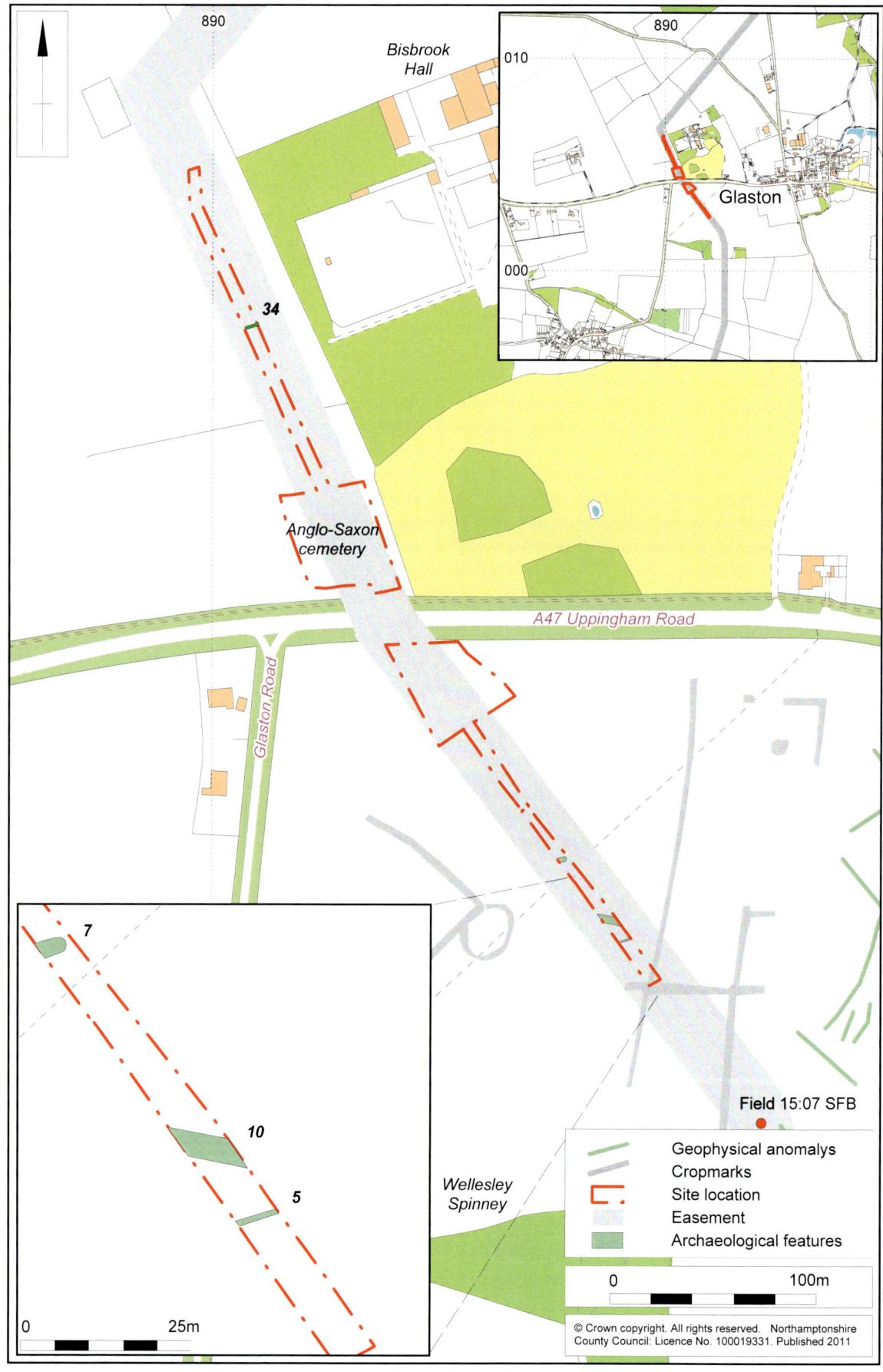

Fig 5.1: Glaston, plan of Roman ditch system

5. Roman Settlement (AD43 - AD450)

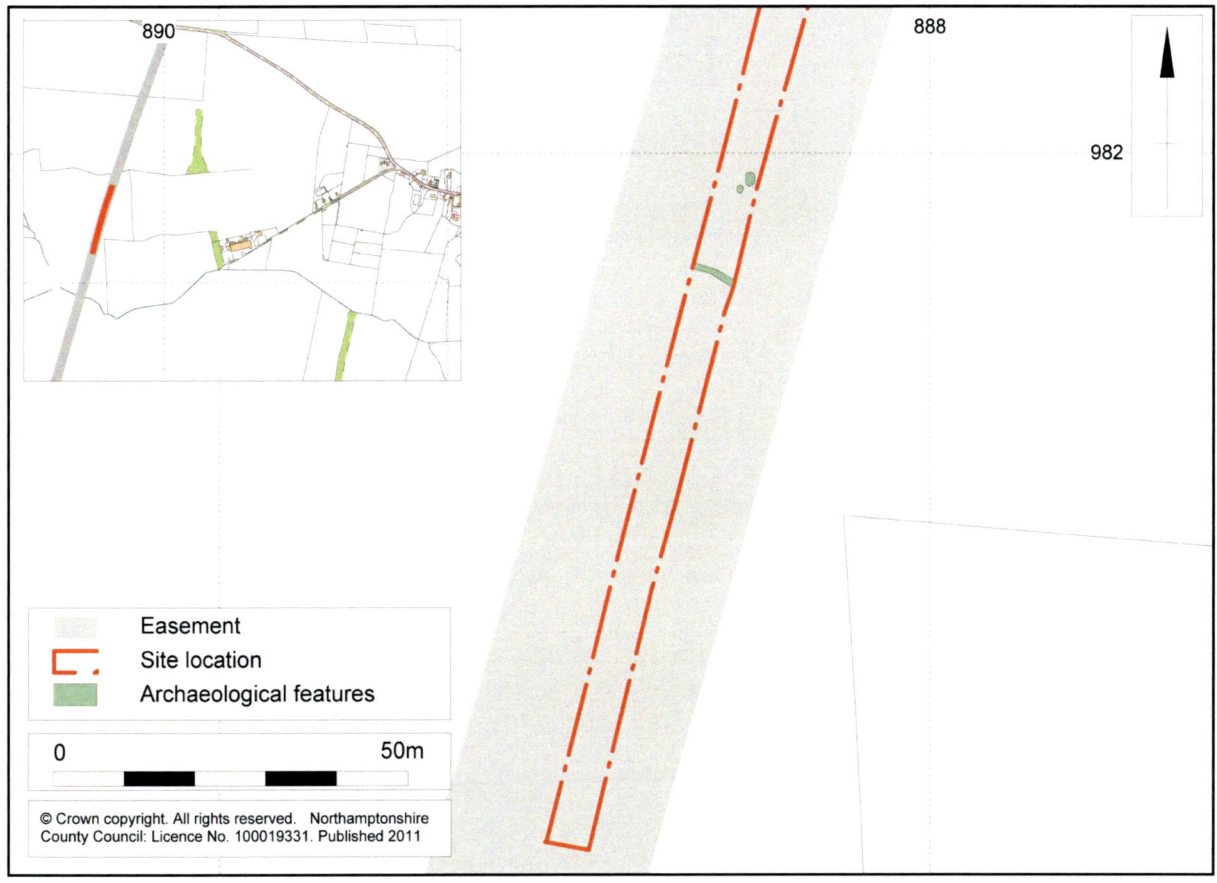

Fig 5.2: Seaton, plan of Roman features

The geophysical survey indicated the presence of a small ditched enclosure, 30m wide, but only the ditch on the western side was located in excavation (Butler 2007, figs 50-51). Ditch 10 was 1.5m wide and up to 0.22m deep, with a fill of mottled mid to dark red-brown sandy clay. The shallowness of the surviving ditch may suggest that the enclosure has been almost ploughed away.

Five metres to the south, ditch 5 was on a slightly different alignment, but of similar dimensions and fill. Roman pottery comprising 16 sherds dating from the 2nd to 4th centuries AD was recovered from both ditches.

Roman cremation burials

Single cremation burials were identified: burial 14 just south of ditch 5 and burial 8, 5m north of ditch 10. The cremation deposits were in small pits, *c*.0.6m in diameter and up to 0.18m deep. Burial deposit 14 comprised grey-black charcoal-rich soil containing less than 1g of bone, indicating that the deposit had been heavily truncated. There were some 70 iron nails in the deposit, but not hobnails from a shoe or boot. Burial 8 had a similar soil matrix containing 107g of bone, indicating that it was less severely truncated, and 13 iron nails. In both instances it would appear that much of the deposit comprised pyre debris, with token bone deposits placed above this. A few small sherds of Roman pottery recovered from the soil deposits as residual finds are dated to the 2nd century AD.

A further cremation burial, Burial 55.01, was recovered to the north of the palaeochannel during the watching brief (Fig 5.3). This too was in a shallow pit, 0.5m in diameter and 0.15m deep, with a fill of pyre debris including 40g of cremated bone.

Examination of the geophysical survey for this area (Butler 2007, figs 50-51), indicates the presence of a scatter of small pits across the area to the east of the palaeochannel, one of which coincides with the cremation burial located in the watching brief. There is also a sparser scatter to the west as well, in and around the ditched enclosure. It is likely, therefore, that the three excavated burials are part of a larger more extensive cremation cemetery, but with the burials apparently quite widely spaced, with several metres between each deposit.

This cemetery perhaps served a nearby farmstead or settlement. A Roman date has been suggested on the basis of the residual pottery and the absence of any Anglo-Saxon grave goods, but the pottery dated to the 2nd century AD does provide only a *terminus post-quem*, and a later date, perhaps even Anglo-Saxon, is possible.

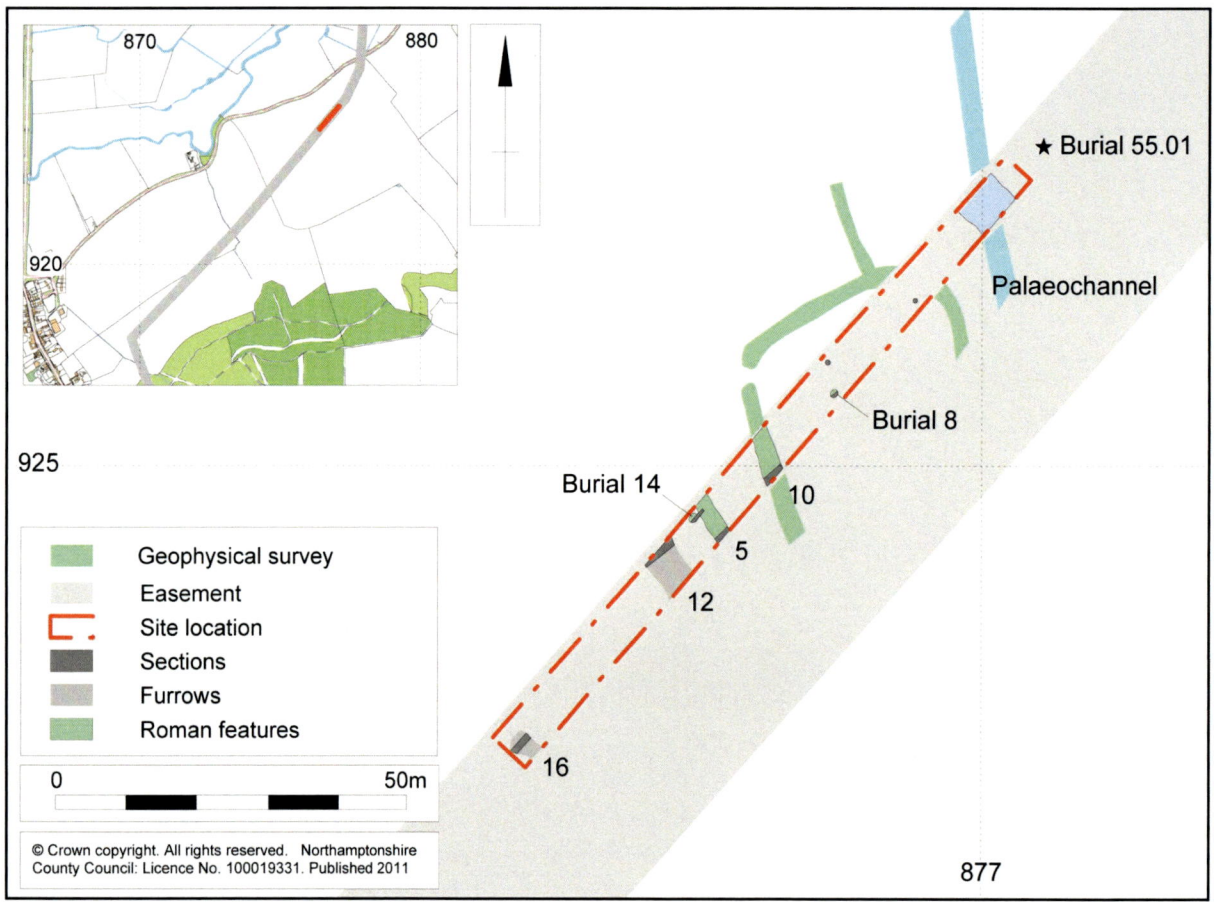

Fig 5.3: Gretton Road, plan of Roman features

A Roman pit at Swinawe Barn, Corby

At the northern end of the Iron Age enclosure, ditch 92 was cut by a large, sub-angular pit, 134, 3.6m in diameter and 0.84m deep (see Fig 4.9). It was largely filled with a homogeneous mid grey-brown silty clay (133), from which Roman grog-tempered ware and greyware pottery dating to the 2nd century AD were recovered (T Hylton pers comm), and animal bone. The upper fill was mid red-brown silty clay (132). Roman pottery was also recovered from one of the medieval furrows.

Roman enclosures at Rushton

This site was situated on the north bank of the River Ise, at c.89m aOD, approximately 0.5km to the north-east of the village of Rushton (NGR: SP 8476 8308; Fig 5.4). The small pottery assemblage of 40 sherds suggests a date in the late 1st to 2nd centuries.

The ground slopes gently to the south-east, levelling off at the foot of the slope onto the alluvial deposits of the floodplain. The geology on the upper slope is Northampton Sand and Ironstone, and on the lower slope Upper Lias Clay (BGS 1976).

Geophysical survey had detected a complex of enclosure and boundary ditches within the easement and in an evaluated area to the north of the easement (Butler 2007, figs 70-71). A Roman villa is known to lie to the west, and these settlement remains may be associated with the villa estate and a possible Iron Age predecessor. A pair of tweezers and part of a pin provide may suggest that an Anglo-Saxon settlement lies nearby.

The enclosure: ditches 12 and 21

The enclosure was roughly sub-rectangular in plan and measured 21m north-west to south-east and c.16m north-east to south-west. The south-eastern arm of the enclosure, ditch 21, was 2.6m wide by 0.8m deep (Fig 5.5, Section 5). The primary fill (20), which had largely accumulated against the northern slope and base, was light yellow-brown mottled silty clay (20) with occasional ironstone pebbles and charcoal flecks. This deposit probably derived in part from a possible interior bank. The secondary fill was dark brown silty clay (19) containing occasional charcoal flecks, animal bone including several large cattle bones and Roman pottery. The upper fill was light brown clay (18). The opposing north-western arm, ditch 12, was less substantial, 1.3m wide by 0.5m deep.

5. ROMAN SETTLEMENT (AD43 - AD450)

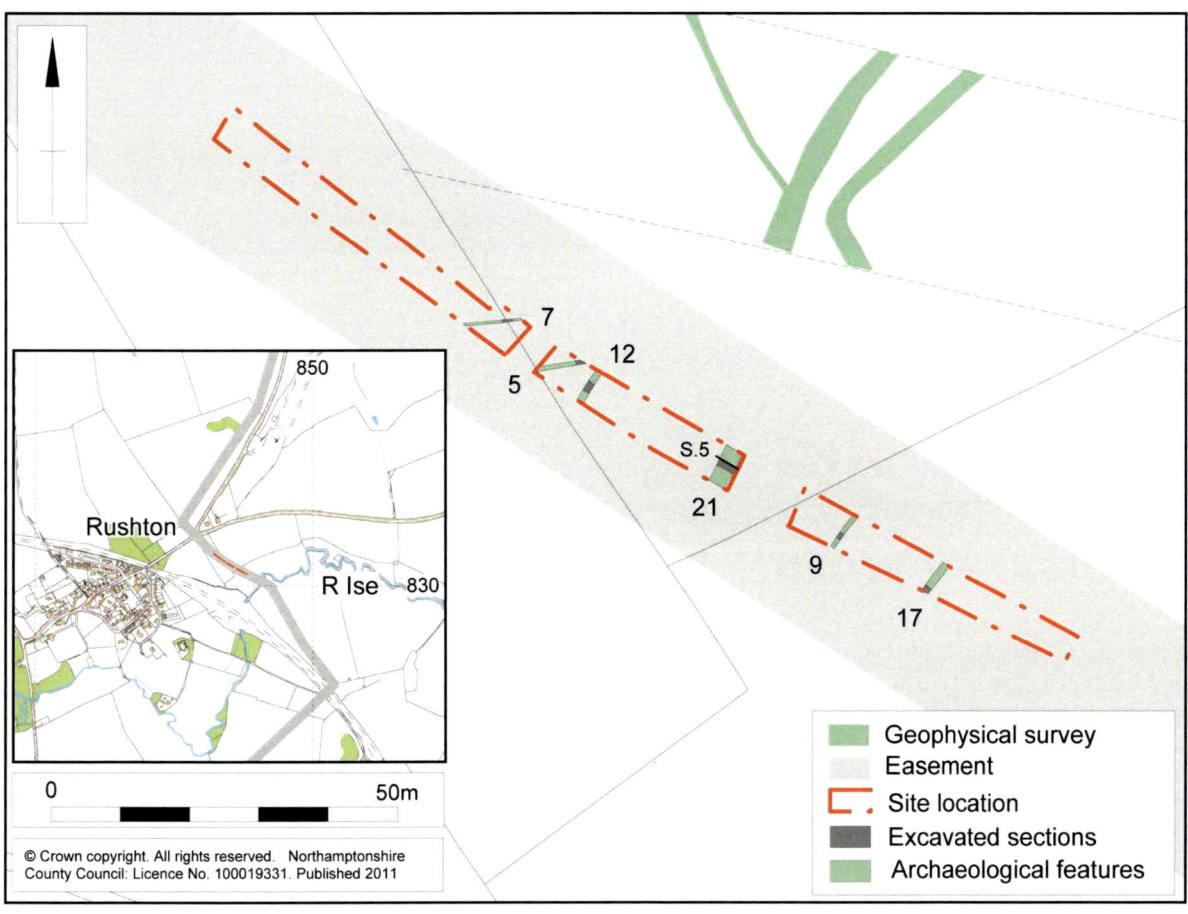

Fig 5.4: Rushton, plan of Roman ditch system

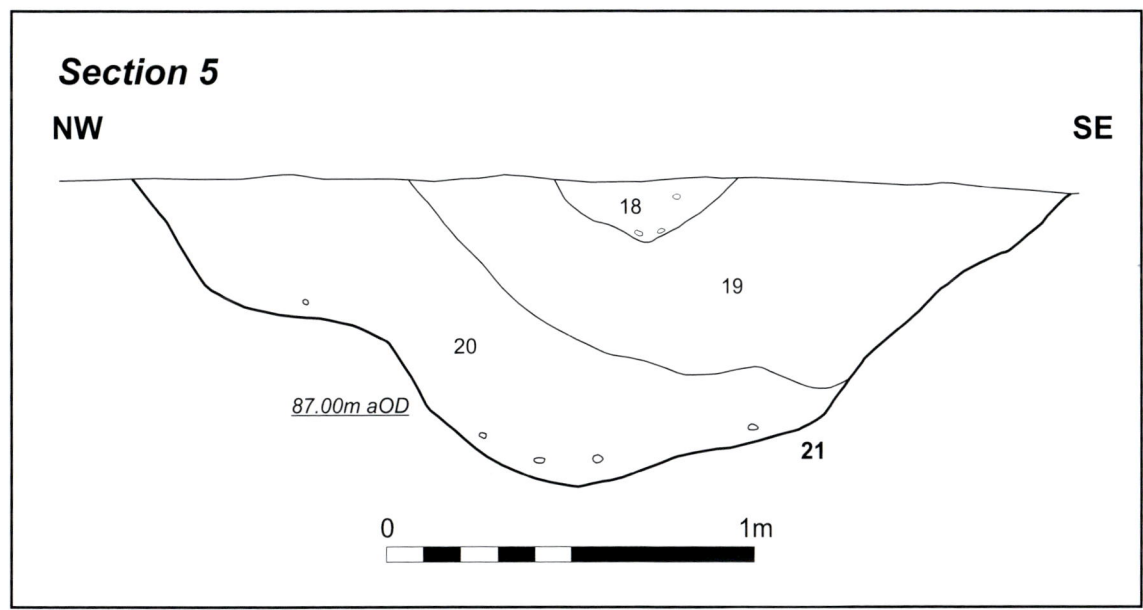

Fig 5.5: Rushton, Section of ditch 21

The droveway: gullies 5 and 7

From the geophysical survey, parallel ditches, perhaps flanking a droveway, lay to the north of the enclosure, running west to east and turning to the north-east at the northern corner of the enclosure. Within the easement, the two parallel gullies, 5 and 7, were spaced 6.5m apart, and measured 0.8m wide by 0.26m deep, with fills of mid brown silty clay.

Gullies 9 and 17

On the alluvium at the edge of the floodplain, at the southern end of the site, two parallel gullies, 9 and 17, both 0.4m wide by 0.3m deep, were aligned north-east to south-west. Iron Age pottery, probably residual, and a fragment of copper alloy rod, possibly Anglo-Saxon in date, were recovered from gully 9, and Roman pottery and animal bone came from gully 17.

A Roman ditch system at Violet Lane

Approximately 2km to the south of Rushton, three small ditches roughly followed the contours of a steep, south-facing slope, between 90.8m and 89.0m aOD, overlooking Slade Brook to the west of Violet Lane (NGR: SP 8406 8076; Fig 5.6). They may be part of a small settlement or field boundary ditches.

The geology on the upper slope is Northampton Sand and Ironstone, on the lower slope Upper Lias Clay (BGS 1976); deposits of colluvium (hill-wash) were encountered near the foot of the slope.

The northernmost ditch, 6, had a steep-sided, V-shaped profile, 1.1m wide by 0.62m deep, with a fill of mottled grey silty clay (5) overlain by mid grey-brown silty clay (4). Approximately 10m to the south, ditch 8, 0.6m wide by 0.20m deep, had steep sides and a flat base. The fill of mid grey-brown silty clay (7) contained Roman pottery.

Ditch 19, a further 13m downslope, had a steep-sided, V-shaped profile, *c* 0.8m wide and 0.46m deep (Fig 5.7). A recut ditch, 15, which truncated the southern edge of ditch 19, was both wider and deeper, 1.3m wide by 0.65m deep. Roman pottery was recovered from the upper fill of the recut ditch.

Roman settlement near Thorpe Malsor

The Roman settlement near Thorpe Malsor was situated at the edge of a plateau of high ground at *c.*99m aOD, approximately 50m south of Iron Age ditches on the lower slope (Thorpe Malsor, Chapter 4). Within the easement, the geophysical survey shows a T-shaped arrangement of two large ditches and a cluster of large pits (Butler 2007, figs 78-79), all of which were investigated by excavation

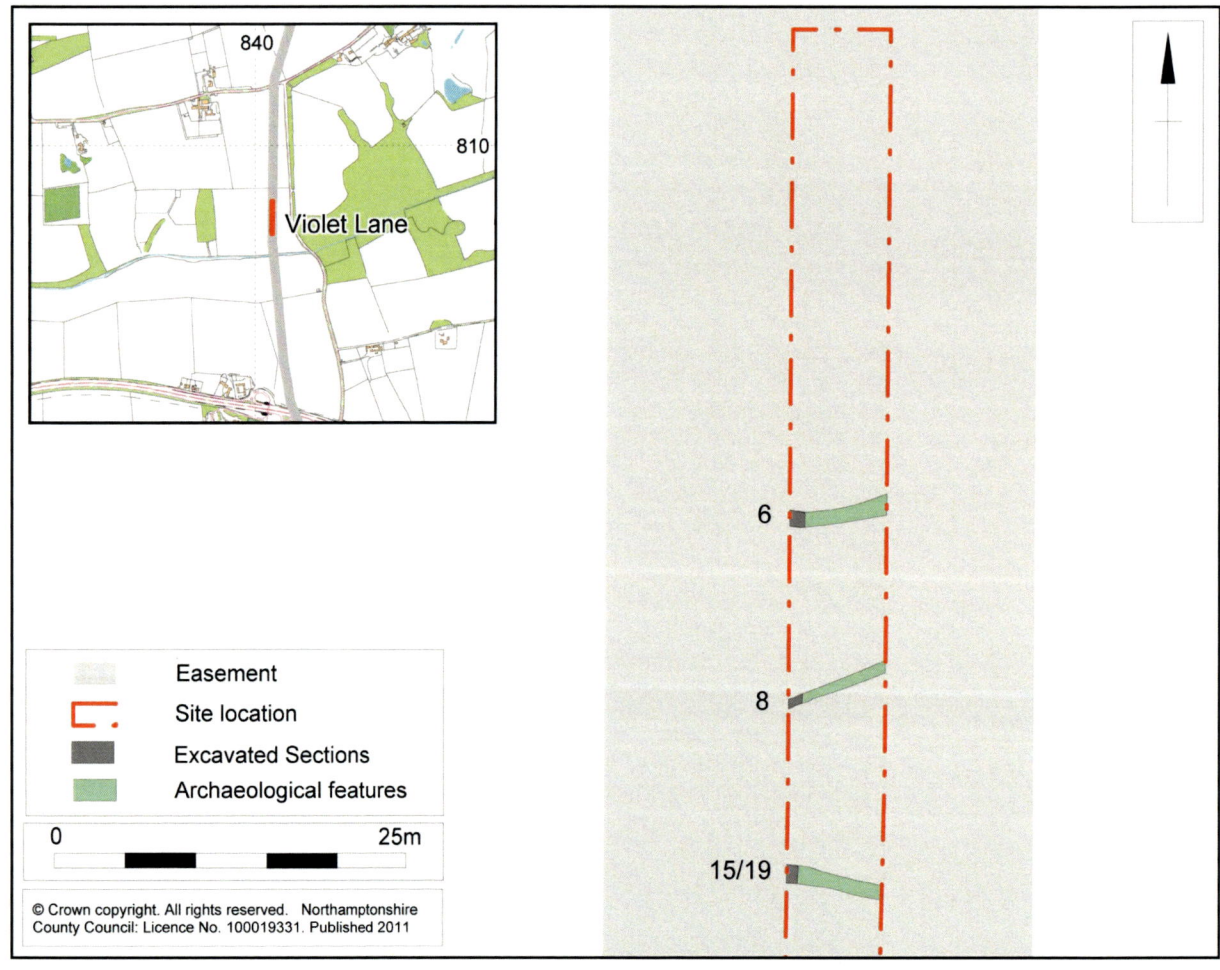

Fig 5.6: Violet Lane, plan of Roman ditch system

5. Roman Settlement (AD43 - AD450)

Fig 5.7: Violet Lane, Roman ditches 15 and 19, looking east (Scale 1m)

(NGR: SP 8404 7913; Figs 5.8 and 5.9). The further extent of the settlement is unknown.

The site produced a substantial assemblage of pottery, 4,200 sherds, as well as a range of other finds, with a broad date range from the early 1st century AD to the 3rd centuries AD. The earliest pits and minor ditches appear to have been in use in the later 1st to early 2nd centuries AD, with the main ditch system dating to the mid-2nd century and continuing in use, being recut in the 3rd century AD.

The geology is Northampton Sand and Ironstone of the Inferior Oolite Series (BGS 1976).

Earlier features, ditches 61, 63 and 128 and pit 67

Ditches 61, 63 and 128, and pit 67, preceded the establishment of the larger ditch system in the middle of the 2nd century AD. Ditches 61 and 128, spaced *c*.17m apart, may have formed the northern and southern arms of a small enclosure, with the western arm removed by the later ditch system.

Ditch 63 was curvilinear, with its southern terminal cut by ditch 61. A nearby pit, 67, largely truncated by ditch 61, may have been contemporary. The pit was 0.8m in diameter by 0.12m deep, with a fill of dark brown silty sand flecked with charcoal (66), containing possible 2nd-century Roman pottery. Ditch 61 had a shallow, concave profile, 0.7-1.0m wide by up to 0.20m deep. The fill of mid to dark brown silty sand (60), contained Roman pottery, possibly dating to the 2nd century, and animal bone.

Ditch 128 had a relatively steep-sided, V-shaped profile, 1.0-1.5m wide by 0.46m deep. The primary fill of slightly stony, dark brown silty clay (127), was overlain by a similar though less stony deposit (126) containing Roman pottery dating to 2nd century, and animal bone.

The major ditch systems

In the middle of the 2nd century AD, two large ditches were excavated, forming a T-junction. They probably formed part of an extensive enclosure complex but the full extent is unknown as they continue beyond the easement and the limits set for the geophysical survey.

The ditch was aligned north-south and was 50m long with a central entrance 4m wide. Ditch 12/94, south of the entrance, had a steep-sided V-shaped profile, 3.4m wide by 1.74m deep, with a narrow flat base (Fig 5.10). At the base of the ditch there was a thin layer of light grey silt (93), overlain by stony mid grey mottled silty clay (92). After the stabilisation of the ditch sides, the

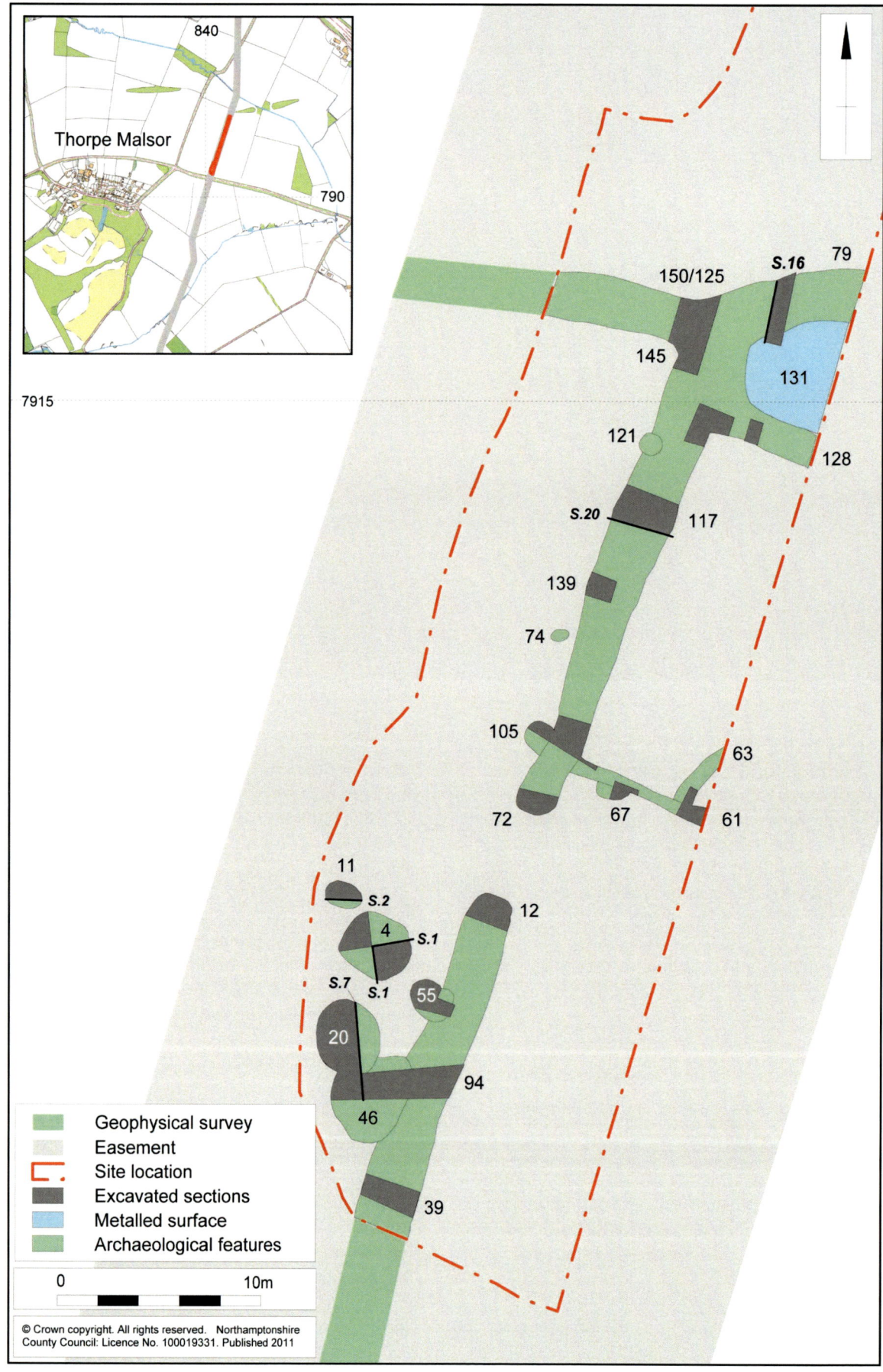

FIG 5.8: THORPE MALSOR, PLAN OF ROMAN SETTLEMENT

5. Roman Settlement (AD43 - AD450)

FIG 5.9: THORPE MALSOR, GENERAL VIEW OF THE SITE, LOOKING SOUTH

ditch silted up almost entirely with far less stony mid grey silty clay (91), which contained Roman pottery.

Towards the end of the 3rd century AD the ditch was recut, although the new ditch did not extend as far north as the original terminal. The recut, ditch 151, c.3.0m wide by 0.68m deep, had a fill of stony mottled mid grey-brown silty clay (90), overlain with mottled mid brown-grey clay (89). Roman pottery and animal bone were recovered from both deposits.

Ditch 72/117, north of the entrance, had a steep-sided, V-shaped profile, 3.0m wide by 1.6m deep, with a narrow concave base (Fig 5.11, Section 20). The surviving primary fill (116) of the original ditch comprised light brown silty clay, with remnants of mid grey-brown silty clay secondary fills (118) also surviving. There was a shallower recut, ditch 119, with a similar profile. The recut, ditch 119, was 1.05m deep. The primary and secondary fills were a homogeneous deposit of mid brown-grey silty clay (115). On the eastern side of the ditch there was a thin layer of hearth waste, comprising charcoal-rich dark grey silt (114), and the upper fill of mid grey-brown silty clay (113) contained large quantities of limestone and ironstone rubble, probably as a deliberate dump. Similar dumps of rubble were noted in the upper fills of Roman ditches at White Hill Lodge (see below). Roman pottery, fragments of Roman glass and animal bone were recovered from these deposits.

The northern arm of the ditch system was possibly misaligned, with the eastern half, ditch 79, curving northwards, perhaps suggesting that they were not contemporary, although they were of similar size and profile, with similar sequences of fills to those of ditch 117 to the south. Both ditches had steep-sided, V-shaped profiles, 2.0m wide by 1.3m deep (Fig 5.11, Section 16). Primary fills of grey- or orange-brown silty clay (149/78) were succeeded by more gradual accumulations of mid brown silty clay (144/77) containing domestic refuse, including Roman pottery, animal bone, a fragment of a quern and hearth ashes.

To the west, ditch 125, was recut by a broader, shallower ditch, 150, offset slightly to the north, 2.8m wide by up to 0.87m deep with a fill of mid brown silty clay (148). The evidence for a recut to the east was less conclusive.

FIG 5.10: THORPE MALSOR, NORTHERN TERMINAL OF DITCH 12, LOOKING SOUTH (SCALE 2M)

Pebbled surface 131

In the northern corner of the enclosed area, between ditches 117 and 79, there was a spread of limestone and ironstone pebbles forming a metalled surface. It stopped abruptly at the edges of the two large ditches, 79 and 121, but was embedded into the upper fills of the earlier ditch 128.

The pit group

To the south there was a group of five large pits, which contained quantities of domestic and industrial refuse.

Pit 46 was the largest and possibly the earliest pit in the group, truncated by ditch 94 and pit, 20. It was 4.5m in diameter by 0.85m deep, with steeply-sloping sides and a broad, flat base (Fig 5.12, Section 7). The secondary fill of mid brown silty clay (44) and the final fill of mid brown-grey silty clay (43) both produced Roman pottery, animal bone and pieces of slag, while the upper fill also contained the partial remains of an infant burial.

Pit 20 was 2.8m in diameter and 1.3m deep, with steep sides and a narrow, pointed base (Fig 5.12, Section 7). The accumulated silts of mid brown silty clay (41), mid grey-brown silty clay (19) and mid brown-grey silty clay (40), contained quantities of animal bone, Roman pottery, iron-working slag and a Roman coin probably in circulation into the 3rd century.

Pit 55 was 2.0m in diameter and 0.49m deep, with steep sides and a concave base. The fills of red-brown silty clay (54) and mid grey-brown sandy silt (53), which contained Roman pottery, also had very high ironstone content, accounting for up to half their volume, suggesting that the pit had been deliberately backfilled. The pit cut ditch 72 but had been truncated by recut, 151, dating to the 3rd century.

Pit 4 was 3.3m in diameter by 0.87m deep, with a near vertical slope to the north and a more gradual slope to the south (Fig 5.12, Section 1). The lower fills comprised several localised dumps of domestic debris, with the illustrated section showing only a little of the complexity of the sequence of deposition. It was one of the most productive pits in terms of pottery, other finds and charred plant remains from any of the excavated Roman sites.

Near the base of the pit there were deposits of mid grey-brown ashy silt, (22, 27 and 28) containing pottery, burnt bone, oyster shells, charcoal lumps, a very worn Roman coin, possibly of Hadrianic date, and burnt cobbles. Against the eastern wall of the pit there were thin layers

5. Roman Settlement (AD43 - AD450)

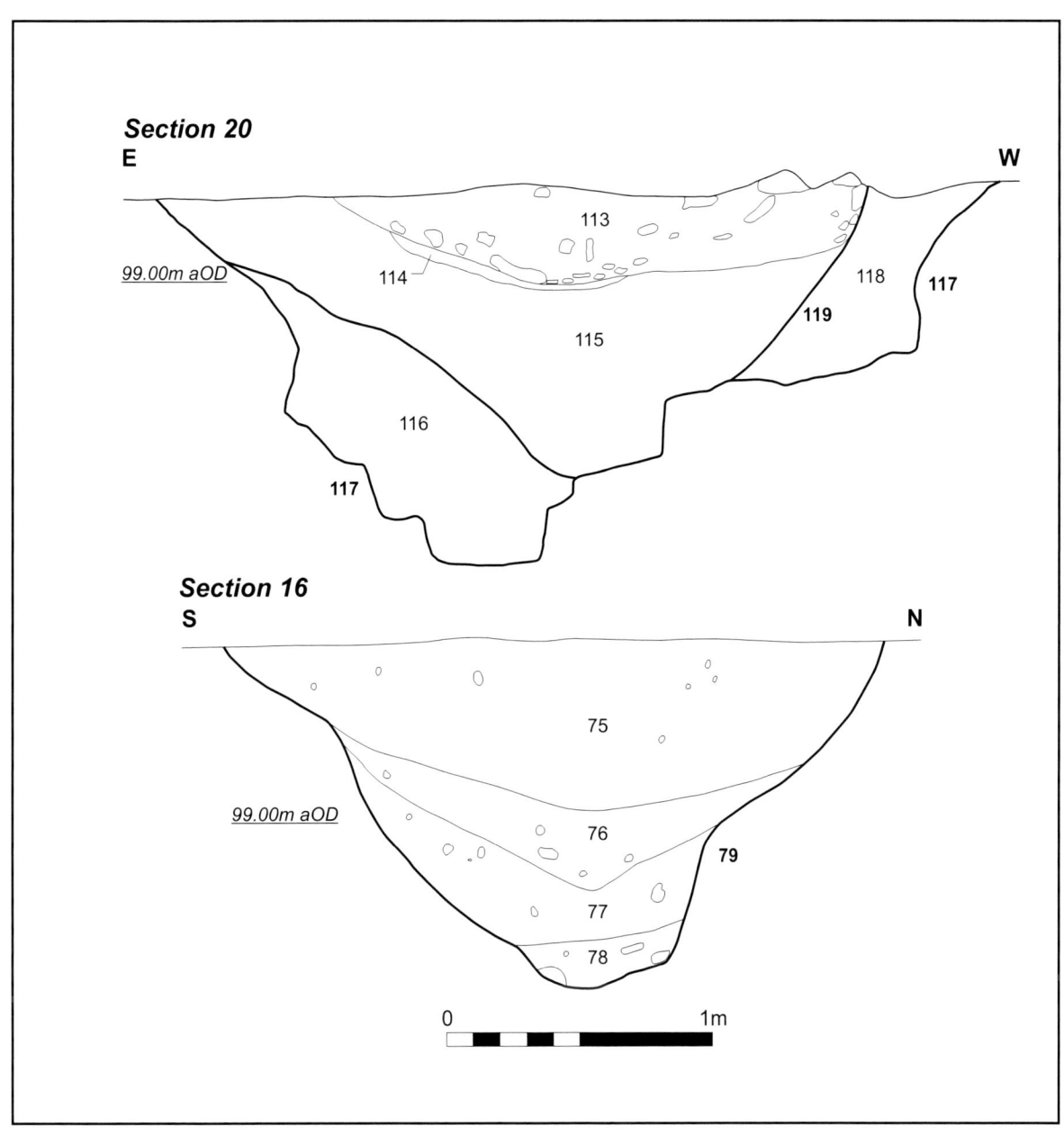

Fig 5.11: Thorpe Malsor, Sections of ditches 117/119 and 79

of grey-brown clayey silt, (9 and 7), separated by a thin layer of orange-grey clay (8), sealed by a larger dump of grey-brown ashy silt (6), from which was recovered a quantity of Roman pottery. Overlying these deposits there was cessy, greenish-grey mottled sandy clay (21) that contained further domestic waste, including pottery, animal bone, burnt cobbles and hearth ashes. The lower layers of domestic waste were sealed by a dumped layer comprising grey-brown and orange-brown silty clay and ironstone rubble (25); the only deposit in the pit to contain no cultural material. The upper fills, (24 and 23), also comprised a mixture of cess-like deposits and clayey silts containing ironstone rubble, ash, charcoal, animal bone, oyster shells, pottery, part of a quern and a fragment of human femur.

The total of nearly 18kg of pottery was the largest assemblage from the site, and included sherds from some 16 samian ware vessels (see Fig 5.22). The assemblage has a date range from the late 1st to the late 2nd/early 3rd centuries AD. Worked bone, fragments of glass, a bronze pin, iron nails and an iron blade were also recovered from these deposits.

The fills of this pit also produced the largest quantity and range of charred cereal and plant remains from any of the Roman sites, with the material comprising waste from a late stage of cereal processing and including a batch of burnt litter or fodder.

Pit 11 was oval and the smallest pit in the group, 1.45m long by 1.05m wide and 0.47m deep, with near vertical sides and a flat base (Fig 5.12, Section 2). The fill of mid grey-brown ashy clay, (10), contained several lenses of charcoal, perhaps the disposal of hearth waste. The pottery dates to the mid to late 1st to early 2nd centuries AD.

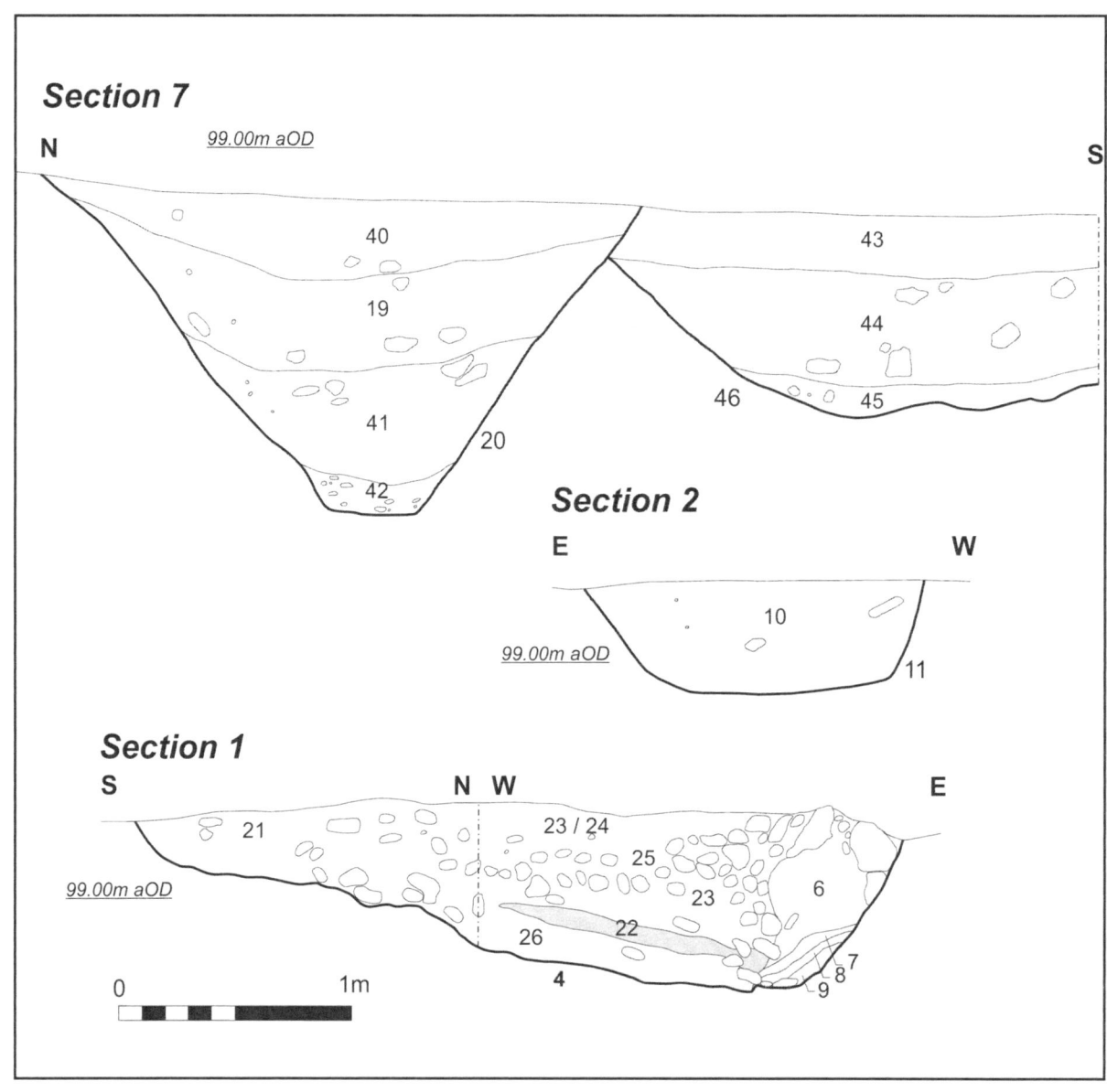

Fig 5.12: Thorpe Malsor, ditch and pit sections

Other pits/postholes 74, 105 and 121

There were three isolated pits or postholes.

Posthole 74 lay close to the western edge of ditch 117. It was sub-rectangular, 0.67m long by 0.41m wide and 0.09m deep, with near vertical sides and a flat base. The fill was charcoal-rich mid to dark grey silt (73) and the edges of the cut were scorched pink, suggesting that the post had been burnt *in situ*.

Pit 105 was cut into the fills of ditch 117, but had been truncated by the recut of the ditch, 119. It was 1.6m in diameter by 1.15m deep, with near vertical sides and a flat base. Against the western side of the pit was a sequence of deposits suggestive of deliberate dumping. These fills comprised red-brown silty sandy clay (104), a thin layer of dark grey silty clay (103), and a thicker deposit of mid brown-grey silty clay (102) containing Roman pottery and animal bone, a layer of mid to dark brown silty clay (101) and a final stonier fill (100).

Pit 121, which also cut the fills of ditch 117, was 1.3m long, 0.6m wide and 0.18m deep. The fill of mid to dark brown-grey silty clay (120), contained some domestic waste, including pottery, animal bone and charcoal.

Roman settlement at White Hill Lodge

A Roman ditch system lay between the villages of Thorpe Malsor and Great Cransley, approximately 0.4km to the north-east of White Hill Lodge (NGR: SP 8371 7799;

5. Roman Settlement (AD43 - AD450)

FIG 5.13: WHITE HILL LODGE, GENERAL VIEW OF ROMAN DITCHES, LOOKING SOUTH

Figs 5.13 and 5.14). It was situated on a spur of high ground between two small streams, at *c*.107m aOD, and the underlying geology is Northamptonshire Sand and Ironstone (BGS 1976). The site of the Roman settlement near Thorpe Malsor could be seen from this location.

Geophysical survey had identified part of an extensive grid-like pattern of linear ditches (Butler 2007, figs 82-83), but it is not possible to determine the structure and character of the settlement due to the limits of the survey area within the pipeline easement. A moderate number of *tesserae* recovered during the watching brief on the initial topsoil strip, deposits of limestone in the enclosure ditch, and two small lumps of tufa, suggest that the remains of a Roman building, and perhaps a bathhouse may be located nearby, and a metal detector survey prior to excavation found two Roman brooches in the subsoil. The small pottery assemblage indicates activity throughout the Roman period.

A ditched enclosure system

Within the excavated area there was the probable northern corner of a rectangular enclosure, ditch 47/62,

and further similar ditches to the south, 28 and 21/25, may have formed either sub-divisions or modifications to the plan form, but too few relationships could be established to provide any sequence of development.

The north-eastern arm of the enclosure, ditch 62/65, had a steep-sided, V-shaped profile, 1.8m wide by 1.0m deep. The fills all contained quantities of small pieces of ironstone, although the upper fill also contained a number of larger limestone cobbles, up to 500mm long, which may have been rubble from the demolition of a nearby Roman building. The north-western arm, ditch 47, had a similar profile and similar fills, but was wider and slightly deeper, at 2.5m wide by 1.1m deep (Fig 5.15, Section 11; Fig 5.16). There may have been a narrower and shallower recut, 44, through the relatively stone free upper fill, (45), although this impression may have been formed through the accumulation or dumping of quantities of larger limestone rubble (43) in the centre of the ditch. Roman pottery and animal bone were recovered from the ditch.

Ditch 28, the larger of the two ditches to the south, had a U-shaped profile, 1.9m wide by 0.93m deep (Fig 5.15, Section 6). The primary fill (27) was stony mid yellow-brown silty clay, and the upper fill (26) of mid to dark orange-brown silty clay, contained Roman pottery and animal bone. There was a narrow recut, 57, along the southern edge, 0.9m wide by 0.43m deep, with a fill of stony mid brown silty clay (56).

Ditch 21/25 was 1.0m wide by 0.50m deep (Fig 5.15, Section 5), with fills of stony mid grey-brown silty clay, containing Roman pottery and animal bone.

There were a few pits and gullies within the enclosed area. To the south, pit 9, largely truncated by ditch 5, was 1.6m in diameter by 0.32m deep. The fill of mid to dark grey-brown silty clay (8) contained Roman pottery. A further pit to the west was not excavated. Ditch 5 was 0.7m wide by 0.26m deep, with a fill of mid to dark brown-grey silty clay (4), charcoal-flecked and

EXCAVATIONS ALONG THE EMPINGHAM TO HANNINGTON PIPELINE 2008-2009

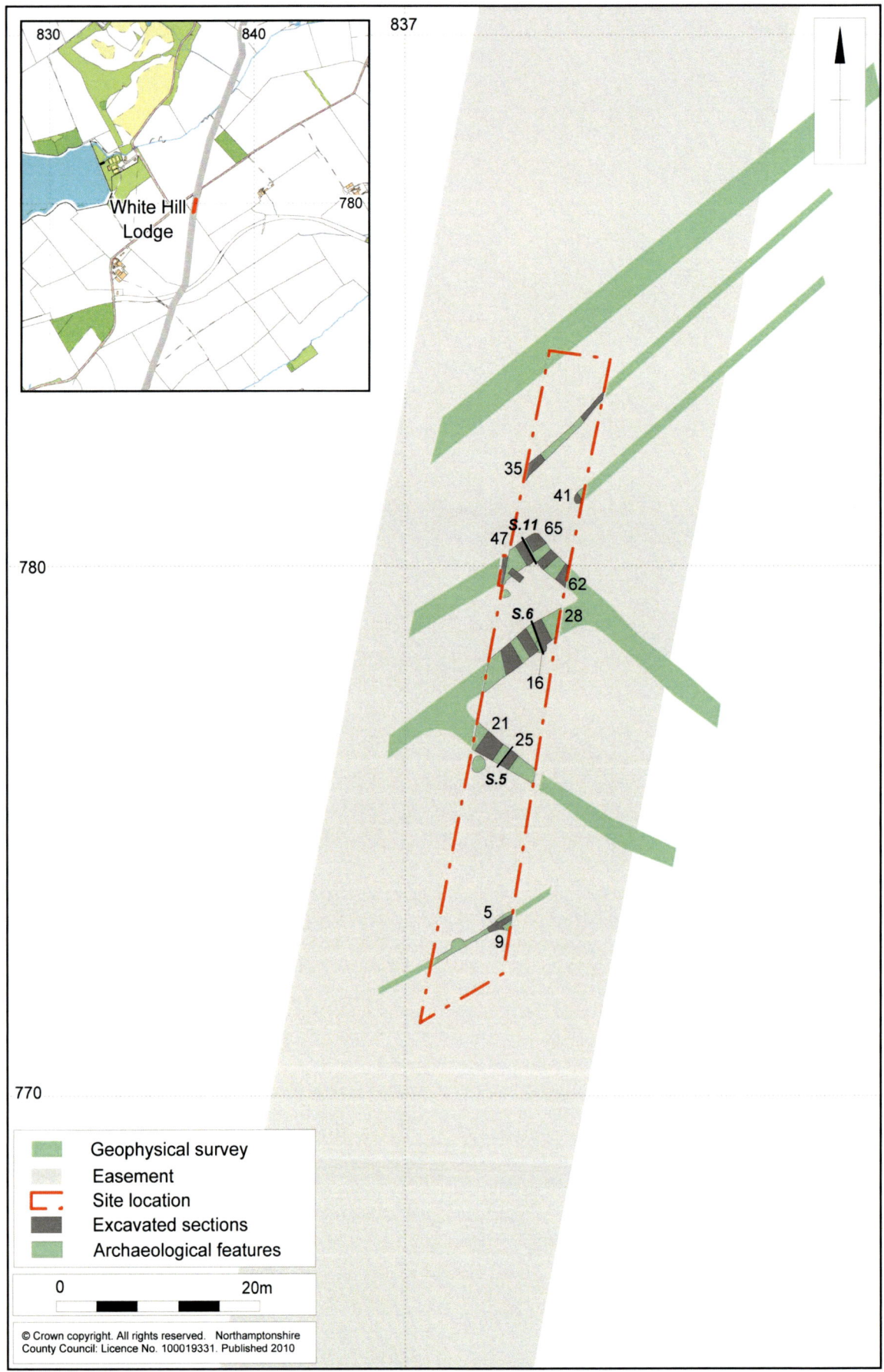

FIG 5.14: WHITE HILL LODGE, PLAN OF ROMAN SETTLEMENT

5. Roman Settlement (AD43 - AD450)

containing Roman pottery and animal bone. This was probably a minor internal division.

Further north, the eroded upper edge of pit 16 cut the fills of ditch 28. The pit was oval with steep to near vertical sides and a flat base, 1.2m long by 1.0m wide and 0.58m deep (Fig 5.15, Section 6). The primary fill of dark grey-green silt (15), was overlain by a similar though more extensive deposit that was more brown-green in colour (14). The distinctive greenish appearance of these fills suggests the deposition of cess, implying that areas of habitation lay nearby. A layer of mid grey-brown clayey silt (13) contained small pieces of burnt clay. The upper fill of charcoal flecked mid brown-green/grey clayey silt (12) had an ashy appearance, and contained burnt pebbles, small pieces of burnt clay and Roman pottery.

Droveway: ditches 35 and 41

Two parallel ditches, 35 and 41, to the north of the enclosure and 5m apart, may have flanked a droveway extending north-eastwards from the enclosure, although the geophysical survey records a further, broader ditch to the west also on a parallel alignment (Fig 5.14).

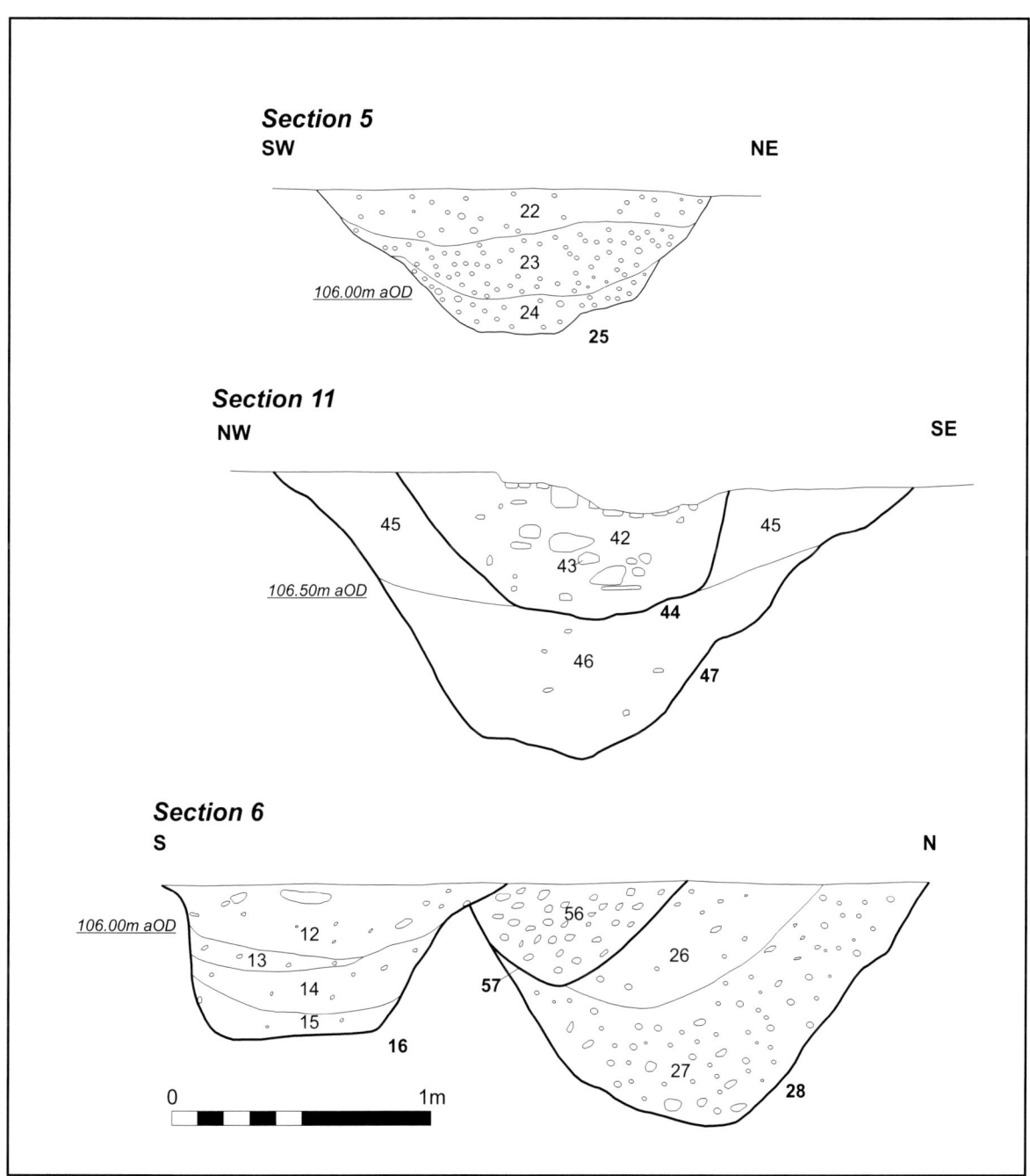

Fig 5.15: White Hill Lodge, ditch sections

Fig 5.16: White Hill Lodge, Roman ditch 44, looking south-west (Scale 2m)

Ditch 35 was up to 0.8m wide by 0.22m deep, but became narrower and shallower to the north-east. The fill of mid to dark brown silty clay (34) contained animal bone and a fragment from a copper alloy object. Only the terminal of ditch 41 was excavated, 1.2m wide by 0.21m deep, with a fill of mid to dark brown silty clay (40).

Roman settlement near Great Cransley

The remains of a Roman settlement were located near the top of a south-east facing slope overlooking a small tributary valley, at c.104m aOD, approximately 0.7km to the north-east of the village of Great Cransley (NGR: SP 8355 7736; Fig 5.17). The settlement had been identified from cropmarks and geophysical survey and comprised several sub-rectangular enclosures to either side of a broad ditched trackway (Butler 2007, figs 84-85). However, the cropmarks were too indistinct and the survey area was too narrow to determine the full extent and morphology of the settlement. The site lay 0.7km to the south-south-west of the Roman settlement at White Hill Lodge; the area between them had been quarried in the 19th century for ironstone.

Ditch 25

The eastern terminal of a small ditch 25, 1.1m wide by 0.35m deep, lay to the west of the trackway on an anomalous alignment. It was cut by enclosure ditch 11, suggesting that ditch 25 may have formed part of an early phase of settlement. The excavated ditch section contained no finds.

Enclosure 1

This lay fully outside the investigated area, but a combination of aerial survey and geophysical survey has defined a sub-rectangular enclosure 45m long by 40m wide, abutting the western side of the trackway.

Enclosure 2: ditches 13 and 17

At the southern end of the complex, and to the west of the trackway, the northern and western arms of a rectangular enclosure, Enclosure 2, at least 30m wide and 40m long, crossed the excavated area.

The northern arm of the enclosure, ditch 13, had a V-shaped profile, 1.6m wide by 0.80m deep (Fig 5.18, Section 5). The fill largely comprised ironstone gravel in a mid brown silty clay matrix (12), mixed with occasional lumps of clay near the base.

The western arm of the enclosure, ditch 17, had a steep-sided, V-shaped profile, 1.9m wide by 0.86m deep (Fig 5.18, Section 2). The primary fill of light brown silty clay (16) was overlain by similar deposits

5. ROMAN SETTLEMENT (AD43 - AD450)

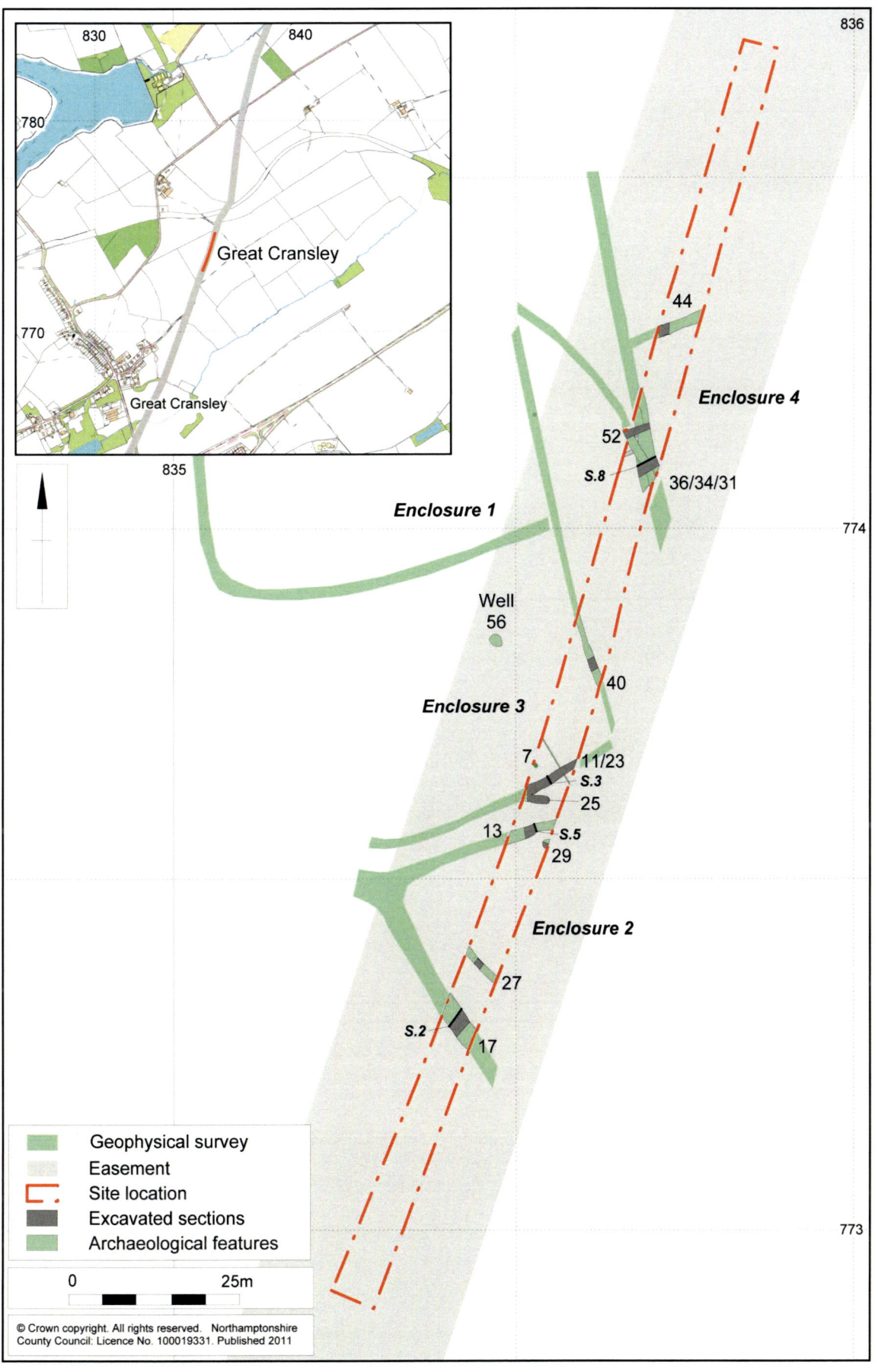

FIG 5.17: GREAT CRANSLEY, PLAN OF ROMAN DITCH SYSTEM

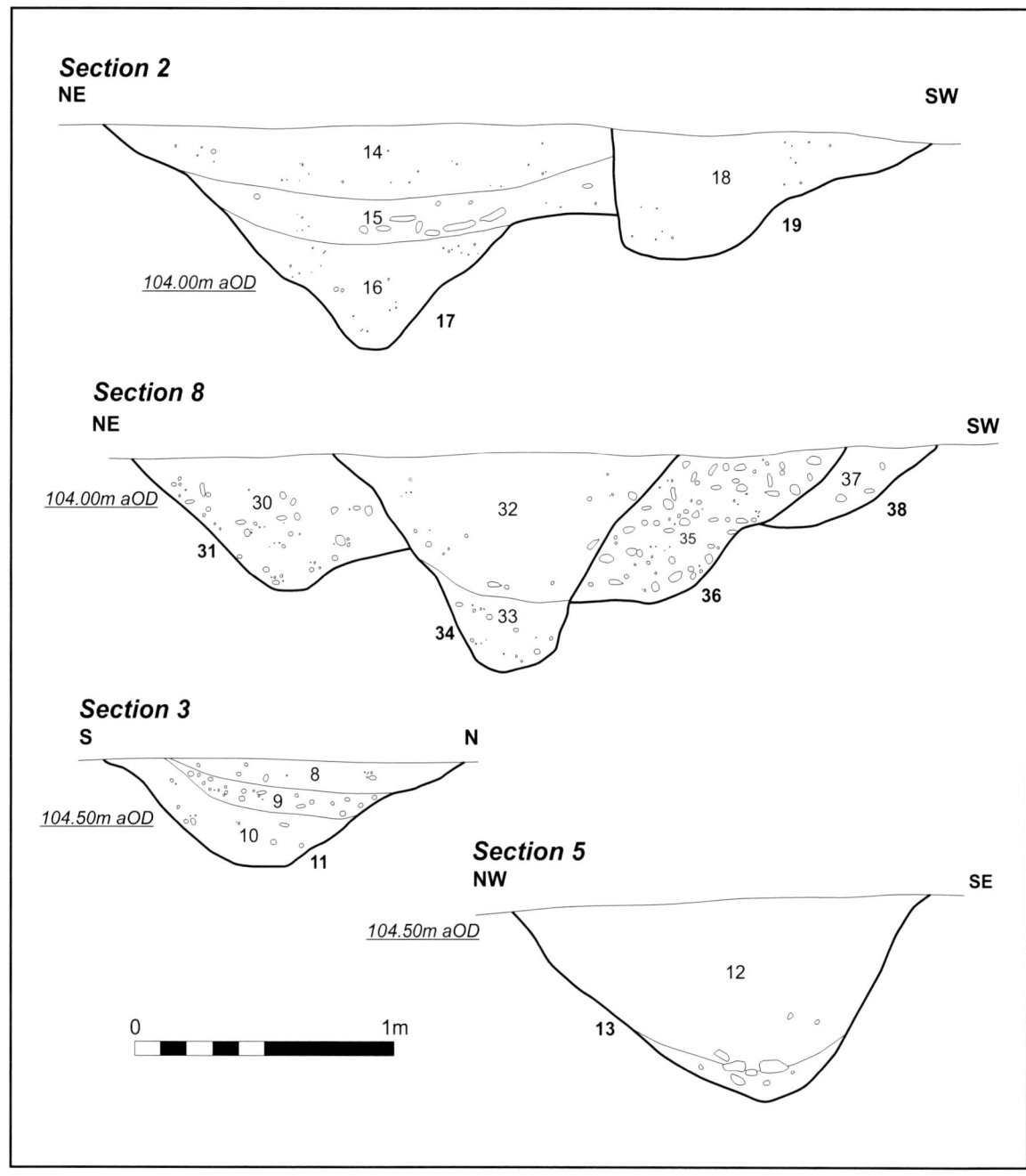

Fig 5.18: Great Cransley, Sections of enclosure ditches

of mid grey-brown silty clay (15 and 14) including Roman pottery, animal bone and fired clay. There was a U-shaped recut, 19, along its outer edge, 1.2m wide by 0.48m deep, with a fill of mid brown-grey silty clay (Fig 5.18, Section 2).

Adjacent to the northern boundary of Enclosure 2, there was a small, sub-rectangular pit, 29, 1.2m wide by 0.31m deep. The fill of mid grey-brown sandy silt (28), contained Roman pottery and debris from a pottery kiln, comprising pieces of burnt clay, possibly from the kiln's superstructure, and fragments of kiln bars.

Enclosure 3: ditch 11

This area was 35m wide, lying between Enclosures 1 and 2. To the west the southern boundary, ditch 11/23, was turning northwards, perhaps to form a western arm.

Ditch 11/23, which formed the southern side of the enclosure, had a broad, V-shaped profile, 1.3m wide by 0.43m deep (Fig 5.18, Section 3). The primary fill, mid brown silty clay (10), was overlain by deposits of stony, mid orange-brown silty clay (9) and mid to dark brown silty clay (8). Both of these contained significant

5. Roman Settlement (AD43 - AD450)

quantities of Roman pottery and animal bone, as well as a hobnail and an iron nail, with this domestic refuse indicating habitation nearby.

To the north of ditch 11, there was an isolated posthole, 7, 0.55m in diameter by 0.15m deep, with a fill of dark brown sandy clayey silt (6), containing Roman pottery, burnt clay, animal bone and an iron nail.

A stone-lined well, 56, within Enclosure 3, lay to the west of the excavated area but within the topsoil stripped easement (Figs 5.19 and 5.20). The well was lined with limestone and ironstone rubble (54), forming a rectangular shaft, 0.55m in diameter. It was not possible to determine the full depth of the well, as excavation was curtailed at *c* 1.5m. At 1.5m there was a deposit of mid to dark brown silty clay (59), over 0.5m thick; when this deposit was removed groundwater rapidly percolated into the well. The overlying deposit, approximately 1.0m thick, was mid yellow-brown silty clay (53) containing pottery, hearth waste, quern fragments and animal bone, including a horse's head. A number of large limestone cobbles in the fill were probably derived from a low wall that had surrounded the well; the foundation course of this superstructure (55), including a revetment of vertically-pitched limestone slabs on the eastern side, survived. The infilled well had been capped with a layer of limestone rubble and mid brown silty clay (57) that contained Roman pottery and quantities of charcoal, probably derived from hearth waste.

The trackway: ditches 40 and 31/36

A linear ditch to the west, ditch 40, and a complex of intercutting linear ditches to the east, ditches 31/34 and 36/52, defined a trackway 14m wide, aligned north-west to south-east.

Ditch 40, 1.2m wide by 0.85m deep, had a steep-sided, V-shaped profile. It was recut by ditch 42, which was narrower and shallower, 0.65m wide by 0.50m deep. Both were filled with mid brown silty clay, with the fill of the recut being far stonier.

The eastern side of the trackway was defined by ditch 31, which had a V-shaped profile, *c* 0.9m wide by 0.41m deep (Fig 5.18, Section 8). The fill of mid brown-grey silty clay (30), contained a large quantity of ironstone pebbles, suggesting it had been deliberately backfilled, at least in part, with previously excavated material. The recut, ditch 36, offset to the south-west by *c*.1.2m, had a similar profile but was slightly wider and deeper. Roman pottery and animal bone were recovered from the fills of both ditches. There was limited evidence for a further cut of the ditch, 38, although this only survived as a truncated remnant at the western edge of ditch 36.

At a later date the trackway must have fallen out of use as a curvilinear ditch, 34/52, was cut diagonally across it. Ditch 34/52 had a steep-sided, V-shaped profile, 1.3m wide by 0.82m deep, with fills of mid grey-brown silty clay (33) overlain by mid grey silty clay (32). The fills contained Roman pottery and animal bone, perhaps suggesting that the reorganisation occurred in the later Roman period.

Enclosure 4: ditch 44

Projecting from the north-east side of the trackway, ditch 44 may have formed an enclosure, Enclosure 4, to the east of the trackway. Ditch 44, had a steep-sided, V-shaped profile with a narrow concave base, 1.65m wide by 0.88m deep, with a fill of stony mid orange-brown silty clay (43), with Roman pottery.

Colluvium 58

At the northern end of the site there was a layer of colluvium, filling a natural depression in the slope. It comprised relatively stoneless mid orange-brown silty clay (58) and contained several sherds of Roman pottery. A machine-dug slot excavated through the deposit showed that it was over 1.0m deep.

Finds from the Roman settlement:

Roman pottery
by Rob Perrin with J M Mills

Nine sites produced Roman pottery but the assemblages from only two of these, Thorpe Malsor and Great Cransley, were considered of sufficient size to warrant analysis beyond the assessment stage (Perrin 2010).

Methodology

The pottery was recorded using simple fabric classifications based on principal inclusion or firing technique, together with the identification of some known regional ware types (eg Lower Nene Valley wares) and some imported wares, for example samian ware. Comments on the samian ware have been provided by J M Mills, and comments on a mortarium stamp are by K F Hartley. At assessment stage the pottery was quantified by sherd count and weight (g) within fabrics. Rim and base percentages were later added for the groups which merited further analysis, but only the rim percentages have been used to calculate the estimated vessel equivalents (EVE) used in the report. No attempt was made to identify joins, other than where certain features of fabric, colour, decoration etc made this obvious.

The main fabrics on all the sites are grogged, shell-gritted, grey and oxidised. A number of sub-types occur in the

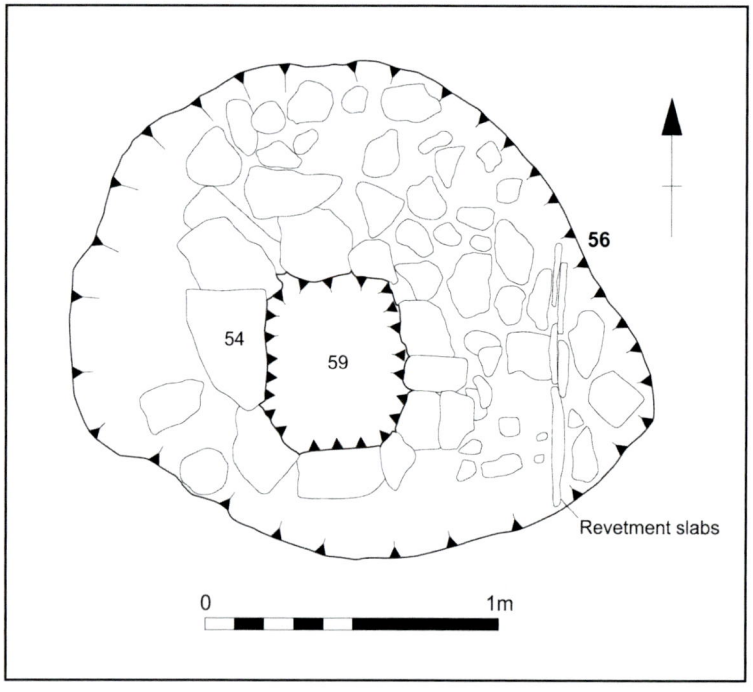

FIG 5.19: GREAT CRANSLEY, PLAN OF ROMAN WELL 56

grogged wares, some of which are likely to have been manufactured in the 1st century AD. Two distinctive grogged wares, a hard cream ware and a usually less hard pink ware, occur on most sites in the area with occupation spanning the later 1st to 2nd centuries AD. Local production is probable, although the source(s) are as yet undiscovered. Pottery in shell-gritted ware was produced locally in the Iron Age and throughout the Roman period.

The main regional and imported wares are Lower Nene Valley colour-coated (LNVCC) and cream wares (LNVCW), South and Central Gaulish samian ware, Mancetter-Hartshill (mortarium), Black burnished ware (BB1 and BB2) and Lower Rhineland (LRCC), Central Gaulish (CGCC) and, possibly, Colchester colour-coated ware. There are a few vessels in mica-dusted ware and London ware in forms imitating samian ware.

FIG 5.20: GREAT CRANSLEY, ROMAN WELL 56, LOOKING SOUTH (SCALE 1M)

5. Roman Settlement (AD43 - AD450)

The grey wares are by far the most abundant and were used throughout the Roman period. They comprise a range of fabrics with varying visual characteristics, but these are likely, in the main, to reflect varying firing conditions and may not therefore be especially meaningful in terms of date or source. A large number of kiln sites which produced grey wares are known in Northamptonshire, including some, Kettering, Rushton, Weekley and Geddington, which are within 10km of the excavated sites. It is likely that a large proportion of the oxidized wares were also produced locally. Some oxidized ware sherds with painted and incised decoration from Thorpe Malsor are probably products of kilns at Rushden (Woods and Hastings 1984).

The vessel types were recorded using simple form codes. The vessel forms comprise various types of jars, bowls and dishes, together with a few lids, flagons, mortaria and beakers. There are no amphorae, although a large handle in oxidized ware (from Thorpe Malsor) is reminiscent of those found on amphorae and may be from one of the amphora-like vessels produced at Verulamium (Symonds 2003). Overall, and in the selected groups, jars of various types comprise at least half of the recognizable vessel forms, with bowls and dishes accounting for around another quarter.

Lid-seated jars occur in both the hard cream and pink grogged fabrics, grey ware, oxidized ware and shell-gritted ware, indicating both the popularity and longevity of this vessel type. Jars with curved rims occur mainly in grey ware, though in many different sizes and forms. Jars with narrow mouths occur in both the hard cream and pink grogged fabrics, grey ware and oxidized ware, but are not common in shell-gritted ware. Other jar forms represented include storage jars, some very large, mainly in grogged or shell-gritted ware, jars with everted rims, mainly in grey ware and smaller jars or beakers, again mainly in grey ware. The BB1 sherds include a cooking pot.

There are a number of wide bowls, with external grooves near the rim, in both hard cream and pink grogged fabrics. Grey ware bowls include carinated vessels with grooved, flat-topped or flanged rims, vessels with beaded or triangular rims, flanged bowls and imitation samian ware vessels. The grey ware dishes are mainly plain, beaded or triangular rimmed and there are also a few plain or triangular rimmed dishes in oxidized ware. There are also sherds from a triangular-rimmed dish in BB2 and a plain-rimmed dish in BB1. The few flagons are mainly from ring necked types with a prominent top ring or bead, though there is one with more of a disc rim, where the 'rings' are vestigal. The mortaria include bead and flange and wall-sided types. The lids include one from a cheese press.

The LNVCC includes sherds from a flagon or narrow mouthed jar, a curved sided dish with a triangular rim, a plain rimmed dish, wide-mouthed jars or bowls, castor boxes, an imitation Dr 36 and funnel neck and plain rimmed beakers, including some with underslip barbotine decoration and overslip painted decoration, and a fragment of a 'Hunt cup'. The Lower Rhineland colour-coated ware and possible Colchester colour-coated ware comprise beakers with roughcast decoration and the Central Gaulish colour-coated sherds are from a beaker with underslip barbotine decoration.

Overall, the lack of fine wares and forms, of non-local and imported material and the preponderance of jars could indicate a fairly utilitarian range of activities and a fairly low status. Similarly, the limited range of samian ware vessel forms, coupled with a low frequency of decorated vessels and also an absence of mortaria, is often seen as typical of Roman 'small towns' and rural settlement in general, but the assemblages are really too small to draw any firm conclusions. An essentially rural nature to the activity is also supported by the animal bone assemblages, which are largely dominated by cattle, followed by sheep/goat and by the probable cereal processing waste, with a quern found in a pit at Thorpe Malsor.

The Roman pottery from Thorpe Malsor (Figs 5.21-5.22)

The site produced a sizeable assemblage of nearly 4,200 sherds with a combined weight of over 62.5kg, giving an average sherd weight of 15g. The features from which pottery was recovered comprised a posthole, pits, ditches and gullies. Table 5.1 shows the pottery assemblage by principal fabric type. Some of the grogged wares may belong to, or have been produced in the Iron Age and the Roman pottery appears to span the whole Roman period. The few dateable small finds are of the 2nd and 3rd centuries AD, while the glass suggests a date from the late 1st to the 3rd century AD.

Fabric	Number	%	Wt (g)	%
Hard cream grog	890	21.3	19110	30.5
Grog	233	5.6	4352	7.0
Pink grog	188	4.5	3826	6.1
Shell	404	9.7	8875	14.2
Grey	1547	37.1	18009	28.8
Oxidised	346	8.3	5628	9.0
LNVCC	50	1.2	558	0.9
LRCC	12	0.3	72	0.1
Colchester?	23	0.6	52	0.1
BB1	19	0.5	408	0.7
BB2	8	0.2	70	0.1
London	21	0.5	158	0.3
Samian	48	1.2	483	0.8
Total	4171		62623	

Table 5.1: Thorpe Malsor, Roman pottery assemblage by principal fabrics

Selected assemblages:

Eight assemblages from Thorpe Malsor were chosen for more detailed analysis and illustration (Table 5.2). These are thought to represent specific episodes of deposition with a limited time span but, as the features are of an 'open' nature, it is not surprising that they also contain later material. The illustrated sherds have been selected to give an idea of the range of pottery fabrics and types occurring in each group and are augmented by vessels of intrinsic interest from other contexts (Figs 5.21 and 5.22).

Feature	Number	Wt (g)	EVE
Ditch 39 (=12 & 94)	236	2766	1.7
Ditch 94 (=12 & 39)	135	3050	4.1
Ditch 112 (= 72, 139, 117 & 145)	216	3194	3.0
Ditch 117 (= 72, 112, 139 & 145)	199	3729	4.7
Ditch 139 (= 72, 112, 117 & 145)	530	10565	14.1
Ditch 145 (= 72, 112, 139 & 145)	198	2751	3.2
Ditch 150 (= 125)	193	2683	3.8
Pit 4	1198	22237	20.8

TABLE 5.2: THORPE MALSOR, QUANTIFICATION OF SELECTED ROMAN POTTERY ASSEMBLAGES

Ditch 39 (part of ditch system with ditches 12 and 94, see below)

The date range for the pottery from this ditch appears to be mid-1st to late 2nd century AD. The earliest material comprises a sherd from a samian form 18 dated to *c* AD50-100 and sherds from a globular vessel with incised and painted decoration. The fabric, form and decoration, with incised 'basketwork' design, banding and 'horizontal ladder' painted decoration, can be paralleled at the kilns at Rushden (Woods and Hastings 1984, 22 & 24), while vessels with panels containing painted lattice work are known from Brixworth and Bannaventa (Woods 1972, fig 39, 275-78). The main Rushden production is dated to *c* AD 45-60, but some of the vessel forms continued to be produced into the 2nd century AD and painted wares are known from other local kiln sites (*op cit* 36-8). The latest pottery from ditch 39 comprises grey ware dishes with a plain rim and a triangular/bead rim. The range of fabrics is expressed as a percentage of the principal fabrics by count, weight and rim EVE (Table 5.3). The jars occur with curved and lid-seated rims, in both shell-gritted and grey wares (Fig 5.21, 1 and 2). The total rim EVE for ditch 39 is just 1.7, mostly jars, with bowls and dishes accounting for 10% and lids 5% of the vessels by rim EVE.

Ditch 94 (part of ditch system with ditches 12, see above, and 39)

The total rim EVE for ditch 94 is a little over 4. Jars comprise just over three-quarters of the vessels by rim EVE with bowls and dishes, and lids around a further 10% each. The jars in grey ware are types with curved rims, everted rims and lattice decoration or with narrow mouths. Narrow mouthed jars also occur in hard cream grog and oxidised wares and lid-seated jars and lid in hard cream grog (Fig 5.21, 3) and shell-gritted wares. The grey ware dishes and bowls include a vessel with a bead rim.

Fabric	No (%)	Wt (%)	EVE (%)
Hard cream grog	2.1	1.2	--
Pink grog	6.4	9.7	8.8
Misc grog	4.7	3.8	--
Shell	31.4	48.6	31.2
Grey	41.1	24.2	48.8
Misc oxidised	6.4	3.8	11.2

TABLE 5.3: THORPE MALSOR, DITCH 39, PERCENTAGES OF PRINCIPAL FABRICS

These vessel forms, together with the overall proportions of grey and hard cream grogged wares would indicate a date in the 2nd century AD for the fills of this ditch. This is supported by the presence of a samian form 18/31 of Hadrianic-Antonine date, a sherd of LRCC and a triangular-rimmed dish with lattice decoration in BB2. The range of fabrics is expressed as a percentage of the principal fabrics by number, weight and rim EVE (Table 5.4).

Fabric	No (%)	Weight (%)	EVE (%)
Hard cream grog	25.2	31.0	34.6
Pink grog	1.6	7.5	10.7
Shell	6.0	8.7	11.4
Grey	54.0	37.4	27.6

TABLE 5.4: THORPE MALSOR, DITCH 94, PERCENTAGES OF PRINCIPAL FABRICS

Ditch 112 (part of ditch system with ditches 72, 139, 117 and 145)

The total rim EVE for ditch 112 is around 3. The presence of a complete ring necked flagon rim accounts for the high EVE figure for oxidised ware (Table 5.5). Jars comprise 58% and bowls and dishes a further 12%, of the vessels by rim EVE. Lid-seated jars occur in hard cream grog, pink grog and shell-gritted wares and curved rim jars in hard cream grog and grey wares (Fig 5.21, 4).

Fabric	No (%)	Weight (%)	EVE (%)
Hard cream grog	8.3	8.0	6.9
Pink grog	16.7	11.0	24.0
Shell	7.9	29.7	14.1
Grey	34.3	23.9	13.2
Oxidised	15.3	9.5	33.6

TABLE 5.5: THORPE MALSOR, DITCH 112, PERCENTAGES OF PRINCIPAL FABRICS

5. Roman Settlement (AD43 - AD450)

The flagon has a large top ring, suggesting a date in the mid-2nd century AD or later. Other pottery from the feature dating to the 2nd century AD includes a grey ware carinated bowl, some sherds of BB1 and the base of a Central Gaulish samian form 27, dated *c* AD120-60. The curved-sided flanged bowl, which probably originally had mica-dusted surfaces, may also date to the 2nd century AD. Sherds from a South Gaulish samian ware form 27, dated *c* AD50-70, also occur and, together with the overall fabric proportions, suggest the assemblage may have a wider date range from the mid to late 1st century AD to mid to late 2nd century AD.

Ditch 117 (part of ditch system with ditches 72, 112, 139 and 145)

The total rim EVE for ditch 117 is around 4.6. Jars account for three quarters of the vessels by rim EVE but bowls and dishes only 14%, owing to the presence of a beaker (2%), mortaria (4%) and a lid (5%). Lid-seated jars occur in hard cream grog, pink grog and shell-gritted wares and curved rim jars in hard cream grog, shell-gritted, oxidised and grey wares (Fig 5.21, 5). Dishes or bowls with bead rims occur in grey and oxidised wares and the grey ware also includes a lid and a carinated bowl with a grooved rim (Fig 5.21, 6). The mortaria comprise sherds from a Lower Nene Valley wall-sided type with ironstone grits and from a bead and flange type of Mancetter-Hartshill origin. The beaker rim is from a funnel necked type produced in the Lower Nene Valley and another beaker sherd is probably from a vessel made in Colchester.

The assemblage contains some pottery which was probably produced in the later 1st century AD but the fabric proportions suggest most dates to the 2nd century AD or later. The dishes or bowls with bead rims are likely to date to the 2nd to 3rd centuries AD and Central Gaulish samian ware dated *c* AD120-60 and AD120-200 also occurs. The mortaria and the funnel necked beaker date to the 3rd century AD. The range of fabrics is expressed as a percentage of the principal fabrics by number, weight and rim EVE (Table 5.6).

Fabric	No (%)	Weight (%)	EVE (%)
Hard cream grog	35.7	42.9	33.7
Pink grog	5.5	3.2	2.6
Shell	12.1	18.2	7.5
Grey	31.2	21.6	42.1

TABLE 5.6: THORPE MALSOR, DITCH 117, PERCENTAGES OF PRINCIPAL FABRICS

Ditch 139 (part of ditch system with ditches 72, 112, 117 and 145)

Ditch 139 contained over 10kg of pottery, the second largest assemblage from the site; the total rim EVE for ditch 139 is over 14. Jars are again the predominant vessels by rim EVE (72%), but bowls and dishes (15%), flagons (7%), a mortarium (2%), lids (2%) and beakers (1.5%) are also represented. Lid-seated jars occur in hard cream grog, pink grog and shell-gritted wares and curved rim jars in hard cream grog and grey wares. Other jar forms are storage jars in hard cream grog and grog wares, narrow mouthed jars in hard cream grog and grey wares, a hard grog ware globular, neckless jar with burnished lattice decoration in zones between grooves, a small fine grey ware jar or beaker, decorated with barbotine 'lozenges' and a handled jar, also in grey ware (Fig 5.21, 8). Other grey ware forms represented are dishes or bowls with triangular and bead rims, curved sided dishes with plain or bead rims, a plain rim dish and a carinated bowl with a grooved rim (Fig 5.21, 9). The assemblage also includes a large wide bowl in hard cream grog ware and other fabrics occurring are LNVCW (two sherds), BB1 (one sherd) and sherds from a 'London' ware imitation samian form 30, a colour-coated roughcast ware beaker (Fig 5.21, 11), a fine oxidised ware disc-necked flagon (Fig 5.21, 7), an oxidised ware lid and a bead and flange Mancetter-Hartshill mortarium (Fig 5.21, 12).

Two samian ware form 18/31s, one from Les Martres de Vere, and one Central Gaulish, are dated *c* AD100-25 and *c* AD120-60, respectively. The mortarium has a potter's stamp dated *c* AD120-60 (130-50). Much of the pottery would fit a Hadrianic-Antonine date and the overall fabric proportions also point to a date in the 2nd century AD. The range of fabrics is expressed as a percentage of the principal fabrics by number, weight and rim EVE (Table 5.7).

Fabric	No (%)	Weight (%)	EVE (%)
Hard cream grog	38.1	43.9	38.2
Pink grog	5.1	5.7	3.0
Shell	7.2	9.3	2.3
Grey	30.0	19.2	33.1
Oxidised	5.9	3.1	10.8

TABLE 5.7: THORPE MALSOR, DITCH 139, PERCENTAGES OF PRINCIPAL FABRICS

Ditch 145 (part of ditch system with ditches 72, 112, 139 and 117)

The total rim EVE for ditch 117 is around 3.2. Jars account for around two-thirds with bowls and dishes a further 31% of the vessels by rim EVE. There are no lid-seated jars in any fabric in this assemblage but curved rim jars occur in both grey and shell-gritted wares. Other grey ware vessels comprise a narrow mouthed jar, a wide mouthed jar or bowl, a bowl with a flat or bead rim and part of a cheese press lid (Fig 5.21, 13).

An indented beaker in grey colour-coated ware might be a Lower Nene Valley product. Definite colour-coated ware from these kilns includes a plain rim dish, sherds from a Castor box lid and some fragments of beakers with overslip paint and underslip barbotine scrolls and dots.

Vessels in other fabrics are a BB1 plain rim dish with burnished wavy lines on the interior and exterior of the base (Fig 5.21, 14), a shallow dish in mica-dusted ware (Fig 5.22, 27) and a Central Gaulish samian ware cup. The latter is dated *c* AD120-200 and the grey colour-coated indented beaker, the Lower Nene Valley sherds and the BB1 dish all definitely date to the 3rd century AD and possibly later, though the assemblage contains earlier material.

The range of fabrics, is expressed as a percentage of the principal fabrics by number, weight and rim EVE (Table 5.8).

Fabric	No (%)	Weight (%)	EVE (%)
Hard cream grog	6.1	2.9	--
Grog	11.6	6.8	--
Shell	19.7	17.6	31.7
Grey	40.9	56.6	48.1
BB1	2.0	7.0	9.6
Oxidised	1.0	1.0	3.4
LNVCC	8.1	3.3	7.1
Mica dusted	3.5	1.4	--
Grey CC	6.1	1.2	--

TABLE 5.8: THORPE MALSOR, DITCH 145, PERCENTAGES OF PRINCIPAL FABRICS

Ditch 150 (north end of site, aligned west-east)

The total rim EVE for ditch 150 is just under 3.8. Jars account for 70% of the vessels by rim EVE, with bowls and dishes (24%) and beakers (6%) making up the remainder. There are again no lid-seated jars in any fabric but curved rim jars occur in oxidised, grey and shell-gritted wares. Other grey ware vessels comprise a bowl with a flat or bead rim (joins 144) and a dish or bowl with a bead rim. Additional sherds of the indented beaker in grey colour-coated ware and the mica-dusted ware dish (Fig 5.21, 15) found in 144 also occur in this assemblage. A small wide mouthed jar or bowl, a beaker with a funnel neck (Fig 5.21, 16) and a beaker sherd with underslip barbotine scroll decoration are all Lower Nene Valley products.

The grey colour-coated indented beaker and the Lower Nene Valley sherds are again all definitely dated to the 3rd century AD and possibly later, though the assemblage contains earlier material, including the CGCC beaker which is of Antonine date.

The range of fabrics is expressed as a percentage of the principal fabrics by number, weight and rim EVE (Table 5.9).

Fabric	No (%)	Weight(%)	EVE (%)
Hard cream grog	6.7	8.1	--
Shell	8.8	10.2	9.0
Grey	72.5	69.8	67.7
Mica dusted	3.6	5.6	9.5
LNVCC	3.1	1.9	8.5

TABLE 5.9: THORPE MALSOR, DITCH 150, PERCENTAGES OF PRINCIPAL FABRICS

Pit 4

Pit 4 contained 22.2kg of pottery, the largest assemblage from the site; the total rim EVE for pit 4 is nearly 21. In analysis, layer 21 (Table 5.10), was quantified separately from the other fills (Table 5.11).

The total rim EVE for Pit 4, layer 21 is almost 2.8. Jars account for 83% of the vessels by rim EVE, with bowls and dishes making up the remainder. Lid-seated jars occur in hard cream grog, shell-gritted and grey wares and curved rim jars occur in hard cream grog and grey wares. Other vessel forms in hard cream grog ware are a narrow mouthed jar, a storage jar (Fig 5.22, 17) and a wide bowl, while there are an everted rim jar, a jar base with burnished lattice decoration and dishes with triangular rims in grey ware. A flagon, a flagon handle, a lid and a possible narrow mouthed jar occur in oxidised ware, together with another handle large enough to be from an amphora-type vessel. A rim sherd from a Central Gaulish samian ware Curle 11 also occurs. This is dated *c* AD120-60 and much of the other pottery would fit a date in the 2nd century AD, with little likely to be any earlier.

The range of fabrics is expressed as a percentage of the principal fabrics by number, weight and rim EVE (Table 5.10).

Fabric	No (%)	Weight (%)	EVE (%)
Hard cream grog	42.4	61.3	57.0
Pink grog	2.5	0.6	--
Shell	9.9	9.5	8.3
Grey	31.0	13.5	25.6
Oxidised	13.3	14.2	7.6

TABLE 5.10: THORPE MALSOR, PIT 4, LAYER 21, PERCENTAGES OF PRINCIPAL FABRICS

For the other fills of pit 4, jars comprise 69% of the vessels by rim EVE with bowls and dishes 16.5% and flagons 5.5%; a mortarium (1%), lids (>1%) and beakers (>1%) are also represented. Lid-seated jars occur in hard cream grog, pink grog, shell-gritted, oxidised and grey wares and curved rim jars in hard cream grog, oxidised and grey wares. Other vessel forms in hard cream grog ware are large jars, narrow mouthed jars, a wide bowl

5. Roman Settlement (AD43 - AD450)

and a mortarium. In grey ware there are also large jars, everted rim jars, small jars, narrow mouthed jars, jars with barbotine 'lozenge', rouletted or incised diagonal comb decoration (Fig 5.22, 22), a carinated bowl with a flat rim, a small bowl with a curved rim (Fig 5.2, 24), a bowl with a flat rim, dishes with everted, flat topped, plain, flanged, bead and bead or triangular rims, lids and an indented beaker (Fig 5.22, 23). Other vessels in oxidised ware comprise a ring-necked flagon with a large top bead, a flagon handle, a curved sided dish, a dish or bowl with a triangular rim (Fig 5.22, 20), a dish or bowl with a flat rim, a lid, narrow mouthed jars, small jars or beakers and an unguentarium or amphora-stopper (Fig 5.22, 21). Fragments from 16 samian ware vessels are represented. Recognisable forms are 31, 31R, 33, 37 (Fig 5.22, 18), 38 and Curle 15. Other fabrics that occur are LRCC - cornice rim, roughcast beakers (Fig 5.22, 26), Lower Nene Valley grey colour-coated ware (imitation samian ware form 36 with barbotine leaf), Oxfordshire white ware, Mancetter-Hartshill (mortarium with red, black and grey grits) and roughcast colour-coated ware, possibly of Colchester origin.

The samian ware date ranges are AD120-40, AD120-200, AD140-200 and AD160-200 and much of the other pottery would fit a date in the 2nd century. The Lower Nene Valley grey colour-coated ware, imitation samian ware form 36, is potentially the latest vessel, being reminiscent of vessels produced in the kilns at Stanground, Peterborough, in the early to mid 3rd century AD (Dannell 1973, 140; Dannell *et al* 1993, 90-1). Pit 4 also contains a number of small finds, including a coin of possible Hadrianic date (SF37), a nail cleaner (SF1) which is dated stylistically to 2nd/3rd centuries AD, and two bone pins (SFs 21, 22) with affinities to Crummy type 2, thought to have a terminal date of *c* AD200 (1983, 21). The range of fabrics is expressed as a percentage of the principal fabrics by number, weight and rim EVE (Table 5.11).

Fabric	No (%)	Weight (%)	EVE (%)
Hard cream grog	24.8	35.5	19.6
Pink grog	5.7	7.5	0.8
Shell	7.1	13.2	6.4
Grey	40.2	25.3	39.7
Oxidised	14.2	11.7	19.7

TABLE 5.11: THORPE MALSOR, PIT 4, OTHER LAYERS, PERCENTAGES OF PRINCIPAL FABRICS

Illustrated vessels (Figs 5.21 and 5.22)

1. Jar, curved rim, grey ware, ditch 39, (context 38)
2. Jar, lid-seated, shell-gritted, large shell flecks, ditch 39 (36)
3. Lid, hard cream grog, ditch 94 (90)
4. Bowl, carinated, grey ware, ditch 112 (109, 110) and pit 105 (100)
5. Jar, grey ware, ditch 117 (115)
6. Bowl, carinated, grey ware ditch 117 (115)
7. Flagon, disc-necked, oxidised ware, ditch 139 (133)
8. Jar, handled, grey ware, ditch 139 (136)
9. Bowl, carinated with a grooved rim, grey ware, ditch 139 (133)
10. Dish, grey ware, ditch 139 (136)
11. Beaker, roughcast, ditch 139 (136)
12. Mortarium, Mancetter-Hartshill, ditch 139 (132, 136). Mrs K F Hartley comments, 'The right-facing stamp is virtually complete and reads ICOTASGI retrograde; it is from one of at least nine dies used by the potter Icotasgus who worked in the Mancetter-Hartshill potteries within the period AD120-160, his optimum date being perhaps AD130-150. For details of his activity see Ferris, Bevan and Cutler 2000, 33, 4'.
13. Cheese press lid, grey ware, ditch 145 (144)
14. Dish, BB1, plain rim, burnished, black burnished, ditch 145 (144)
15. Bowl, mica-dusted, ditch 150 (148, 144); (cf ditch 125 (124) CGCC)
16. Beaker, funnel-necked, very dark grey colour coat, ditch 150 (148) (Fig 5.22)
17. Jar, hard grog, pit 4, layer 21
18. Rim sherd from a small form 37 bowl, Central Gaulish samian ware in the style of Geminus of Lezoux, pit 4 (9, 26). The motifs include Geminus' ovolo Rogers (1974) B76 and his untidy wavy line below. The design is repetitive; comprising small double medallions linked with the double astragalus (ibid) R91 used by Geminus and Drusus I, with a small trifid bud (ibid) G113 between. Of the complete medallions one contains a larger trifid leaf, the other rear-facing bird O. 2298. It is probable that these alternate. *c* AD120-140
19. Flagon, ring-necked with a large top bead, oxidised ware, pit 4 (7)
20. Bowl, triangular rim, oxidised ware, pit 4 (22)
21. Unguentarium or amphora-stopper, oxidised ware, pit 4 (23)
22. Jar base, grey ware, lighter core edges, pit 4 (24)
23. Indented jar, grey ware, light grey core, pit 4 (23)
24. Dish, flat rim, grey ware, very dark grey-black,, pit 4 (23, 21 ironstone layer)
25. Small dish, curved rim, grey ware, very dark grey-black, pit 4 (26)
26. Beaker, very dark grey colour-coat; LRCC roughcast, pit 4 (27)
27. Shallow dish, oxidised ware, probably mica dusted, ditch 72 (69), similar to Timby 2004, fig 14, 24

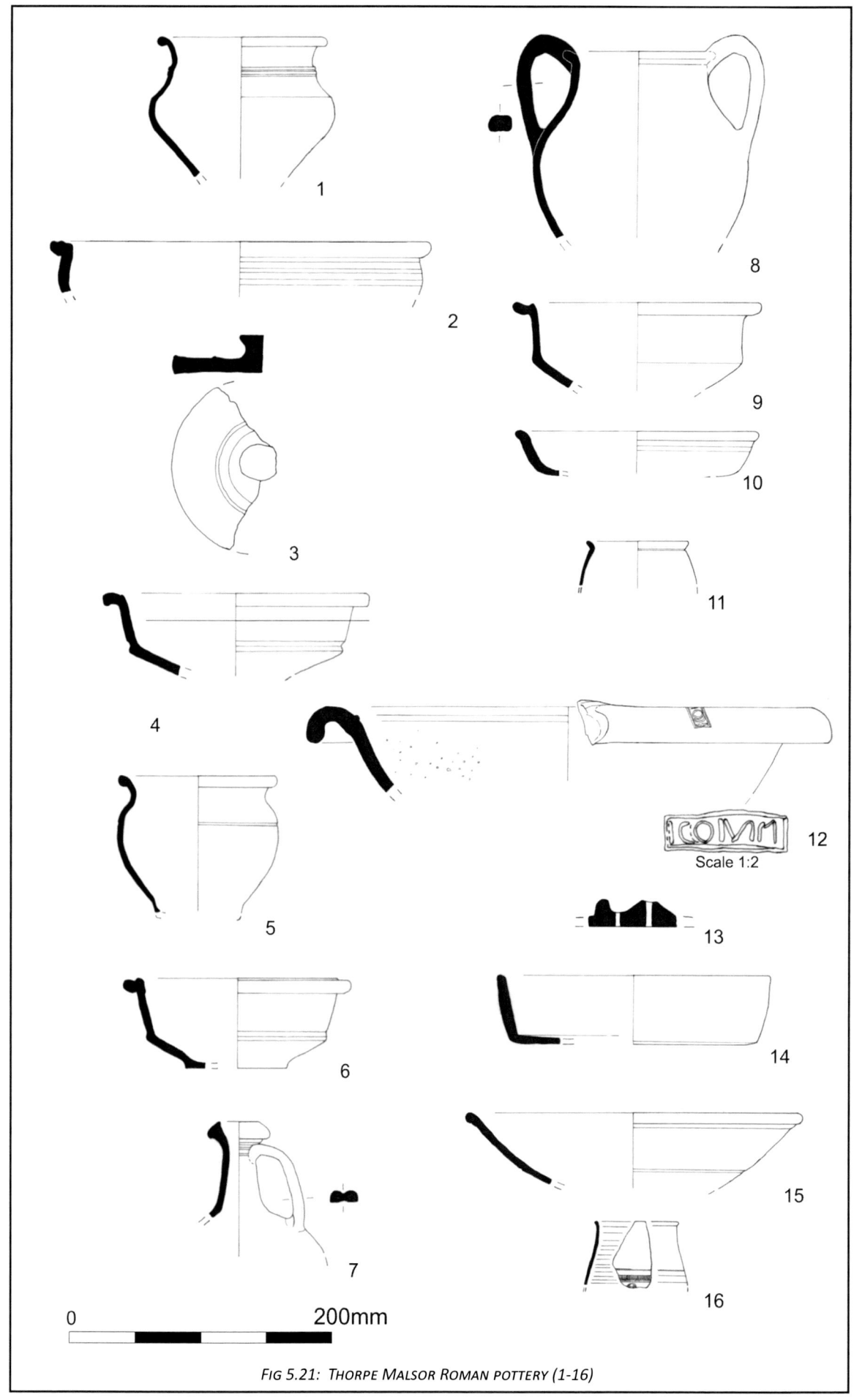

Fig 5.21: Thorpe Malsor Roman pottery (1-16)

5. Roman Settlement (AD43 - AD450)

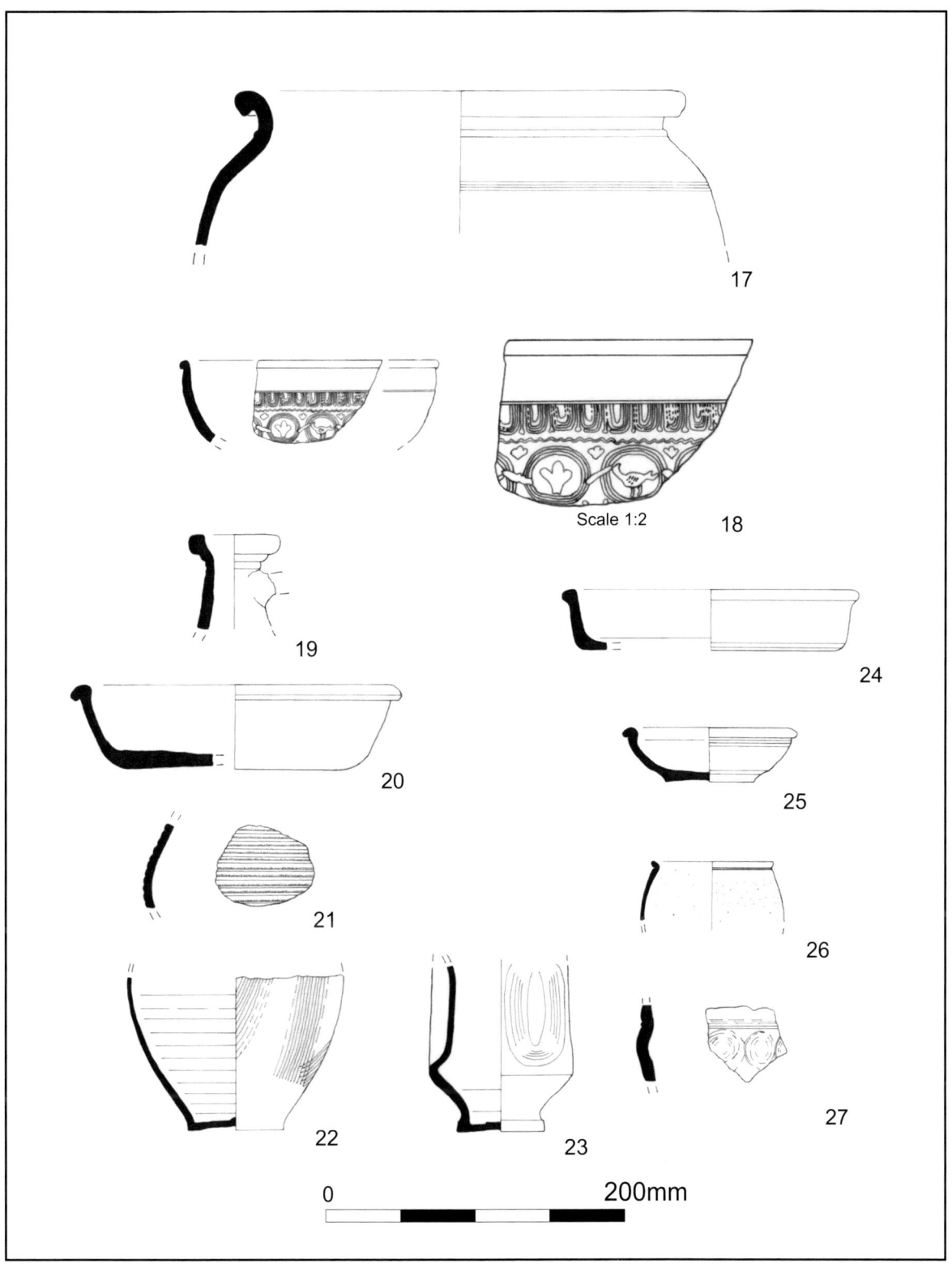

Fig 5.22: Thorpe Malsor Roman pottery (17-27)

Cross-feature joins

A number of joining sherds from different contexts were noted during the recording of the pottery, as follows:

Ditch 94 with Pit 46, intercutting features
Pit 105 with Ditch 112, adjacent sections
Pit 4 with Ditch 79, at opposite end of site
Ditch 117 with Ditch 139, same ditch system
Ditch 145 with Ditch 150, adjacent ditch sections
Ditch 145 with Ditch 125, adjacent ditch sections
Ditch 72 with Ditch 139, same ditch system

In most cases, these can be explained by intercutting features and different sections on the same ditch system. The joining sherds from a Central Gaulish samian ware

Curle 15, found in pit 4 and ditch 79, are more intriguing given the 35m distance between the two features.

The assemblages in these features are secondary, having been discarded as rubbish deriving from activity elsewhere. It is possible, therefore, that the deposit from which the broken samian vessel originated was dumped into more than one feature. If this were the case, other joins between pottery sherds from the different features might be expected, but none were noted, though the assemblages have not been examined together in detail. Interestingly, one of the joining sherds is large (pit 4) and the other is just a small piece from the rim. This raises the possibility of another scenario, one where a small piece escaped the initial collection of larger broken sherds, to become part of another rubbish deposit dumped into a different feature.

Samian ware
by J M Mills

The majority of the small collection of samian from Thorpe Malsor came from Central Gaulish kilns at Lezoux dating to the 2nd century AD, with a single sherd dating to the 1st century AD from Les Martres-de-Veyre and two sherds, both of form 18 (plates), from South Gaul.

The samian is in good condition. Few, if any sherds exhibit signs of excessive wear. A single drilled repair hole was noted on a dish dated to the early 2nd century AD from Les Martres (ditch 139) and a very small footring sherd appears to have had a notch, possibly a mark of ownership, cut across it (ditch 145). Otherwise the collection is unremarkable. Many of the sherds are very small which makes identification difficult; about half of the sherds weigh less than 5g each.

The date range of these sherds, which include a pre-Flavian (AD14-68) form 18 (plate) ditch 112, and forms of the late 2nd century AD, such as Walters 79 (dishes) and Dr 31R (bowls), suggests occupation throughout the 1st and 2nd centuries AD. In such a small collection it is not surprising that no examples from East Gaulish kilns were identified as these, like the products of Les Martres-de-Veyre, usually only form a small percentage of an assemblage. The range of forms is very limited, and only one certain decorated bowl, a form 37 in Geminus' style (pit 4), was identified (Fig 5.22, 18).

The Roman pottery from Great Cransley (Fig 5.23)

The site produced an assemblage of 1,256 sherds with a combined weight of over 17.5kg, giving an average sherd weight of 14g (Table 5.12). Some of the grogged wares may belong to, or have been produced in the Iron Age, and the Roman pottery appears to span the whole Roman period. The features from which pottery was recovered comprised a posthole, a pit, ditches, gullies and a well.

Fabric	No	%	Weight (g)	%
Hard cream grog	84	6.7	1730	9.8
Misc grogs	177	14.1	3282	18.6
Shell	157	12.5	2142	12.2
Grey	634	50.5	7398	42.0
Misc oxidised	158	12.6	2608	14.8
LNVCC	37	3.0	270	1.5
Total	1256		17604	

TABLE 5.12: GREAT CRANSLEY, ROMAN POTTERY ASSEMBLAGE BY PRINCIPAL FABRICS

Selected assemblages:

Five assemblages from Cransley were selected for more detailed analysis (Table 5.13). These are thought to represent specific episodes of deposition which had a limited time span but, as the features from which they are derived are essentially of an 'open' nature, it is not surprising that they also contain later material. The illustrated sherds have been selected to give an idea of the range of pottery fabrics and types occurring in each group and are augmented by vessels of intrinsic interest from other contexts (Fig 5.22).

Feature	No	Weight (g)	EVE
Ditch 11, E3	675	9778	12.7
Ditch 17, E2	213	3312	2.5
Ditch 23, E3	137	1648	1.7
Ditch 52, late boundary	128	1582	1.6
Pit 29, E2	47	652	0.8

TABLE 5.13: GREAT CRANSLEY, QUANTIFICATION OF SELECTED ROMAN POTTERY ASSEMBLAGES

Ditch 11, Enclosure 3, southern arm (same as ditch 23)

The assemblage from ditch 11 is by far the largest from the site with an overall weight approaching 10kg; the total rim EVE for ditch 11 is just under 13. Three-quarters of the vessels by rim EVE are jars, with bowls and dishes accounting for the rest. Lid-seated jars occur in hard cream grog, shell-gritted and oxidised wares and curved rim jars in hard cream grog (Fig 5.23, 28, 29), grog, shell-gritted, oxidised and grey wares (Fig 5.23, 30). Other jar forms present are storage jars in grog and shell-gritted wares, narrow-mouthed jars in grey and oxidised wares and a shell-gritted ware jar with a curved, undercut rim. The grey ware also includes bowls (Fig 5.23, 31) or dishes with bead, downturned, everted flat, triangular and flanged rims and dishes with plain rims (Fig 5.23, 32), flat and flanged rims. Other vessels occurring are an imitation samian ware form 36 (dish), and curved-sided dish with a triangular rim, a hunt cup and a flagon or narrow mouthed jar in LNVCC, a LNVCW mortarium with ironstone grits and the base of an indented beaker in oxidised ware (Fig 5.23, 34).

5. Roman Settlement (AD43 - AD450)

Four Central Gaulish samian ware vessels also occur in ditch 11. A form 31 (bowl) is dated *c.*AD140-200, a form 33 (cup), *c.*AD120-200, a possible Déchelette 72 (beaker), *c.*AD140-200 and a bowl, *c* AD120-200. The low proportion of grogged wares and the amounts of grey ware and LNVCC suggest material is derived from activity in the later 2nd and 3rd centuries. The LNVCC from the ditch includes an indented beaker with barbotine scale decoration, dating to the 3rd century AD, and an imitation samian form 36, which could date to the 3rd or 4th centuries AD. A shell-gritted jar with an undercut rim and a mortarium with ironstone trituration grits also date to the 3rd or even the 4th century AD. The narrow mouthed jar with painted decoration is very similar in form and decoration to cream oxidized ware vessels made in the Lower Nene Valley (cf. Perrin, 1999, fig 49, 328), but the fabric of this example is a sandy reddish-yellow, which suggests a different, perhaps more local, origin (Fig 5.23, 33). The range of fabrics is expressed as a percentage of the principal fabrics by number, weight and rim EVE (Table 5.14).

Fabric	No (%)	Weight (%)	EVE (%)
Hard cream grog	6.2	9.2	4.9
Grog	6.8	8.0	5.1
Shell	13.8	10.3	10.9
Grey	51.0	49.3	64.8
Misc oxidised	17.8	20.6	12.0
LNVCC	3.9	2.0	1.1

TABLE 5.14: GREAT CRANSLEY, DITCH 11, PERCENTAGES OF PRINCIPAL FABRICS

Ditch 17 (Enclosure 2, southern arm)

The total rim EVE for Ditch 17 is around 2.5, of which 82% are jars and 18% bowls. The relatively few recognisable vessels are a lid-seated jar and a jar with deep external rilling in pink grogged ware, curved rim jars in grey ware, a large wide bowl in pink grogged ware (Fig 5.23, 36) and a small grey ware curved-sided lid-seated dish or bowl.

The high percentage of grogged wares in ditch 17 would appear to indicate a date range of late 1st to 2nd century AD, despite the quantities of grey ware vessels, which are mainly jars with decoration typical of the later 1st or 2nd centuries AD, such as close combing, rouletting and zonal burnishing. Ditch 17 did not contain any LNVCC. The range of fabrics is expressed as a percentage of the principal fabrics by count, weight and rim EVE (Table 5.15).

Ditch 23 (Enclosure 3, southern arm, same as ditch 7)

The total rim EVE for ditch 23 is just 1.7, of which 85% comprises jars, 10% beakers and 5% the mortarium. Lid-seated jars occur in hard cream grog and grey wares and

Fabric	No (%)	Weight (%)	EVE (%)
Hard cream grog	0.9	3.0	--
Grog	2.8	1.9	--
Pink Grog	33.8	57.1	1.1
Grey	59.6	35.7	1.4

TABLE 5.15: GREAT CRANSLEY, DITCH 17, PERCENTAGES OF PRINCIPAL FABRICS

there are also curved and everted rim jars in grey ware. The other jar form present is a large jar in grey ware. The LNVCC from ditch 23 includes a plain rimmed beaker and an indented funnel neck beaker. The layers also contain sherds from a large mica-dusted vessel, which may be either a jar or flagon and a Mancetter-Hartshill mortarium which appears to be a bead rim, grooved flange type.

The proportion of grogged wares of the late 1st to 2nd centuries AD is quite high in ditch 23, though there are none in the pink grogged fabric. The grey wares form less than half the assemblage, again perhaps indicative of an earlier date range. Both LNVCC vessels are types from the 3rd century AD, while the large mica-dusted vessel is likely to date to the 2nd century. The range of fabrics is expressed as a percentage of the principal fabrics by count, weight and rim EVE (Table 5.16).

Fabric	No (%)	Weight (%)	EVE (%)
Hard cream grog	18.3	27.3	0.2
Grog	12.4	9.5	0.2
Shell	2.9	6.6	--
Grey	43.8	37.7	1.1
Misc oxidised	16.8	15.2	--
LNVCC	5.8	3.8	0.2

TABLE 5.16: GREAT CRANSLEY, DITCH 23, PERCENTAGES OF PRINCIPAL FABRICS

Ditch 52 (late boundary, cutting trackway ditches, eastern side)

The total rim EVE for ditch 52 is just 1.6, all from jars, comprising carinated and curved rim jars in grey ware and plain jars in shell-gritted ware (Fig 5.23, 36). The range of fabrics is expressed as a percentage of the principal fabrics by count, weight and rim EVE (Table 5.17).

Fabric	No (%)	Weight (%)	EVE (%)
Grog	2.3	0.9	-
Pink Grog	3.1	8.7	-
Shell	43.8	57.4	-
Grey	50.8	33.0	1.6

TABLE 5.17: GREAT CRANSLEY, DITCH 52, PERCENTAGES OF PRINCIPAL FABRICS

Shell-gritted ware and grey ware dominate this assemblage, in which the amount of grogged ware is relatively low. The shell-gritted ware is almost entirely from two vessels, both of which have cut holes in their bases; however, no rims were recovered. The grey ware is all from jars, one of which is substantially complete. Ditch 52 does not contain any LNVCC and the assemblage appears to date mainly to the 2nd century AD.

Pit 29, Enclosure 2

The total rim EVE for pit 29 is less than 1 (0.8), again all from jars, comprising jars with curved or everted rims in grey ware and a grey ware jar with external burnished lattice decoration.

Pit 29 does not contain any pink grogged ware, shell-gritted ware or LNVCC and the hard cream grogged ware comprises sherds from a jar. The grey ware jar with external burnished lattice decoration appears to be imitating black burnished ware. The oxidised ware is mainly from a small jar in a cream oxidised fabric of a form which is more common in grey ware (Fig 5.23, 37); there is also a sherd, probably from a flagon, with a cream slip over a reddish-yellow fabric. A stamped Central Gaulish samian ware form 31 base, dated c.AD170-90 occurs in the pit and the assemblage as a whole appears to date mainly to the 2nd century. The range of fabrics is expressed as a percentage of the principal fabrics by count, weight and rim EVE (Table 5.18).

Fabric	No (%)	Weight (%)	EVE (%)
Hard cream grog	29.8	42.9	0.6
Grey	40.4	22.1	--
Misc oxidised	23.4	20.2	0.2
Misc	4.6	12.6	--

TABLE 5.18: GREAT CRANSLEY, PIT 29, PERCENTAGES OF PRINCIPAL FABRICS

Illustrated vessels (Fig 5.23)

28. Jar, hard cream grog, ditch 11 (10)
29. Jar, feint external rilling, hard cream grog, ditch 11 (8)
30. Jar, beaded rim, grey ware, ditch 11 (9)
31. Bowl, grey ware with lighter core, ditch 11 (8)
32. Dish, grey ware, ditch 11 (8)
33. Narrow mouthed jar, oxidised ware, sandy reddish-yellow painted decoration, ditch 11 (9)
34. Indented jar/beaker, base, oxidised ware, possible kiln product, ditch 11(8)
35. Wide bowl, hard cream pink grogged ware, enclosure 2, ditch 17 (15)
36. Jar, grey ware, late boundary ditch 52 (50)
37. Jar, cream oxidised ware, possible kiln product? pit 29 (28)

Pit 29 also contained some kiln bars, associated with kilns of the 1st to 2nd centuries AD (Shaw 1979). There are no wasters or other certain indicators of possible local production amongst the pottery from Great Cransley. However, pit 29 did contain a small jar in a cream oxidised fabric which is a form that is more common in grey ware (Fig 5.23, 37). The only other 'candidates' from Cransley for possible local production are a substantially complete reddish-yellow oxidised indented beaker from ditch 11 and grey ware jars from ditch 17 and ditch 52, both substantially complete (not illustrated), which have a mixed grey/reddish-yellow colour.

Samian ware
by J M Mills

Sherds from four vessels came from ditch 11 and from one vessel in pit 29. The sherds are in good condition and, as might be expected of sherds from pits and ditches, the sherd size is, with the exception of the body sherd from a Déchelette 72 (beaker), quite large. All of the samian dates to the 2nd century, probably from the workshops at Lezoux in Central Gaul. Each feature produced part of a form 31 base (bowl), a form usually dated to the Antonine period (AD138-192). One of the bases bears a partial stamp of Tituro of Lezoux (AD136-200). It is not possible, or wise, to draw any conclusions from only five vessels, although their presence may help to refine the overall ceramic dating and interpretation of the site.

Other sites

Roman pottery was recovered from a number of other sites on the route of the pipeline (Table 5.19). The totals from Caldecott and Thorpe by Water are insignificant, and are low for the others; Glaston, Bisbrooke, Gretton, Rushton, Seaton, and White Hill Lodge. Little meaningful can be said about these assemblages.

The Glaston site was an early Anglo-Saxon cremation cemetery, and the Roman pottery came from nearby ditches. The LNVCC in this group comprises forms dating to the 4th century AD. At the Gretton ditches contained pottery spanning the 2nd to 4th centuries AD pottery, including a LNVCC form of the 4th century, and three cremation burials contained residual sherds dating to the 2nd century AD. At Rushton pottery from ditches and gullies appears to date to the 1st to 2nd centuries AD. A similar date is probable for the Roman pottery from Seaton, which came from a small ditch. At White Hill Lodge the pottery was from 17 features, each containing only a few sherds, with the group as a whole indicating activity throughout the Roman period.

5. Roman Settlement (AD43 - AD450)

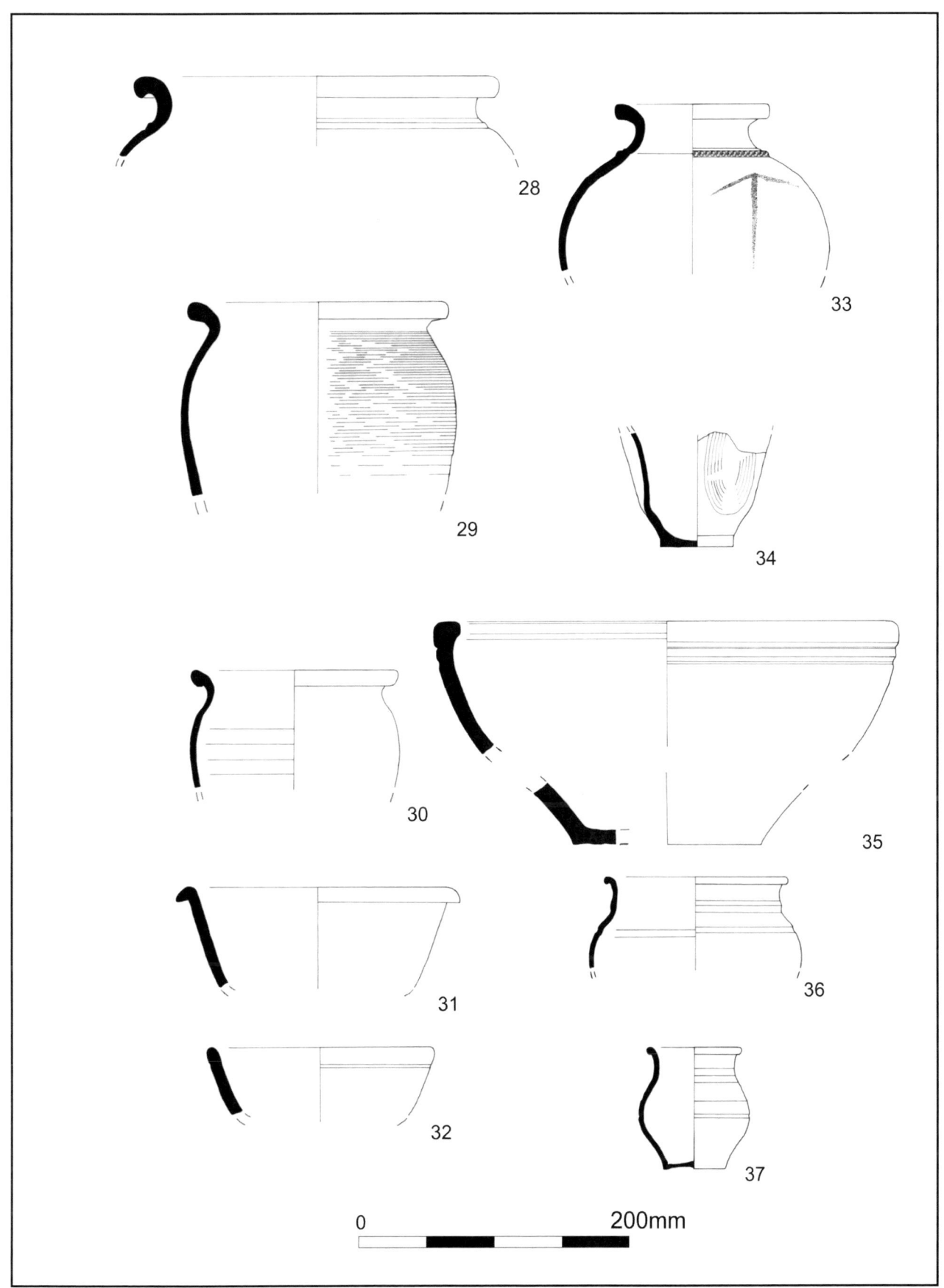

FIG 5.23: GREAT CRANSLEY ROMAN POTTERY (28-37)

Fabric	Caldecott No (wt) (g)	Glaston No (wt) (g)	Gretton No (wt) (g)	Rushton No (wt) (g)	Seaton No (wt) (g)	Thorpe by Water No (wt) (g)	White Hill Lodge No (wt) (g)
Hard cream grog	--	--	1 (16)	8 (104)	--	--	17 (330)
Grog	1 (2)	1 (8)	3 (20)	8 (40)	3 (20)	--	24 (312)
Shell	--	--	1 (4)	--	--	--	10 (276)
Grey	--	19 (104)	5 (46)	15 (120)	1 (6)	1 (2)	12 (165)
Oxidised	--	5 (36)	3 (8)	8 (60)	4 (24)	--	4 (16)
LNVCC	--	24 (341)	3 (26)	--	--	--	2 (86)
CGS	--	--	--	1 (2)	--	--	-
Total	1 (2)	49 (489)	16 (120)	40 (326)	8 (50)	1 (2)	69 (1185)

TABLE 5.19: SUMMARY OF ROMAN POTTERY FROM OTHER SITES

Roman fired clay and ceramic building material
by Pat Chapman

Seaton

There are 37 fragments of fired clay, weighing 329g, from pit 7 and ditch 13. The majority are fine silty clay, orange and buff with occasional black, irregularly-shaped. The rest are either dark red, sub-rounded and slightly sandy, or soft fine pale brown.

Gretton Road

All the material came from the topsoil. Four small sherds of Roman tile made from a fine slightly soft orange fabric with small grog or small gravel, but with no features to define the type of tile.

Rushton

Twelve sherds of unstratified Roman tile, weighing 740g, are small and very abraded. Four are roof tile sherds, two from the flat *tegula* identified by the flange, and two from the curved *imbrex*; the remainder are undiagnostic body sherds. The *tegulae* fabric is a fine hard orange clay, and three other sherds have a soft orange surface. One small undiagnostic sherd is made in the local regional pink grog type.

Thorpe Malsor

One *tegula* sherd came from ditch 125; the body 15mm thick, and the flange 45mm high from base to top and 20mm wide. The fabric is fine pinkish-orange and black clay with some shell and small gravel and voids from leached organic or calcareous material. The other *tegula*, from ditch 150, has lost most of its surface and flange, just leaving a rough hard pale orange-pink and white body, 13mm thick. A possible body sherd, 15mm thick, from pit 4, is made from hard fine reddish-orange clay with occasional shell and gravel.

A short kiln bar fragment *c* 38mm square came from ditch 112, and five oven plate fragments from pit 4. The plates are 20-35mm thick, with curved edges, made in hard fine orange clay, containing quite dense large shell, with dull grey smooth but uneven surfaces. This furniture is associated with kilns of the 1st to 2nd centuries AD (Shaw 1979). A further 54 fragments, weighing 622g, come from pit 4 and ditches 72 and 112. They are all in hard fine orange and reddish to black fabric, containing dense shell up to 12mm long, have smooth uneven surfaces and could be the remains of oven plates.

White Hill Lodge

There are 33 *tesserae*, 30 unstratified and three from ditch 65. They have been cut from tiles, 20-25mm thick, made from fine sandy clay with tiny gravel inclusions, fired to bright orange-brown, sometimes with a mid-grey core. Most of the edges and corners are abraded, apart from two in ditch 65. Their presence suggests there was a tessellated pavement somewhere in the vicinity.

Fourteen pieces of fired clay, weighing 225g, came from pit 16. They are typically 15-20mm thick, with one smooth but uneven and slightly vitrified surface, while the rest is fine slightly soft orange with tiny grit and grog, a fabric similar to some Roman tile. These fragments are probably the debris from the lining of an oven or hearth.

A large, irregular piece of fired clay came from ditch 21, and an unstratified piece with one smooth surface may be from a tile, but it is too small and broken to be certain.

Two lumps of tufa from ditch 65, each about 90 x 50 x 40mm, may suggest there was a bathhouse lined with tufa blocks in the neighbourhood.

5. Roman Settlement (AD43 - AD450)

Great Cransley

Forty-one fragments, weighing 2.1kg, from kiln bars, came from pit 29. They have a rectangular section, typically 85-90mm wide and 40mm thick, tapering to 20mm thick at one end. In fine orange clay with few inclusions, they are either slightly soft and friable or hard. One smooth flat highly-fired piece from ditch 42 may be the flattened end of a bar.

There are similar bars from pottery kilns in Caldecotte, Milton Keynes (King 1994) and Camp Hill, Northampton (Shaw 1979). The kilns at Caldecotte were described as La Tène III-derived kilns using portable kiln furniture before and after the Roman conquest. Those kiln bars were up to 350mm long with tapering ends. The pottery from the Camp Hill kilns was dated to the mid -1st to 2nd centuries AD.

Roman querns
by Andy Chapman

Thorpe Malsor

Fragments of five stones, with a total weight of 11.3kg, probably come from four flat-topped querns typical of the Roman period, in three distinct geologies (Table 5.20).

The smallest stone (SF25-26), only 300mm in diameter, is a distinctive sandstone conglomerate containing dense large quartz pebbles, Old Red Sandstone from the Forest of Dean (Shaffrey 2006). It has a small central eye, only 50mm in diameter, and the surfaces are smooth, but retain no tool marks. A thin band of surface iron-staining, 10-15mm thick, encircles the circumference of the stone, indicating the former presence of an iron band to which the turning handle was probably attached, making it easier to rotate such a small diameter stone. The stone diameter is accurate as the central eye survives, but the surviving length of circumference has a flattened curvature, suggesting that it comprised a number of flattened facets, perhaps to prevent the encircling iron band from slipping. An example of a complete upper stone with an iron band attached has been recovered from Chester's Fort on Hadrian's Wall (Watts 2002, 38 & fig 11b), and a similar quern in Old Red Sandstone also with an encircling band of iron staining, has been found at a Roman settlement at Milton Ham, near Northampton (Chapman 2010b, 26-27 & fig 20).

There is a slightly larger diameter quern (45) in fine-grained sandstone, 420mm diameter. This has a large central eye, 150mm diameter, and had been heavily used, with the stone only 26mm thick at the central eye. The upper surface and the circumference are worn smooth but retain some scattered shallow dimpled tool marks, while the grinding surface has a denser pattern of small dimpled tool marks.

The largest stone (8), in Millstone Grit, is 600mm in diameter, up to 110mm thick and 90mm thick at the circumference, with a very large central eye, 200mm in diameter. This stone lies at the upper end of the size and weight range for hand rotation, as the complete stone would have weighed around 40kg, which suggests that this was probably a small millstone rather than a hand-turned rotary quern. The other two pieces (30 and 44), probably come from the same stone.

Context Feature (small find, SF)	Geology	Diameter/ Thickness Completeness	Comments
76, ditch 79 (SF25-26)	Sandstone conglomerate (dense quartz up to 35mm) Old Red Sandstone	Curvature 450mm Diameter 300mm Eye 50mm Thickness 40-65 Completeness 20%	Upper stone Plain surfaces, band of iron-staining around circumference
13, ditch 12 (SF30)	Millstone Grit (Coarse, quartz 5-10mm)	Thickness 100mm	Irregular fragment, no surfaces survive
9, pit 4 (SF8)	Millstone Grit	Diameter 600mm Eye 200m Thickness 65-90mm Completeness 15%	Upper stone Smooth surfaces, no tool marks
21, pit 4 (SF44)	Millstone Grit (Coarse, quartz 5-10mm)	Thickness 110mm	Irregular fragment, Full width survives Probably same as SF30
21, pit 4 (SF45)	Sandstone (fine grained)	Diameter 420mm Eye 150mm Thickness 26-42mm Completeness 10%	Upper stone Dimpled surfaces

TABLE 5.20: THORPE MALSOR, QUANTIFICATION OF QUERNS

Great Cransley

There are fragments from three flat rotary querns in Millstone Grit, typical of the Roman period; two of these, along with part of a sharpening stone, came from the well, 56 (Table 5.21).

Two partial upper stones (7 and 8) are similar in form but show extreme contrasts in usage. Both are from flat-topped upper stones around 600mm in diameter, and they are plain, with no tool marks surviving. The thicker stone (7) has a central eye 100mm in diameter. However, while stone (7) is near its original thickness, at up to 88mm thick, the other (8) has been worn down to a minimum of only 19mm thick. The thicker stone has also had its outer circumference hacked away, and it is possible that this may have been a deliberate act of "killing" an almost new stone. The surviving fragment of this stone weighs 7.2kg, so the complete stone would have weighed $c.$36kg. A third small fragment of an upper stone (10) may be one of the fragments hacked from the circumference of stone (7).

A grinding/sharpening stone (9) is a roughly rectangular block of fine-grained sandstone, at least 142mm long, 100mm wide and 50-85mm thick. The broad upper surface is worn to a smooth concave surface, and one adjacent side is also worn to a similarly smooth concave surface. It seems most likely that it was used as a whetstone for the honing of metal implements.

Other Roman finds
by Tora Hylton

Glaston

An iron nail, Manning type 1b nail (1985, fig 32) and a rod fragment (possibly a nail shank) came from ditch 34. A Roman coin from the topsoil, perforated and extremely worn, is a 3rd-century radiate, c AD275 (Ian Meadows pers comm). The perforation, presumably for suspension, suggests that the coin may have been reused as a pendant during the Anglo-Saxon period. A piece of molten lead was recovered from ditch 10 in the field to the south of the A47.

Gretton Road

The assemblage comprises numerous nails and nail fragments from cremation burials 8 and 14. From burial 8 there are nine flat sub-circular nail heads, up to $c.$10mm in diameter, and four nail shank fragments. There are no complete examples. Over 70 individual fragments were recovered from burial 14, including 29 nails with heads but not the entire shank and one complete nail, 34mm long. All the nails appear to have the same sized heads; flat, sub-circular, and 11mm in diameter; similar to Manning Type 1b (1985, fig 32). None appear to be hobnails, and it is possible that they originated from the material used to construct the pyre.

Thorpe Malsor

The majority of artefacts date to the Roman period and form a small assemblage comparable with those from other small rural sites of a similar date.

Coins

A sestertius, possibly of Hadrian (AD117-138), comes from pit 20, and a possible second example from pit 4. These two coins are both worn; the example from pit 4 is almost smooth denoting an extended period in circulation. Coins of this period were kept in circulation, so a coin date in the early-mid 2nd century is unlikely to indicate the date of deposition, which could be in the later 2nd century or even the 3rd century AD.

A corroded coin, possibly of Magnentius, issued AD350-53, from the spoil heap and has limited value in dating the site.

Context/ feature (small find SF)	Geology	Diameter/ Thickness Completeness	Comments
53, well 56 (SF7)	Millstone Grit	Diameter >570mm Thickness 88mm Eye 100mm 20%	Upper stone Same stone as SF10?
53, well 56 (SF8)	Millstone Grit	Diameter c 600mm Thickness 19-34mm 5%	Well worn, upper stone
53, well 56 (SF9)	Fine-grained sandstone	Length (broken) 142mm Width 100mm Thickness 50-85mm	Sharpening stone
20, ditch 23 (SF10)	Millstone Grit	85mm thick	Irregular fragment Same stone as SF7?

TABLE 5.21: GREAT CRANSLEY, QUANTIFICATION OF QUERNS

5. Roman Settlement (AD43 - AD450)

Copper alloy objects

The five copper alloy objects comprise a nail cleaner, a pin, a rivet and two undiagnostic fragments of sheet metal. The nail cleaner, from pit 4, has a stylised blade with a broad, almost circular upper section decorated with ring and dot, which tapers to form a long, narrow, parallel-sided blade, which terminates in a double point. The suspension loop is on the same alignment as the blade and there are decorative mouldings (spool and reel) at the junction with the blade. Two of the raised ridges are decorated with opposing oblique incisions, giving a rope effect. It displays similarities to Crummy's Type 2b, which dates to the 2nd/3rd centuries AD (1983, fig 62, 1872). The pin, also from pit, 4, is complete, 106mm long, with a simple head with double groove (reel) beneath a conical/sub-oval moulding; the shank is circular-sectioned and tapers to a point. Typologically, it falls within Cools Group 2, Sub-group B (knob on cordoned head), a style of pin used throughout Roman period (1990, fig 2, 9). One of the undiagnostic fragments of sheet metal is pierced by a short square-sectioned rivet.

Copper casting debris
by Andy Chapman

A cylinder of copper alloy, 24mm in diameter and 10mm high, has a concave top and expands outwards at the bottom into three lobes, all fractured near the top leaving uneven surfaces. It is suggested that this piece is casting debris, probably the fill of a cylindrical sprue cup that had fed three separate runners. It was recovered from layer 31 above ditch 39, and was not securely stratified in a Roman deposit.

Iron

There are 11 individually or group recorded iron objects; two undiagnostic fragments and nine nails. The nails comprise four Manning Type 1b for light structural fixings (1985, fig 32); one Type 10, a hob nail for shoes, one Type 3 with a T-shaped head; and one Type 4 with an L-shaped head. The latter two types could have been driven into the wood to conceal the head.

Lead

There is one piece of lead, a waste molten fragment from pit 4.

Worked bone

There are three incomplete bone pins. Two are furnished with transverse grooves beneath a globular head. The head of one is ornamented with two transverse grooves, while the other has three transverse grooves, both stylistically similar to Crummy's Type 2 (1983, fig 18). There is also a pointed terminal from the shaft of a pin.

Glass

Twenty-one fragments of Roman glass were recovered from stratified deposits (Table 5.22). Much of the assemblage comprises body sherds with curved profiles, too small to provide any detail of the vessel form, but the fineness of the glass suggests that they originated from fine tablewares. There are vessel fragments in blue-green, colourless and yellow-brown glass, and decorative techniques include indents and trails. Part of a convex cup in pale green glass decorated with indents, is a form of decoration occurring throughout the Roman period (Price and Cottam 1998, 32-33). A colourless undiagnostic fragment decorated with a horizontal trail, is possibly from a beaker, and a fire-rounded out-turned rim fragment is probably from small flask or unguent bottle. The assemblage probably dates to late 1st to 3rd centuries AD.

Context/feature	Colour	Description
9/4	Colourless	Undiagnostic body sherd, curved profile, bubbles in matrix (SF7)
	Pale green	Rim fragment, fire-rounded out-turned rim, probably from small flask or unguent bottle (SF6)
22/4	Colourless	Undiagnostic, curved profile, translucent with iridescent surfaces (SF36)
	Blue-green	Undiagnostic, curved profile with iridescent surfaces (SF36)
23/4	Yellow-brown	Six fragments, undiagnostic with curved profile. Poss. shoulder from flagon (SF16)
	Blue-green	Two undiagnostic sherds with curved profile (SF16)
	Colourless	?Beaker – curved profile, vestige of trailed decoration on ext. surface (SF16)
110/112	Pale green	Six fragments (five joining) Convex cup (Dia. C.90mm), Out-turned fire-rounded rim with indentations (SF 31)
115/117	Blue-green	Undiagnostic, surface blistered/spald (SF33).
136/139	Pale green	Base sherd – faint horizontal polishing marks on surface (SF41)

TABLE 5.22: THORPE MALSOR, ROMAN GLASS

White Hill Lodge

Parts of three Roman brooches were recovered. A hybrid Colchester type brooch (SF2), dating to AD60-90, is from the subsoil. It is a large brooch, 64mm long, with part of the spring and catchplate missing/damaged. The bow is almost round in section and tapers to a point. The catchplate, although incomplete, appears to be triangular-shaped, a British trait (MacKreth 1994, 287).

A round plate brooch (SF1), 32mm in diameter, is from the subsoil. It is divided into two zones by concentric ribs, and the inner collar secures an applied conical copper alloy boss, now loose (Fig 5.24). The outermost ring contains blue enamel and inner ring white enamel, now discoloured. The underside is furnished with a hinge mechanism, comprising a spring of three turns set between two lugs with an iron axial rod, and a catch plate; the pin is missing.

A Colchester derivative brooch (Nene Valley group), dating to the 1st and 2nd centuries AD, comes ditch 35. It is incomplete, in four pieces, with the wings and part of the pin missing. There is a crest on the upper part of the bow, otherwise it is plain.

FIG 5.24: GREAT CRANSLEY, CIRCULAR COPPER ALLOY PLATE BROOCH (SF1) (SCALE 10MM)

There are three nails and several corroded objects that are unidentifiable.

Great Cransley

Part of a Dolphin brooch (Polden Hill type), dating to the late 1st to mid-2nd century AD, was recovered from the subsoil.

Eight iron nails were recovered from posthole 7 and ditch 11. There are four hobnails, presumably from footwear, Manning types Type 10 (1985, 134ff), and four nails with flat sub-circular heads and up to 44mm long (Type 1b), probably used for light structural fixings.

Faunal and environmental remains from the Roman settlements:

Human bone
by Sarah Inskip

Cremation burials from Gretton Road

Two Roman cremation burials associated with iron nails, were recovered from the excavation at Gretton Road, and a third was recovered nearby during the watching brief in Field 55:01.

The cremated bone mainly consists of white fragments and some grey pieces, with the high quantity of white fragments indicating temperatures exceeding 600°C (Brickley and McKinley 2004). The low quantities of material in these deposits (Table 5.23) indicates that they represent very incomplete individuals, since adult cremations weigh between 1-3kg and juveniles around 0.5kg (Trotter and Hixon 1974).

The cremated bone from burial 8 contains a number of identifiable elements, including temporal, frontal and vault fragments from the skull, seven occipital tooth roots (including a lower permanent incisor and a possible premolar), cervical vertebra, a manual phalange and long bone fragments. The bone elements from Burial 55:01 include skull, long bone fragments, bones of the toe and some tooth roots. Burial 14 contained no identifiable fragments.

The bone provides little information for determining the age or sex of the individuals. Fused phalanges from Burials B55:01 and 8 indicate individuals over 14 years

Burial	Weight	Weight by bone size (10-1mm)				Maximum
		>10	>5	>2	>1	
B8	107g	4g	47g	56g	<1g	18.1mm
B14	<1g	-	<1g	-	-	7.8mm
B55:01	37g	2g	17g	18g	-	not recorded

TABLE 5.23: GRETTON ROAD, QUANTIFICATION OF CREMATED BONE

of age (Scheuer and Black 2000, 466) but more concise estimates cannot be provided as the major indicators of age (pubis, auricular surface and the occlusial surfaces of teeth) are missing, as are the critical sexually dimorphic regions. There are no notable pathologies.

Infant burial from Thorpe Malsor

An infant burial was recovered from the upper fill (43) of pit 46, dated to 2nd to 3rd centuries AD. Over 90% of the cortical bone survived and the bones are in excellent condition, with the skeleton 50-75% complete. No skull bones were recovered and the hands and feet are absent. Out of the spinal column, only three lumbar vertebrae are present. Seventeen ribs are present but the scapulae are absent. Out of the long bones, only the left clavicle, ulna and fibula are absent. As no teeth were recovered, age estimates were obtained from long bone measurements (Mays 2011, 1), using data produced by Fazekas and Kosa (1978) and presented in Scheuer and Black (2000) (Table 5.24).

Long bone	Maximum length (mm)	Age
Right humerus	65.8	40 weeks +
Right radius	52.8	40 weeks +
Right femur	78.6	40 weeks +

TABLE 5.24: GRETTON ROAD, HUMAN INFANT LONG BONE LENGTHS AND EQUIVALENT AGES

All the long bones are slightly greater than the average measurement for 40 weeks gestation, but they fall in the normal range for a full term infant. Accordingly, the evidence suggests that the infant is likely to have died around the time of birth or in the immediate post-natal period.

The burial of infants during the Roman period in Britain

Many infants appear to have been buried separately from other members of society during the Roman period where burials took place in extramural cemeteries from the 1st and 2nd centuries AD (Jupp and Gittings 1999, 51). Infant burials commonly appear in a number of different locations including under floors, in walls, in pits and near buildings. Examples can be found at Beddingham Villa, Sussex (Waldron *et al* 1999), Bozeat villa (S Carlyle, pers comm) and Silverstone Fields Farm (Mudd 2008), Northamptonshire. While it is very easy to jump to the conclusion that the burial of these tiny individuals in such unusual places suggest foul play, Mays (1993, 883) cautions that there are many examples of societies where infants are accorded different burial rites. However, documentary evidence highlighted by Taylor (2010, 94) indicates that the Romans did practice infanticide for many reasons, including limitation of family size and the birth of a daughter as opposed to a more preferred son.

Although archaeologically a problematic concept, Mays (1993) does suggest that infanticide may have occurred in Britain, but without direct evidence of trauma it is impossible to pinpoint the individuals that may have been victims of the practice. As no evidence of trauma is observed on the Thorpe Malsor infant, it is not possible to say whether the infant died as a result of infanticide or simply of one of the natural causes invisible to osteological examination.

Animal bone
by Matilda Holmes

Animal bone was recovered from several Roman settlements investigated along the route of the pipeline, although only three of the assemblages, from Thorpe Malsor, White Hill Lodge and Great Cransley, Northamptonshire, were sufficiently large to permit further analysis beyond the assessment stage (Deighton 2010). These assemblages have been fully recorded and analysed to provide an indication of the animal husbandry practices adopted at the settlements (Tables 5.25-5.27).

Site	Date	NISP
Thorpe Malsor	Late Iron Age and Roman	490
White Hill Lodge	Roman	85
Great Cransley	Roman	75

TABLE 5.25: ROMAN ANIMAL BONE ASSEMBLAGES BY SIZE (NISP)

Site Condition	Thorpe Malsor	White Hill Lodge	Great Cransley
Excellent (1)	1	0	0
Good (2)	122	8	0
Fair (3)	190	12	20
Poor (4)	35	4	14
Bad (5)	3	9	4
Total	351	33	38

TABLE 5.26: ANIMAL BONE CONDITION BY BONE NUMBER

Site/ Taphonomy	Thorpe Malsor	White Hill Lodge	Great Cransley
Butchery	9%	6%	3%
Gnawing	23%	12%	7%
Fresh break	30%	27%	16%
Burning	3%	0	0
Refit	48 (184)	7 (164)	6 (64)
loose teeth: mandibles*	55:13	5:3	16:1

* mandibles with 2 or more molars present

TABLE 5.27: ANIMAL BONE TAPHONOMY BY PERCENTAGES

Thorpe Malsor

Animal bone was recovered from ditches and pits, with a few remains from smaller gullies and postholes (Table 5.28). Due to uncertainties over the nature of the sites, the potential for inter-site comparisons is limited. However, the assemblage is large enough for some idea of the nature of the deposits and animal husbandry to be gained.

Feature	No. bones
No feature	39
Ditch	325
Gully	3
Pit	270
Posthole	3
Total	**640**

TABLE 5.28: THORPE MALSOR, NUMBER OF IDENTIFIED ANIMAL BONES

Carcass representation and butchery

Samples are small but, nevertheless, they are generally indicative of the deposition of all parts of cattle and sheep carcasses (Table 5.29). Butchery marks were recorded on cattle, sheep and pig bones in the form of chop and cut marks, on limb bones in areas consistent with the disarticulation of the carcass to make joints of food. Two horse metapodia had been chopped through at the proximal end, which may suggest the removal of skin or the use of bone for the manufacture of objects. In general, the assemblage is typical of the deposition of carcass parts from all stages of processing.

Species representation and diet

The assemblage is dominated by cattle, present in over half the assemblage (Table 5.30). Sheep/goats were the next most common species, then pig and horse bones in similar, but smaller quantities, and a few fragments of dog and domestic fowl. Within this assemblage, beef would have been the most common meat, then mutton, pork and possibly horse.

Animal husbandry

The majority of ageing data was recovered from the fusion of limb bones, although a few mandibles were complete enough to be used for the calculation of tooth wear data. Nearly all cattle had reached 3-4 years of age, at which point over 80% were culled; of those remaining, a small number were alive until maturity. Older animals were apparent from the tooth wear data, where the majority were alive until maturity (stage G-I). Taken together, this suggests that a large proportion of cattle were culled when they were just full grown, to give the

Anatomy	Cattle	Sheep	Pig	Horse
Horn Core*	3	-	-	-
Occipitale	4	-	1	-
Zygomatic	2	-	-	-
Mandible**	6	8	3	1
Scapula	2	1	3	1
Humerus P	1	-	-	-
Humerus D	5	-	1	2
Radius P	4	2	-	1
Radius D	2	1	-	1
Ulna	1	-	-	-
3rd Carpal	1	-	-	-
Pelvis	6	1	1	-
Femur P	2	-	1	1
Femur D	4	1	2	
Tibia P	3	1	1	1
Tibia D	5	2		2
Calcaneum	2	2	1	1
Metacarpal P	2	1	-	2
Metacarpal D	1	-	-	1
Metatarsal P	5	1	-	-
Metatarsal D	4	1	-	-
1st Phalange***	1	1	-	1
2nd Phalange***	1	-	1	1
3rd Phalange***	1	-	-	-
Atlas	3	-	-	-
Axis	-	2	-	-
Cervical	3	2	-	-
Thoracic	2	-	-	-
Lumbar	10	-	-	-
Sacrum	1	-	-	-
Total	**87**	**27**	**15**	**16**

TABLE 5.29: THORPE MALSOR, REPRESENTATION OF BONE ELEMENTS (EPIPHYSIS COUNT)

maximum meat to cost ratio, and another group of cattle were kept alive until old age, presumably for secondary production, either milk or traction.

Both the fusion and tooth wear data for the sheep assemblage are similar, suggesting that there was a steady cull of animals from one year of age. There was also evidence for a neonatal animal, suggesting that they were bred in the vicinity. This indicates that some animals were kept for secondary products, and excess animals were culled from the flock for meat as necessary.

There was little evidence for pigs over one year of age from the fusion data; this was reflected in a mandible

5. Roman Settlement (AD43 - AD450)

Species	No	%
Cattle	264	54
Sheep/ Goat	135	28
Sheep	2	-
Pig * skeletons count as 1	37*	7
Horse	35	7
Dog	11	2
Domestic fowl	4	1
Human	1	-
Total Identified	**490**	
Unidentified mammal	551	-
Large mammal	611	-
Medium mammal	228	-
Small mammal	10	-
Bird	2	-
Total	**1892**	-

TABLE 5.30: THORPE MALSOR, ANIMAL BONE SPECIES (NISP)

at wear stage C (after Hambleton 1999), yet the other two mandibles gave wear stages of E, indicative of older animals up to 2.5 years of age. Two nearly complete, extremely young pig skeletons were recovered from pit 20, one of which displayed evidence of a massive infection surrounding a fractured tibia prior to the animal's death.

All horse bones were fused, consistent with their importance for secondary products (ie draught and transport).

White Hill Lodge

Nearly all bones were recovered from ditches dated to the Roman period (Table 5.31). The sample was very small and will only be considered in terms of the species represented, as it lies well below the minimum 300 fragments suggested by Hambleton (1999) for an assemblage to be suitable for inter-site comparisons.

Feature	No
Ditch	93
Gully	1

TABLE 5.31: WHITE HILL LODGE, NUMBER OF IDENTIFIED ANIMAL BONES

Despite the small size of the assemblage, there were a surprising variety of species present both from the hand-recovered and soil sample material (Table 5.32). As well as the main domesticates (cattle, sheep/goat and pig), this included horse, dog, a pigeon or dove and the only fish bone from the entire project: two eel vertebrae. Oyster shell was also present.

Species	Hand-collected
Cattle	41
Sheep/Goat	13
Pig	3
Horse	19
Dog *articulated fragments count as 1	5*
Pigeon/ dove	2
Eel	1
Total Identified	**85**
Unidentified mammal	66
Large mammal	109
Medium mammal	9
Total	**269**

TABLE 5.32: WHITE HILL LODGE, ANIMAL BONE SPECIES (NISP)

The animal bone group from ditch 44 came from the head and vertebrae of an adult dog. There were no signs of butchery.

Great Cransley

The animal bones were recovered from the enclosure ditches and the well (Table 5.33). Again, the sample was small, with fewer than 100 elements identified to species, so it will only be considered briefly.

Feature	No
Ditch	17
Enclosure Ditch	83
Well	3
Gully	1

TABLE 5.33: GREAT CRANSLEY, NUMBER OF IDENTIFIED ANIMAL BONES

A more restricted suite of species was recorded at this site, the assemblage being dominated by the bones of larger mammals, cattle and horse, with a few sheep/goat bones also recorded (Table 5.34).

Species	Hand collected
Cattle	58
Sheep/Goat	5
Horse	10
Amphibian	2
Total Identified	**75**
Unidentified Mammal	137
Large Mammal	112
Medium Mammal	19
Total	**343**

TABLE 5.34: GREAT CRANSLEY ANIMAL BONE SPECIES (NISP)

Of greatest interest were the well deposits, which included a number of background species: water vole, shrew, frog (amphibian), mouse, vole and a cattle skull, without mandibles, possibly a deliberate deposition to mark the disuse of the well. The deposition of complete vessels, skulls and animals have been recorded from a number of Roman wells (Fulford 2001, 202), although these are more commonly dogs, such as at Staines, where at least 16 dogs were placed in a Roman well on top of infill material (Chapman and Smith 1988). However, the dumping of a large quantity of animal bones in a well at Oakridge, Basingstoke (Maltby 1994) included a predominance of cattle head, tail and foot bones, described as primary butchery waste, which were not considered to be of ritual nature, but merely the opportune dumping of refuse.

Discussion

These sites provide an interesting view of the animal husbandry and diet of several settlements in a relatively small geographical area. The emphasis on cattle in all phases is notable, although the poor preservation of the assemblage may have biased the survival of bones towards the larger fragments of cattle and greater destruction of smaller fragments such as sheep and pigs.

Data from the Roman settlement near Thorpe Malsor indicates a similar husbandry strategy, where animals were kept for meat, but there is also an emphasis on secondary production. The two smaller assemblages from the Roman sites to the south were very different in character, despite the small size of the assemblages. White Hill Lodge had a wide variety of species that may indicate a wealthier settlement, whose inhabitants dined on wild and domestic mammals as well as birds and fish. This provides a contrast with the other assemblages, which were limited to the main domesticates, none more so than the site at Great Cransley, which was dominated by cattle and horse. A cautionary note must be sounded against making judgements on the character of a settlement from small samples. For example, it has been shown previously that the bones of larger mammals are more likely to be disposed of at the periphery of a site (Wilson 1996), and if the assemblage from Great Cransley was from boundary ditches, this could explain the predominance of cattle and horse. Nonetheless, the diversity of species at White Hill Lodge is very different to that recorded from the other, contemporary sites, and does imply that the inhabitants enjoyed a more varied diet.

Charred plant remains
by Val Fryer

At five sites of Roman settlement and activity, a total of 63 bulk soil samples were taken for assessment and analysis. Only the assemblages from Thorpe Malsor, and in particular those from a single Roman pit at that site, merited further work.

Thorpe Malsor

The assemblages are from the fills of three Roman ditches, a posthole (Table 5.35) and a pit (Table 5.36). The three fills from the pit are of especial note as they all contain moderate to high densities of cereal chaff/grains and seeds of common segetal weeds. It would appear most likely that all are derived from one or more small deposits of charred cereal processing waste. Preservation was variable; the grains/seeds within some assemblages were severely puffed and distorted, probably as a result of combustion at very high temperatures, whilst other remains were very well preserved.

Occasional to moderate quantities of grains/seeds are recorded within all seven samples and include barley (*Hordeum* sp), wheat (*Triticum* sp) and oat (*Avena* sp), with wheat and barley occurring most frequently. The wheat grains were mostly of an elongated 'drop' form typical of emmer (*T. dicoccum*) or spelt (*T. spelta*), although a small number of more rounded hexaploid type forms were also noted. Spelt chaff was predominant but bread wheat (*T. aestivum/compactum*) type rachis nodes were also recovered from pit 4 (see below).

The assemblage from ditch 117 is also of note as, although small, it is almost entirely composed of silica 'skeletons' of cereal awn. Such assemblages are formed when chaff is burnt in a well aerated fire at a very high temperature, leaving only the silica skeletons of the original plant remains.

Seeds of common weeds and wetland plants, and tree/shrub macrofossils were present, mostly at a low density. Weed seeds, often occurring as single specimens within an assemblage, included: broom (*Bromus* sp), grass (Poaceae), knotgrass (*Polygonum aviculare*), dock (*Rumex* sp), goosegrass (*Galium aparine*), corn gromwell (*Lithospermum arvense*), henbane (*Hyoscyamus niger*) and vetch/vetchling (*Vicia/Lathyrus* sp). Nutlets/fruits of wetland plants, namely sedge (*Carex* sp) and spike sedges (*Eleocharis* sp) were also recorded along with single examples of hazel (*Corylus avellana*) nutshell and damson/bullace (*Prunus domestica* ssp *insititia*) type fruit stones. Charcoal/charred wood fragments were present and were frequently the major component of the assemblage.

Pit 4

Of the nine samples, only the three from the fills of pit 4 merited further analysis (Table 5.36). All three contained moderate to high densities of charred plant material, much of which appeared to be derived from either cereal processing waste or from burnt fodder or litter. It was

5. Roman Settlement (AD43 - AD450)

Sample	6	7	9	10
Context	73	114	137	144
Feature	74	117	139	150
Feature type	posthole	ditch	ditch	ditch
Cereals				
Avena sp. (grains)	x	-	-	-
Hordeum sp. (grains)	x	-	xcf	xcf
Triticum sp. (grains)	-	-	x	x
(glume bases)	-	x	x	-
T. spelta L. (glume bases)	-	x	-	-
Cereal indet. (grains)	x	xfg	x	-
(silica skeletons)	-	xxxx	-	-
Herbs				
Anthemis arvensis L.	-	-	-	x
Hyoscyamus niger L.	xcf	-	-	-
Lithospermum arvense L.	-	xfg	-	-
Small Poaceae indet.	-	-	x	-
Raphanus raphanistrum L. (siliquae)	-	-	-	xfg
Rosaceae indet.	-	x	-	-
Rumex sp.	-	x	-	-
Stellaria media (L.)Vill	-	-	-	x
Tripleurospermum inodorum (L.) Schultz-Bip	-	x	-	-
Vicia/Lathyrus sp.	-	-	x	-
Wetland plants				
Carex sp.	-	-	-	x
Eleocharis sp.	-	-	-	-
Tree/shrub macrofossils				
Prunus domestica ssp. *insititia* (L.) Bonnier & Layens	xfg	-	-	-
Other plant macrofossils				
Charcoal <2mm	xxxx	xx	xx	xx
Charcoal >2mm	xx	-	x	x
Indet.culm nodes	-	-	-	x
Indet.seeds	-	-	x	x
Indet.thorn *(Rosa* type)	-	x	-	-
Volume of flot (litres)	<0.1	<0.1	<0.1	<0.1
% flot sorted	100%	100%	100%	100%

Key to Tables
x = 1 – 10; xx = 11 – 50; xxx = 51 – 100 specimens and xxxx = 100+ specimens; cf = compare; fg = fragment; coty = cotyledon

TABLE 5.35: THORPE MALSOR CHARRED PLANT REMAINS

hoped that analysis of these assemblages would provide a clearer understanding of the interaction of settlement and environment during the earlier Roman period within this area of Northamptonshire.

Cereal grains, chaff elements and seeds of common segetal weeds and grassland herbs were present at varying densities within all three assemblages. Preservation was poor to moderate, with a high density of the grains and seeds being severely puffed and distorted, probably as a result of combustion at very high temperatures.

Oat (*Avena* sp), barley (*Hordeum* sp) and wheat (*Triticum* sp) grains were present within all three assemblages. Wheat was predominant throughout (60% of the total assemblage of identifiable grains), with most specimens being of an elongated 'drop' from typical of spelt (*T spelta*). Spelt wheat glume bases were also present within all three assemblages, being especially abundant within fills (6-9) and (23), where they accounted for approximately 53% of all the identifiable plant remains. A small number of the wheat grains appeared to be of a rounded form more typically seen within the free-threshing hexaploid varieties, but as most specimens were poorly preserved, close identification was not possible. Barley and oat grains accounted for respectively 26% and 13% of the total assemblage of identifiable grains, but in both instances preservation was especially

Sample	2	3	4
Fill	6-9	23	26
Cereals			
Avena sp. (grains)	6	6+12cf	4cf
(awn frags.)	12	8	2
(floret bases)	-	2	-
Hordeum sp. (grains)	8	30+2cf	12+2cf
(rachis nodes)	-	34	6
Triticum sp. (grains)	44	40+6cf	30+6cf
(glume bases)	240	42	2
(spikelet bases)	140	16	4
(rachis internodes)	72	12	2
T. spelta L. (glume bases)	944	128	14
Cereal indet. (grains)	42	90	56
(detached sprout frags.)	12	-	2
(silica skeletons)	xx awn		
Herbs			
Aphanes arvensis L.	-	2cf	-
Asteraceae indet.	4	4	4
Brassicaceae indet.	-	2	-
Bromus sp.	2cffg	4cf	4fg
Caryophyllaceae indet.	2	-	-
Centaurea sp.	-	-	2
Chenopodium album L.	2	-	-
Chenopodiaceae indet.	18	10	6
Fallopia convolvulus (L.) A.Love	2+2tf	-	-
Galium aparine L.	-	10+8fg	-
Lithospermum arvense L.	4	-	12+10fg
Medicago/Trifolium/Lotus sp.	16	4cf	2cf
Papaver sp.	8	136+6m	2
Persicaria maculosa/lapathifolia	-	2	-
Plantago lanceolata L.	4	4	-
Small Poaceae indet.	16	102	36
Large Poaceae indet.	-	2	4
Polygonum aviculare L.	40	2	2
Polygonaceae indet.	24	-	-
Potentilla sp.	-	2	-
Prunella vulgaris L.	-	2cf	-
Ranunculus sp.	-	2cf	-
R. flammula L.	-	2cf	-
Raphanus raphanistrum L. (siliquae)	2+22fg	10+32fg	4fg
Rumex sp.	2	14	2
R. acetosella L.	-	4	8+4cf
Rumex/Carex sp.	4	-	-
Tripleurospermum inodorum (L.) Schultz-Bip	50	14	20
Urtica dioica L.	2cf		
Vicia/Lathyrus sp.	18+22coty	10+16coty	6coty

TABLE 5.36: THORPE MALSOR, CHARRED PLANT REMAINS, PIT 4 (1)

5. Roman Settlement (AD43 - AD450)

Sample	2	3	4
Fill	6-9	23	26
Wetland plants			
Carex sp.	6	6	-
Eleocharis sp.	2	10	-
Tree/shrub macrofossils			
Corylus avellana L.	-	2cffg	2cffg
Other plant macrofossils			
Charcoal <2mm	xxxx	xxxx	xx
Charcoal >2mm	xxx	xxx	xx
Charcoal >5mm	xx	xx	x
Charred root/stem	x	x	x
Indet.culm nodes	-	-	4
Indet.seeds	46	40+2m	30
Indet.thorns (*Prunus* type)	2	-	-
Sample volume (litres)	10	10	10
Volume of flot (litres)	0.2	0.1	<0.1
% flot sorted	100%	100%	100%

TABLE 5.36: THORPE MALSOR, CHARRED PLANT REMAINS, PIT 4 (2)

poor. Oat floret bases were noted within the assemblage from context 23, but as all lacked the diagnostic bases, it was not possible to ascertain whether cultivated or wild varieties were present.

Seeds of common segetal weeds and grassland herbs were present throughout, although subtle differences in composition were noted within the assemblages from the three pit fills (see discussion). Segetal taxa included brome (*Bromus* sp.), fat hen type (Chenopodiaceae), goosegrass (*Galium aparine*), corn gromwell (*Lithospermum arvense*), poppy (*Papaver* sp.), knotgrass (*Polygonum aviculare*), wild radish (*Raphanus raphanistrum*) and scentless mayweed (*Tripleurospermum inodorum*). Grass (Poaceae) fruits were moderately common within all three assemblages; other grassland herbs included medick/clover/trefoil (*Medicago/Trifolium/Lotus* sp.), ribwort plantain (*Plantago lanceolata*), dock (*Rumex* sp.), sheep's sorrel (*R. acetosella*) and vetch/vetchling (*Vicia/Lathyrus* sp.). Nutlets of sedge (*Carex* sp.) and spike-rush (*Eleocharis* sp.), both of which are commonly found in areas of damp grassland, were noted within the assemblages from pit fills (6-9) and (23), and possible hazel (*Corylus avellana*) nutshell fragments were recorded from fills (23) and (26). Charcoal/charred wood fragments were present throughout along with pieces of charred root or stem. Other plant macrofossils were scarce, but did include indeterminate culm nodes and thorns of sloe (*Prunus* sp.) type.

The fragments of black porous and tarry material noted within all three assemblages, but particularly common within fills 6-9, were all probable residues of the combustion of organic remains (including cereal grains) at very high temperatures. Other remains occurred very infrequently, but did include fragments of bone and eggshell, small mammal bones (some of which were burnt) and vitreous concretions, with the latter again possibly indicative of high temperatures of combustion.

Pit 4 from which the samples were taken was large (3.3m diameter and 0.87m deep) and contained a mixture of domestic waste, cess and other refuse including pottery, animal bone and several artefacts.

Although the three plant macrofossil assemblages are broadly similar in composition, there are differences, which may indicate that materials from different sources were being deposited within the pit; this would be entirely consistent with its use as a general refuse 'dump'. The assemblage from fills (6-9) is particularly chaff rich, and although cereals are present, the chaff to grain ratio is approximately 14:1. Seeds of common segetal weeds are also moderately common, probably indicating that this assemblage is primarily derived from charred cereal processing waste. Wheat grains/chaff are predominant, suggesting that this was the main crop in this instance, with the oats and barley being present as contaminants. As wheat is best suited to production on slightly heavier soils than those present around the site, it is possible that these are the remains of an imported crop, which was stored as whole ears or spikelets and then processed immediately prior to storage/consumption. This was regular practice during the Iron Age, although it became less common during the Roman period as it proved a very bulky method of storing and transporting grain. The moderate density of 'silica skeletons' within this assemblage almost certainly indicates that after processing, the waste material was burnt in a high temperature fire with a good air supply, as this results in a loss of carbon, leaving only a skeleton of silica.

Cereals and chaff are again present within the assemblage from fill 23, although here, they appear along with a very high density of grass fruits and seeds of weeds commonly seen on either cultivated soils or grassland areas (including cinquefoil (*Potentilla* sp) and buttercups (*Ranunculus* sp). It is, perhaps, most likely that this assemblage is principally derived from a small batch of burnt litter and/or fodder, although some cereal processing detritus may also be present.

Although small (at <0.1 litres in volume), the assemblage from fill (26) is relatively cereal rich, with grains accounting for approximately 70% of the total assemblage. Although weed seeds are relatively scarce, it is possibly of note that many of those present are either of a similar size to the grains (for example the corn gromwell) or would have been present within the original assemblage as intact capitulae or seed heads (for example the scentless mayweed). This may indicate that some or all of the material within this assemblage is derived from either cereal storage detritus or waste from a late stage of processing, as the larger contaminants, which were not separated out during winnowing, were frequently stored along with the grain, only being removed by hand immediately prior to consumption.

Conclusions

In summary, although only three assemblages were suitable for detailed analysis, their composition would appear to indicate that a number of distinct activities were being conducted on or near the site at Thorpe Malsor during the Roman period.

Although some cereals were probably being grown locally, others were possibly being imported to the site in an unprocessed state, where they were stored and later processed as required. The processing waste was then burnt at a high temperature in well-oxygenated fires, possibly along with detritus from the stores or granaries. Such structures would have been cleaned regularly to minimise the risk of insect, rodent or fungal damage to the grain. It would appear most likely that grasses and grassland herbs were also being gathered and stored on site, where they were probably used as animal bedding or, mixed with chaff and grain, as fodder. The burnt detritus from these and other activities was then deposited in the pit along with a range of other refuse.

6. Anglo-Saxon burial and settlement (AD450-650)

For the Anglo-Saxon period the majority of the evidence relates to part of a cremation cemetery at Glaston, Rutland, which lay north of an extensive area of Roman settlement. To the south of the Roman settlement, and 300m south of the cemetery, a single sunken-featured building, seen in watching brief, may have been part of the associated settlement (see Fig 5.1). In addition, some Anglo-Saxon finds came from the upper fill of a late Roman ditch at Rushton, Northamptonshire.

An Anglo-Saxon cremation cemetery at Glaston

During topsoil stripping for the construction of a compound on the north side of the A47, Uppingham Road, c.0.4km to the west of Glaston, the remains of an Anglo-Saxon cremation cemetery were found during the watching brief (NGR: SK 8906 0046; Fig 6.1). The site lay within an arable field, at c.124m aOD, to the west of the grounds of Bisbrooke Hall; earthworks of ridge and furrow ploughing within the grounds indicate that the land there has not been subject to modern ploughing, and the cemetery may be reasonably well preserved if it extends to the east, although still subject to medieval plough disturbance, as in the excavated area. The underlying geology comprises fine sands and clays, with low-grade ironstone, of the Grantham Formation (Middle Jurassic), with beds of Northampton Sand to the west (BGS 1978).

The Anglo-Saxon cremation cemetery extended over an area of c.0.42ha, measuring 40m by 45m, and comprised a scattered group of small pits, the majority containing pottery urns holding cremated human bone (Fig 6.2). Many of the vessels had been truncated by medieval ploughing and fragments of pottery and cremated bone had been disturbed and scattered, although several vessels that had been buried a little deeper were almost complete (Fig 6.3). Ten cremation burials were *in situ* within the excavated area and another four were identified from disturbed remains that included bone, burials B5, B8, B13 and B20 (Table 6.1). Two pots *in situ* are identified as accessory vessels, burial B8 and pit 48, and some heavily disturbed features that produced only a few sherds of pottery may have been burials that had lost all of the bone deposit, pits 30, 32 and 40.

The pottery assemblage is representative of styles produced in the 5th and 6th centuries AD, although the one urn dated with some certainty to the 5th century was somewhat worn, suggesting that it may have been quite old when it was buried. A radiocarbon date from the bone of burial B16 of 570-655 Cal AD (95% confidence, 1440+/-30 BP, Beta-293240) provides a date between the late 6th and mid-7th centuries AD, a little later than the range indicated by the pottery, but broadly consistent with the dates of other Anglo-Saxon cremation cemeteries in the region.

The burial pits were approximately 0.3m in diameter and up to 0.19m deep, although many had been severely truncated, leaving only the base of the pit and the base and few other fragments of the urns. The main group lay across the eastern half of the site, with individual burials between 1m and 4m apart, but there were also more widely spaced outliers to the west and perhaps the east, continuing beyond the excavated area.

Analysis of the cremated bone suggests that the temperature of the funeral pyres was between 800-1000°C, high enough to melt glass but relatively low, compared with that of many Bronze Age cremations, for example,. There was no ash or charcoal mixed with the bones, indicating that the bone was carefully collected from the ashes of the pyre and/or cleaned after collection before deposition in the urn (Fig 6.3). The level of care and a lack of deliberate crushing is indicated by the large size of some of the bone fragments, with many long bone fragments measuring 50-100m (Fig 6.4). A few urns were intact and therefore retained the entire bone deposit, and in these instances the weight of bone varies from 300g in burial B6 to 1kg in burial B16. Given that an adult body will produce 1-3kg of bone, it is evident that recovery of bone from the pyre was only partial, and at best perhaps around a third of the available bone was deposited in the urn for burial, probably a lower proportion on average than in early Bronze Age cremation burials. There was no evidence for funeral pyres on the site, indicating that the bodies had been cremated elsewhere.

Demographic analysis of the cremated bone shows that the sampled area contained the remains of eight adults and four juveniles (66% and 33% of the identified remains respectively). There were no young infants (less than 4 years of age), and two burials, B5 and B8 did not contained sufficient bone to determine the age of the individuals. Only two of the burials, B4 and B16, displayed sexually dimorphic features to allow the sex of the individuals to be determined; in both cases, they were possible female adults (Table 6.1).

Four of the urns were decorated. The urn containing burial B16 was the most elaborate and the best preserved, with stamped and incised decoration on the neck and body (Fig 6.4). The vessels containing burials B7, B9 and B11 were also decorated although only small parts of these vessels survived.

Several of the urns contained personal items, including glass beads from burials B6, B7, B9, B11, B14 and B16 (Fig 6.5), a decorated bone mount from burial B7 (Fig 6.6), a copper alloy brooch from burial B14 (Fig 6.7)

Excavations along the Empingham to Hannington pipeline 2008-2009

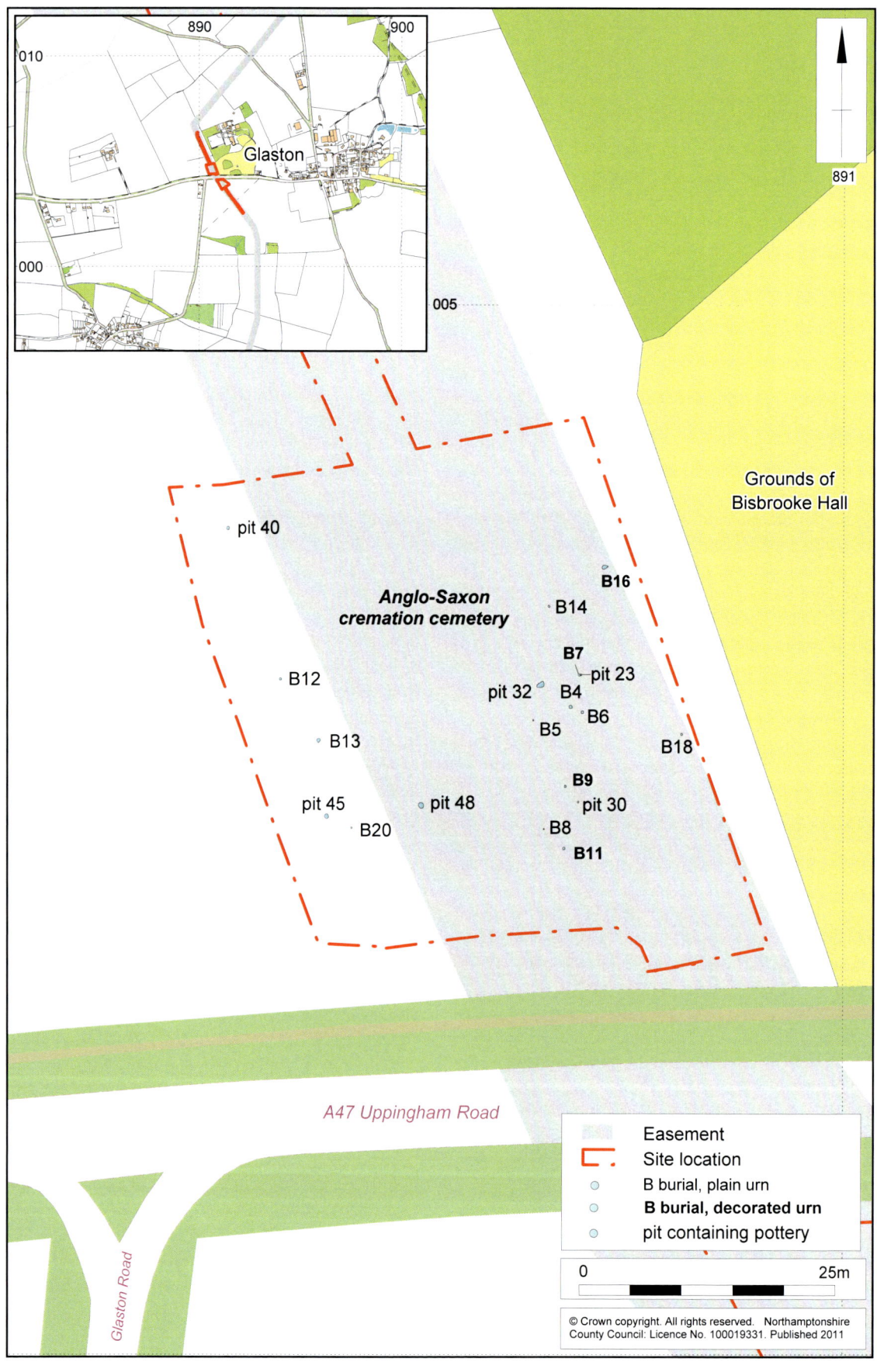

Fig 6.1: Glaston, plan of Anglo-Saxon cremation cemetery

6. Anglo-Saxon burial and settlement (AD450-650)

Fig 6.2: Glaston, excavation of urn, Burial B16

Fig 6.3: Glaston, Burial B6, showing the concentration of large bone fragments (Scale 50mm)

Burial (B)/ feature	Context/ [feature]	Bone wt (g)	Age (years)	Urn	Grave goods
B4	4, 5/[6]	816	Adult (female?)	Large plain urn	---
B5	8	5	?	Urn (base only)	---
B6	10, 11/[12]	311	Adult	Large plain urn	7 glass beads
B7	13, 14/[15]	71	Juvenile (4-5)	Decorated urn	Bone mount, bead ? Cu alloy frag
B8	16, 17/[18]	<1	?	Small accessory vessel	---
B9	19, 20/[21]	78	Juvenile (>10)	Decorated urn	c 5 glass beads
B11	24, 25/[26]	297	Juvenile + Adult	Decorated urn	Glass bead, 6 iron rivets (comb?)
B12	27, 28/[29]	614	Adult (15-18)	Medium plain urn	Cu alloy frags
B13	31	58	Adult	---	Bone comb frags
B14	36, 37, 51/[38]	272	Adult	Small urn (early?)	Quoit brooch, Glass bead
B16	41, 42/[43]	995	Adult (female?)	Decorated urn	Glass bead
B18	49/[50]	86	Adult	Urn base	---
B20	35	14	Juvenile	Body sherd	---
Pit 30	30	---	---	Rim, small cup/bowl	---
Pit 32	32	---	---	Base sherd, probable urn	---
Pit 40	39	---	---	Probable urn sherds	---
Pit 48	47	---	---	Small accessory vessel	---

TABLE 6.1: GLASTON, CATALOGUE OF BURIALS AND GRAVE GOODS

and a bone comb from burial B13. With the exception of the bone mount, all of these items were heat-affected, indicating that they were on the bodies when they were cremated. As the bone assemblages are all the product of only partial collection from the pyre, other objects may also not have been recovered. The distribution of finds and their association with the burials and types of urn shows no apparent pattern, and due to the lack of diagnostic bone information no correlation can be obtained for the classes of objects and the sex/age of the individuals.

Two small pots came from the cemetery area, one associated with burial B8 and the other from pit 48 (Figs 6.11, 3 & 4; 6.9). These pots are both probably accessory vessels that were used in funerary rituals, perhaps to contain offerings of food or drink.

During the watching brief, tentative evidence for Anglo-Saxon settlement in the area was encountered to the south of Uppingham Road, further down the slope from the Roman remains. A shallow rectangular pit, 15:07/5, characteristic of those associated with Anglo-Saxon sunken-featured buildings, was aligned east to west, 4.3m long by 2.8m wide and 0.18m deep. The fill of mid to dark grey sandy silt contained animal bone, a small assemblage of Anglo-Saxon pottery, dated AD450-650, including a complete miniature pot (Figs 6.11, 5; 6.10).

Anglo-Saxon activity at Rushton

There were no features at Rushton that could specifically be dated to the Anglo-Saxon period, but a pair of tweezers from the subsoil and a rod fragment from gully 9, indicate that there was activity in the vicinity at this time.

Finds from the Anglo-Saxon cemetery and other sites:

Anglo-Saxon pottery
by Paul Blinkhorn

The collection of Anglo-Saxon urns included decorated vessels that suggest that the cemetery was in use from the 5th to 6th centuries AD. The assemblage also included an unusual miniature pot and a large stamped

6. ANGLO-SAXON BURIAL AND SETTLEMENT (AD450-650)

FIG 6.4: GLASTON, DECORATED URN AND CREMATED BONE, BURIAL B16 (SCALE 50MM)

FIG 6.5: GLASTON, HEAT DISTORTED GLASS BEADS FROM BURIAL B6 (SCALE 10MM)

FIG 6.6: GLASTON, WORKED BONE MOUNT FROM BURIAL B7 (SCALE 10MM)

vessel which had been decorated with both dies and the foot of a brooch, probably a small-long type. A number of the urns were also accompanied by sherds from other vessels, and while some of these are likely simply to have been 'strays' from earlier activity, at least two were heavily burnt, and may have been placed on the pyre with the body, while others were large enough to perhaps have been used as *ad hoc* lids.

Fabric

The following fabric types were noted:

Fabric F1: Sparse sub-angular quartz and sub-angular calcareous material up to 1mm.

Fabric F2: Sparse fine sub-angular quartz < 0.5mm.

Fabric F3: Moderate to dense sub-angular quartz up to 0.5mm.

Fabric F4: Moderate to dense sub-angular quartz up to 2mm, rare rounded ironstone of the same size.

Fabric F5: Sparse to moderate granite fragments up to 1mm, rare calcareous material of the same size, sparse free mica flakes.

The range of fabric types is fairly typical of the early Anglo-Saxon pottery of the region, and can be paralleled at a number of sites (eg Blinkhorn 2000, 98).

FIG 6.7: GLASTON, COPPER ALLOY QUOIT BROOCH, BURIAL B14, WITH HEAT DISTORTED GLASS BEADS OBSCURING THE PIN (SCALE 20MM)

Chronology and decorative symbolism

The dating of early Anglo-Saxon hand-built pottery is notoriously difficult. Undecorated urns, which on average comprise less than 25% of the vessels used as cremation containers but can make up nearly two-thirds of the urns from a cemetery (Richards 1987, 157), are virtually impossible to date other than to the main period of cremation burial in England, c AD450-650. Decorated vessels have the potential to be more accurately dated, but even these are problematic. Myres' (1977) *Corpus* of most of the urns known at that time attempted to create a typology based on decoration and, to a lesser extent, vessel form, using continental parallels and associated artefacts to provide an absolute chronology, and while his scheme can perhaps be useful at a very broad level, it must be treated with extreme caution. As Richards (1987, 25) noted, '*of the 3471 vessels in the Corpus... only about 100 vessels are listed with associated 'datable' objects... Furthermore, only about half of these are decorated vessels*'.

More recently, Leahy's (2007) excavations at the Cleatham cremation cemetery in Lincolnshire produced an assemblage of urns, many of which had stratigraphic relationships, enabling him to produce a seriated system of five chronological phases which showed that rather than being a linear progression, the trends in the use of the various decorative techniques used on urns was very fluid. There are also social and cultural factors to take into account. Richards (1987) showed that it is very likely that the size, shape and decoration of urns was related to the age, gender and social identity of those contained within them. He also noted that there appeared to be a lot of localized variation in such practice, and that those cemeteries which were quite near to each other showed very different patterns. Leahy was unable to take age and gender into account at Cleatham as he was unable to obtain funding for analysis of the bone from the urns. If this crucial work is ever carried out, a clearer picture will probably emerge. Leahy also did not put an absolute chronology to his sequence, mainly due to a lack of other forms of datable cultural material associated with the cremations.

Thus any dating which is given to the vessels from this group of urns must be regarded as tentative. It will concentrate mainly on the decorated vessels, although any others which have distinctive attributes of form will also be discussed, in all cases using both Myres' and Leahy's work as the main points of reference.

The undecorated urns and other vessels:

Burial B4 (SF3)

Lower part of vessel (weight 880g). Fabric F1. Dark grey fabric with light orange-brown patches on the outer surface. Very friable, somewhat under-fired fabric, meaning that much of the vessel had disintegrated. The rim is entirely missing, and there is no evidence of decoration. The few joining sherds and a large fragment of the lower body, which was reconstructed, suggest that the vessel was originally quite large, and probably shouldered. The size of the vessel corresponds with the fact that the cremated bone is from an adult, possibly a female. This context also produced a rimsherd from a different vessel, in fabric F1. Diameter 200mm, EVE = 0.07. It does not appear large enough to have functioned as a lid, and was not burnt.

Burial B5 (SF4)

Only the base of this vessel remains (weight 134g). Fabric F1. Black fabric with light orange-brown outer surface. There are traces on the inner surface of a burnt residue, so it appears that the pot is a reused cooking vessel.

Burial B6 (SF7)

Complete lower part of vessel (Figs 6.12 & 6.8). Outer surfaces evenly burnished (weight 1244g). Fabric F4. Uniform black fabric. The context also produced a few sherds from the shoulder and rim of a different vessel, but in a similar fabric (F4), weighing 138g. It was possibly used as a lid, and a further sherd in the same fabric with a single impression of a 'hot cross bun' stamp (3g) is also present. The decorated sherd is likely to be from a third vessel. Finally, a fragmented and clearly burnt sherd in fabric F5 occurred (weight 53g). This seems highly likely to have been placed on the pyre along with deceased. The urn also contained glass beads, a strongly female-linked artefact type in inhumations (Lucy 2000, 83-4), but not so in cremations (Richards 1987, 199). The remaining portion of the urn suggests that it was originally fairly large with a rounded profile; it contained the remains of an adult.

Burial B8 (SF6)

Near-complete miniature pot (Fig 6.11, 4). Fabric F1. Dark grey fabric with browner, smoothed and lightly burnished outer surface. Rim diameter 80mm, EVE = 0.35, weight 182g. This is likely to be an accessory vessel rather than an urn.

Burial B12 (SF11)

Lower part of vessel. Upper half and rim entirely missing. No evidence of decoration (weight 535g). Fabric F3. Grey fabric with light orange-brown outer surface. It is difficult to be sure of the original form of the vessel, but there is evidence of a slight waist carination. It is not particularly large, but contained the remains of an adult, aged 15-18 years.

Burial B14 (SF16)

Lower part of vessel, partially fragmented (weight 484g). Fabric F3. Uniform grey fabric. Upper half and rim largely missing, apart from a single rimsherd and two from the neck. Rim diameter 224mm, EVE = 5%. The outer surface is lightly and evenly burnished, but there

6. ANGLO-SAXON BURIAL AND SETTLEMENT (AD450-650)

FIG 6.8: GLASTON, PLAIN-BODIED URN (SF7), BURIAL B6 (SCALE 20MM)

is no other evidence of decoration. Also present was the highly fragmented remains of a single large bodysherd in fabric F1 (weight 231g). Dark grey with a light orange-brown outer surface. It may have functioned as a lid.

This vessel appears fairly small and squat, with a relatively wide mouth for its size. It also has a noticeable waist carination, and was more likely to have been biconical or shouldered than globular. This may be early in date, perhaps 5th century rather than 6th, but this cannot be stated with a great deal of confidence. The size and shape would suggest that the urn was the repository of the remains of a juvenile or young adult female. Analysis of the bone indicates an adult, although the sex of the individual is unknown. The vessel also produced the burnt remains of a bronze quoit brooch. Richards (1987, 198) found that brooches are not correlated with any particular gender- or age-group in cremations, although they tend to occur in urns which have a shouldered profile, or have impressed dot decoration.

Burial B18

Only the base of the vessel remains, weight 301g (Fig 6.12, 11). Fabric F4. Dark grey fabric with variegated orange-brown and dark grey outer surface. There is a hole in the centre of the base which is not recent, and appears to have been made from the inside. It is possible that this is evidence of a deliberate act at the time of burial. Anglo-Saxon urns with perforations are fairly well-known; at Cleatham, where nearly 10% of the urns had been modified in this fashion, and a similar percentage of urns from Spong Hill exhibited evidence of the same action (Leahy 2007, 82). It contained the remains of an adult.

Burial B20 (SF13)

A single, large fragmented bodysherd (weight 132g) from a vessel of uncertain size and shape, associated with the cremated remains of a juvenile. Fabric F1. Black fabric with light orange brown outer surface.

Pit 40

There are two large, non-joining sherds from the rim, body and base (weight 535g) Rim diameter 260mm, EVE = 0.27. Fabric F1. Dark grey fabric with pale orange-brown outer lower body. No evidence of decoration. The vessel is quite thick-walled, and while it is impossible to be certain, it appears fairly squat, with a wide mouth and a globular profile. Heavily disturbed, only fragments of pottery survived; no cremated bone.

Pit 48 (SF 17)

Small jar with the outer surface sooted above the waist, extensive blackening on the inner surface, rim and upper body missing on one side, weight 423g (Figs 6.11, 3 and 6.9). Rim diameter 100mm, EVE = 0.40. Fabric

Fig 6.9: Glaston, accessory vessel from cemetery, pit 48 (Scale 10mm)

F4. Dark grey fabric with light orange-brown surfaces. A single small sherd in fabric F1 was also present (weight 13g). This is one of the smaller vessels from the cemetery, and appears to have been an accessory vessel rather than an urn. The smoke-blackening suggests that it was originally used as a cooking vessel. Disturbed, crushed pot *in situ*; no cremated bone.

Topsoil (1)

A single abraded bodysherd in Fabric F1 occurred (weight 7g).

Field 15:07 (5), SFB

Complete miniature urn, weight 61g (Figs 6.11, 5 & 6.10). Rim diameter 35mm, EVE = 1.00. Fabric F3. Grey fabric with light grey-brown surfaces.

Pit 30

Rim from a small cup or bowl (weight 68g). Rim diameter 80mm, 45% complete. Fabric F4. Orange fabric. Fragments of pottery found, feature not defined.

Pit 32

Sherd from the base of a fairly large vessel (weight 100g). Fabric F4. Uniform dark grey fabric. Pottery sherd found, feature not defined.

Catalogue of illustrated Anglo-Saxon pottery
(Figs 6.11 and 6.12)

1. Decorated urn (SF15), burial B16 (Figs 6.15 &6.16)
2. Decorated urn (SF5), burial B7 (Fig 6.13)
3. Small jar (SF17), pit 48 (Fig 6.9)
4. Small accessory vessel (SF6), burial B8
5. Miniature pot from sunken-featured building in Field 15:07 (and Fig 6.10)
6. Rim of small bowl from Roman ditch 10
7. Decorated urn (SF10), burial B11 (Fig 6.14)
8. Decorated urn (SF10), burial B11 (and Fig 6.14)
9. Decorated urn (SF 10), burial B11(and Fig 6.14)
10. Base of decorated urn (SF8), burial B9
11. Base of urn, burial B18
12. Urn (SF7), burial B6 (and Fig 6.8)

The decorated urns:

Burial B7 (SF5) (Figs 6.11, 2 & 6.13)

Most of the body above the carination and the entire rim are missing (weight 475g). It has a lightly and evenly burnished outer surface with incised cordons on and above the carination, and zig-zag or chevron decoration comprising groups of four lines between the cordons. The outer surface of the vessel is fairly extensively lightly pitted, suggesting that it may have been quite old when placed in the ground. Fabric F5. Uniform dark grey fabric.

The vessel is fairly small with a fairly sharp carination. Vessels with simple incised chevron-and-line decoration are well-represented in the Myres *corpus* (*ibid* 1977, figs 262-74), but exact parallels, where the chevrons are contained within combed bands, are rare. Vessels with a similar squat carinated form are mainly confined to the

Fig 6.10: Field 15:07, miniature pot from sunken-featured building (Scale 10mm)

6. Anglo-Saxon burial and settlement (AD450-650)

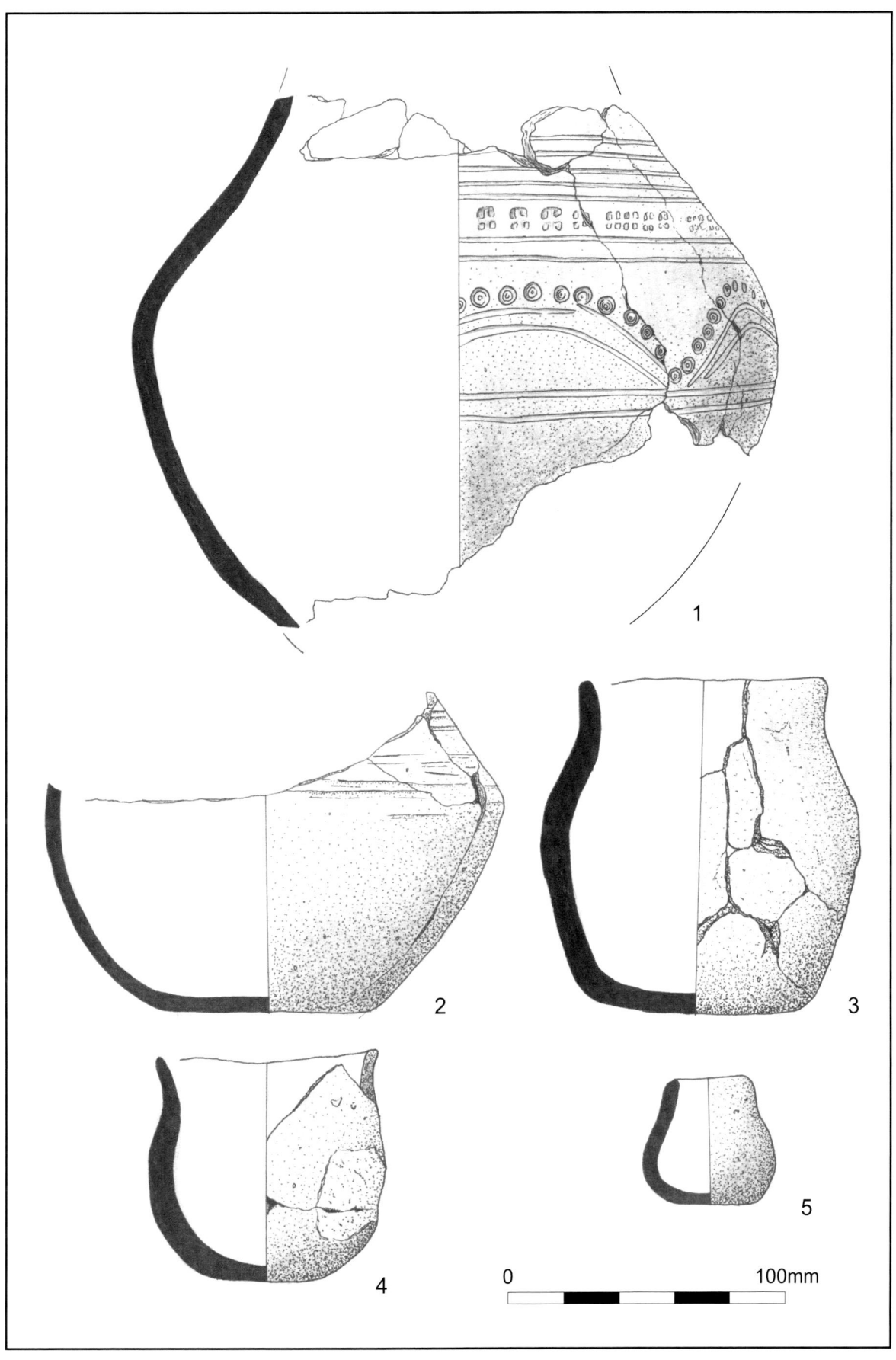

FIG 6.11: GLASTON, ANGLO-SAXON POTTERY (1-5)

Excavations along the Empingham to Hannington pipeline 2008-2009

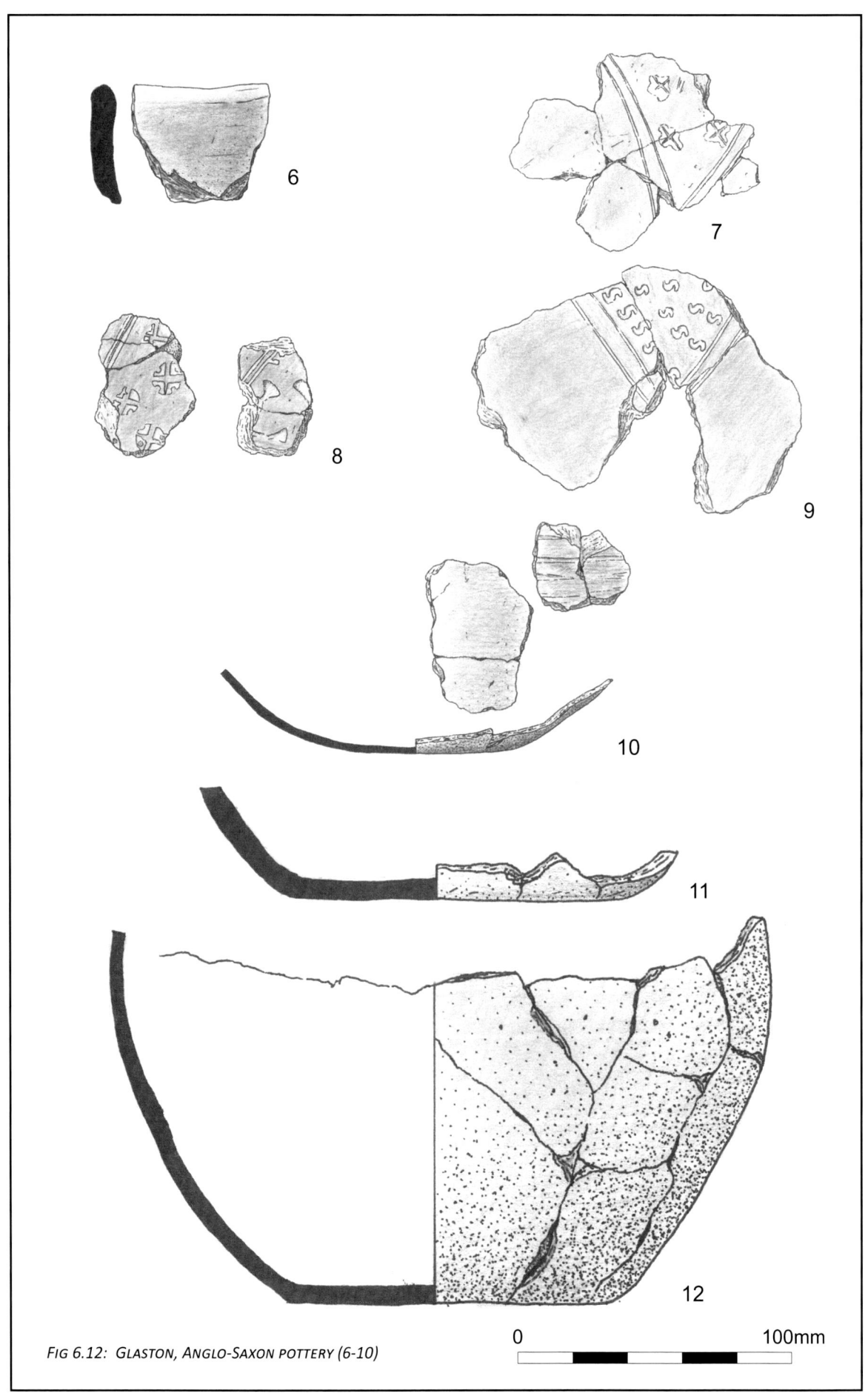

Fig 6.12: Glaston, Anglo-Saxon pottery (6-10)

cemeteries at Sancton in Yorkshire (*ibid* fig 263), with more recent work on the site producing more examples of vessels of this type (eg Timby 1993, fig 29). Myres suggested, on the grounds that there are numerous similar vessels in continental cemeteries, particularly in Schleswig and around the estuaries of the Elbe and Weser, that vessels of this type are likely to date to the 5th century (*ibid* 46 – 48).

Similar vessels occurred at Cleatham, classified by Leahy as Group 10a, and these appear, as Myres suggested, to be early and date to Leahy's Phase 1 (*ibid* 2007, 105-6). There were 49 urns of this type at Cleatham, and one of them, number 459, contained fragments of a 5th-century Frisian barred comb. Leahy also lists vessels of this type with datable artefacts from other sites, and the vast majority date to the 5th century AD (*ibid* 106). A number of such vessels also occurred at Spong Hill (Hills and Penn 1981, fig 35), one of which (*ibid* no 1743) had a fairly large group of artefacts accompanying the bones, including a double-sided bone comb. Richards (1987, 199) noted that bone combs are particularly closely correlated with vessels of this type, and a fragmented bone object did occur in this burial (Fig 6.6), although it does not appear to be a comb.

Given that Richards made a good case for the height of an urn being related to the age of the individual contained within it (*ibid* 1987, 195), it would be perhaps expected that this vessel would have been used to contain the remains of a younger individual, and the skeletal evidence shows that this was indeed the case. The style of decoration indicates that this vessel is most likely to date to the 5th century AD, but, as noted above, the outer surface is quite worn, and could have been an 'heirloom' which was quite old when placed in the ground.

Burial B9 (SF8) (Fig 6.12, 10)

Little of this vessel remains, other than the base, although the few neck fragments present are decorated with horizontal incised cordons (weight 255g). Fabric F1. Uniform black fabric, highly fragmented. A single bodysherd has small fragments of vertical incised lines, but no evidence of stamping, so it appears probable that the vessel originally had a purely linear decorative scheme, although the exact nature of it remains unclear. The fact that some of the upper part of the vessel fell into the urn and was preserved suggests that it originally had a lid or cover of some sort, which prevented soil entering the vessel until the weight of earth crushed the upper part of it. The urn also contained glass beads, a strongly female-linked artefact type in inhumations (Lucy 2000, 83-4), but not so in cremations (Richards 1987, 199).

Fig 6.13: Glaston, urn (SF7), Burial B7, decorated with incised chevrons (scale 20mm)

It is not possible to assess the size of the vessel from what remains, although the relative thinness of the walls indicate that it was not particularly large, which, considering that the remains contained within it were of a juvenile, is perhaps to be expected given the findings of Richards (1987, 195). Dating the vessel is somewhat difficult. Myres (1977) lists numerous varieties of pots with purely linear decoration, and the dating depends very much on the overall scheme, so it is not possible to date the vessel other than to within the broad early Anglo-Saxon period, that is the 5th to 6th centuries AD. The same can be said of the urns in Leahy's sequence (*ibid* 2007, fig 116).

Burial B11 (SF10) (Fig 6.12, 7-9 & 6.14 a, b & c)

Highly fragmented partial remains of a decorated urn (weight 263g). Fabric F2. The body has the remains of at least four incised pendant triangles, each filled with the impressions of a different die. Three are fairly standard Anglo-Saxon die motifs, with two cruciform, one in a cross-shaped field (Fig 6.12, 7 & 6.14, b), the other in a round field, with a dot in each quadrant formed by the cross (Fig 6.12, 8 left & 6.14, a) and one being the S-shaped 'wyrm' stamp (Fig 6.12, 9 & 6.14, c). The fourth, however, is filled with what appears to be impressions of the foot of a cruciform brooch (Fig 6.12, 8 right). The use of brooches and other forms of jewellery is a rare occurrence on Anglo-Saxon pottery, but it is a technique which has been known to archaeologists for some time (Briscoe 1985), and while a direct parallel to the example from this site is not known, the use of the feet of cruciform brooches as dies is well-attested. Their main distribution seems to be in Norfolk, Lincolnshire and the Trent Valley, although a few examples are known from northern Suffolk, Cambridgeshire and south Yorkshire (*ibid*, fig 3).

The presence of a 'wyrm' stamp on this vessel would suggested that the contained individual was not a young adult, as Richards (1987, 201) noted that such stamps rarely occur on pots which contained people of that age group. However, Richards also noted that adults were usually placed in urns which, when stamped, had a fairly simple arrangement, and often, only one die was used.

Furthermore, one of the stamps on this urn is a cross in a cruciform field. Again, Richards (1987) noted that stamps with a field of this type were not often used on pots containing adults. He also noted that cruciform motifs with a raised cross are linked with young adults, and two of the four stamp motifs on this urn are of that type. The fragmentary nature of the vessel makes it difficult to ascertain the size and form of the urn, but it appears to be of fairly average size, and globular in shape.

There thus seems to be a certain amount of conflicting information in the decoration of this vessel, with the weight of evidence suggesting it would have been most appropriate on a container for the remains of a young adult, which perhaps reflects uncertain aging of the skeletal remains, which include those of a juvenile and an adult.

Myres saw globular urns with stamped pendant triangle decoration as being very typical of the 6th century (*ibid*, 1977, 53-4). Such designs are very common, and known from all over Anglo-Saxon England (eg *ibid*, figs 317-326). Very few vessels with stamped pendant triangle decoration occurred at Cleatham, with the closest parallel perhaps being Group 18s, but these were similar rather than identical (Leahy 2007, 116-7). Such pots appear to date to the later part of the Cleatham sequence (*ibid*). This vessel is therefore probably dates to the 6th century AD.

Burial B16 (SF 15) (Figs 6.2; 6.11, 1; 6.15 & 6.16)

Rim missing, base somewhat under-fired, and disintegrated after burial; it could not be reconstructed (weight 1441g). Fabric F1. Black fabric with variegated light orange-brown outer to dark grey surface. The vessel was accompanied by a sherd from another pot, probably in the same fabric (weight 38g), although the sherd has been heavily burnt, and is partially vitrified and distorted, suggesting it was almost certainly placed on the pyre with the deceased.

The upper part of vessel is decorated with incised horizontal cordons and a row of stamps, plus incised *stehende bogen* (standing curves) above the carination, and outlined with ring-and-dot stamps. Vessels with *stehende bogen* decoration are well-represented in the Myres *Corpus*, although examples with incised curves accentuated with stamping and incised and stamped neck collars are extremely rare, and no direct parallels are present. There are a few vessels with a passing similarity; an urn from North Luffenham in Rutland (Myres 1977, fig 341, 842) has hanging curves (*hängende bogen*) outlined with dots, but no stamping on the neck collar, and others from Loveden Hill in Lincolnshire (*ibid*, fig 301. 540) and Caister-by-Norwich in Norfolk (*ibid*, 1843) have incised zig-zags or chevrons outlined with stamps, but again lack stamping on the neck-collar. Myres (1977, 51) saw stamped chevron pottery as largely dating to the 6th century AD. In the case of the vessel from North Luffenham, Myres implied that vessels with *hängende bogen* but without stamping were early, whereas those with it were dated to the 6th century AD, due to the lack of continental parallels and the increased use of stamping by Anglo-Saxon potters at that time (*ibid*, 58-9).

6. ANGLO-SAXON BURIAL AND SETTLEMENT (AD450-650)

Fig 6.14: Glaston, Burial B11, sherds from decorated urn (SF10) showing stamp motifs: a) cruciform in round field, b) cruciform in cross-shaped field, and c) the S-shaped 'wyrm' (scale 10mm)

Fig 6.15: Glaston, the decorated urn, Burial B16 (scale 50mm)

Fig 6.16: Glaston, detail of decoration on urn, Burial B16

The evidence from Cleatham suggests a similar chronological picture for vessels with *stehende bogen* decoration. His Group 12s, 'standing bows with stamp decoration', comprised seven urns; one of which, on stratigraphic grounds could be placed in any of Phases 2, 3 or 4, with Leahy placing it in Phase 4 'on stylistic grounds' (*ibid* 2007, 114). Urns with 'standing bows' but no stamping (Group 12a), of which there were four examples at Cleatham, appear to date to Phase 1 (*ibid*, 109).

This vessel appears likely to have originally been somewhat squat, a form which Richards saw as more typical of the containers for female cremations (*ibid*, 1987, 196), and adult females are, however, more closely linked with *stehende bogen* when compared to male cremations (*ibid*, 201). He also noted when stamped, urns containing adult females are closely linked with stamp designs with a square field, and those comprising concentric circles or ring-and-dot design. The two dies used on this urn are a cross in a square field, and a ring-and-dot type. It would be expected therefore that this urn was the container for the cremated remains of an adult female, and the skeletal remains indicate that this was probably the case. Radiocarbon dating of bone from this urn has given a date of spanning the late 5th to mid 7th centuries AD.

Other Anglo-Saxon pottery

Several sherds of Anglo-Saxon pottery were also recovered from the subsoil and Roman features in the field to the south of the A47.

Subsoil (2)

Plain bodysherd, 6g, fabric F5

Ditch 10 (Fig 6.9, 6)

Three plain bodysherds and rim of a small bowl, rim diameter = 200mm, 8% complete, different vessels, all fabric F1 (total weight = 62g), ditch 10

Discussion

It is unfortunate that so many of the urns from this site were damaged by past activity, presumably ploughing, as this has made any coherent overview of the urns somewhat difficult. Certainly, all the damage appears to be old, as none of the incomplete vessels have fresh breaks on their upper edges. The decorated vessels suggest that the cremation cemetery was in use for most of the early Anglo-Saxon period (ie from the 5th to the

6th centuries AD), so it is likely that it was servicing a small, local community. It should be borne in mind, however, that the only vessel which can be dated to the 5th century AD on the type of decoration on the pot may have been of some age when it was placed in the ground. Generally however, the range of decoration and urn size and shape, where discernable, fits well with Richards' (1987) analysis of such vessels, with the age and sex of the cremated individuals largely reflecting the nature of the pots. A few factors are worthy of further discussion, particularly the miniature pots which appear to have been deposited as grave goods.

Miniature Anglo-Saxon pots are not unknown in a funerary context in the 5th and 6th centuries AD. The Myres *Corpus* includes a fairly large number of such pots (*ibid*, 1977, figs 10, 46, and 47), and some are as small or with the same form as the vessel from the sunken-featured building (Field 15:07). They have a fairly wide distribution, with the geographically closest to this site being two from Rothwell in Northamptonshire (*ibid*, fig 58 no. 2893; fig 73 no. 2896). Most of these are from inhumations however, Richards (1987, 83) noted only two examples of whole miniature pots placed in urns. The small pots from burial 8 and pit 48 have far more parallels. They have a very widespread distribution, and similar vessels are known from Great Casterton, Market Overton and Cottesmore in Rutland (*ibid*, fig 27, 4014; fig 61, 834; fig 63, 1059).

The presence of burnt sherds and large body sherds which may have been used as lids is also worthy of comment. The possibility that some of the large sherds found in association with the urns at this site could have functioned as lids is a trend which has been noted elsewhere. At Spong Hill, urn C2022 appears to have had a sherd functioning in such a manner (Hills and Penn 1981, 49).

Lucy (2000, 110) cites a number of examples where burnt sherds occur in cremation burials, such as at Portway, near Andover in Hampshire, and they were not uncommon at Spong Hill (Hills and Penn 1981, table 7). Richards (1987, 83) notes that sherds in cremations are 'quite a common find' and suggests that they were not complete vessels when placed on the pyre, and functioned as representations of whole pots. Incomplete vessels are known from inhumation burials. For example, at Sewerby in Yorkshire, some of the accessory vessels were incomplete, and 'loose' sherds were found in the fill of some of the graves (Hirst 1985, 92). Hirst also cited earlier work which suggested that sherds were placed in graves as symbolic representations of whole pots (*ibid*, 32). A perhaps more convincing example comes from South Carlton in Lincolnshire, where a crouched inhumation occurred which had one hand placed on a large sherd from an incomplete pottery vessel (Wessex Archaeology 2004,

fig 7). A number of large sherds were carefully placed in inhumations at the Berinsfield cemetery in Oxfordshire (Booth 1995, 101), and many other examples exist.

Anglo-Saxon pottery from a watching brief, Field 15:07/4
by Andy Chapman

There is a small assemblage of pottery, 65 sherds, weighing 1.36kg, in hard and well-fired sandy fabrics, typically grey in colour, but including vessels with patchy light brown external surfaces. The group includes sherds from a thin-walled carinated bowl with burnished surfaces. It is decorated with four shallow incised grooves encircling the neck and short oblique grooved incisions on the carination. There is a coarseware vessel with a boss, a sherd with fine combed decoration and a sherd with deeply scored decoration. There are rims from at least five vessels, all are simple upright rims either rounded or flattened. This feature also contained a complete miniature urn, in a sandy fabric, grey with light grey-brown surfaces (Fig 6.8, 5 & Fig 6.11). It has a rim diameter 35mm and stands 41mm high (see Blinkhorn). The decorated carinated bowl and the boss indicate an early Anglo-Saxon date, AD450-650.

Other Anglo-Saxon finds
by Tora Hylton

Glaston

The burnt remains of 15 individual or grouped finds were recovered from eight of the burials: B6, B7, B9, B11-B14 and B16. The majority of the artefacts had been placed inside the urns, together with the cremated bone. The distorted nature of some of the finds, particularly the glass beads, suggests that the individuals had been dressed as for life when they were cremated. The finds comprise items for personal adornment and grooming and comprise a copper alloy brooch, a range of glass beads, and bone mount and parts of a bone comb (Table 6.1). The range represented may be paralleled by finds recovered from other Anglo-Saxon cemeteries in the south-east Midlands. Typologically the finds suggest a mid 5th to 6th-century date, which corresponds with the dating of the pottery.

Burial B6 (adult, sex unknown)

Some seven glass beads, including two polychrome beads damaged and distorted by heat (Fig 6.5). Originally they would have been cylindrical in shape with circular sections (*c.*25mm long and 12mm diameter), manufactured from red, yellow and green glass. It is difficult to be sure of the original decorative scheme but possibly a streaked example of a 'Traffic Light' bead (cf Brugmann 1996, 34). SF9.

Melted fragment, comprising two or three globular beads in blue glass, flanking an amorphous mass of brown (or red) with flecks of green and yellow. Probably the remains of a single polychrome bead (red/yellow/green). No measurements. SF24.

Amorphous, vesicular fragment of melted red and green glass bead(s), to which has adhered a small fragment of human bone. No measurements. SF25.

Complete, but broken, annular bead, possibly in dark blue glass, but difficult to tell as surfaces vitrified. Diameter: external 9mm; internal 2-3mm. Depth: 4mm. SF33.

Burial B7 (juvenile, 4-5 years, sex unknown)

Broken and incomplete bone mount, distorted bone by the heat and therefore difficult to reconstruct (Fig 6.6). Hollow, thin-walled cylindrical mount; the exterior surface is decorated with worn incised horizontal grooves. Two marginally placed circular perforations, both display signs of wear. The function of this piece is undefined, but as it was recovered from a juvenile there is a possibility that it was a part of a child's toy. Height: 24mm. SF 22.

Elongated undiagnostic fragment of clear glass with curved profile and irregular sub-circular section. Nature of object impossible to determine, but possibly the remains of a melted bead. Length: 50mm; width: 7mm. SF23.

Nodule, copper alloy. Sub-circular. Diameter: 4mm. SF31.

Burial B9 (juvenile, greater than 10 years old, sex unknown)

Amorphous piece of melted glass, comprising approximately five individual beads fused together. Although difficult to be certain, there appears to be two red beads, two blue beads (annular) and one white bead. Measurement: 16 x 15 x 10mm. SF29.

Burial B11 (adult and juvenile, sex unknown)

Melted fragment of black glass, probably a globular bead, but difficult to be sure. Measurements: 10 x 9mm. SF27.

Seven small fragments of iron. The X-ray reveals that six of the fragments have circular sections (diameter: 2mm) and of those five are parallel-sided and *c* 10-11mm long, and one is 7mm long. Two pieces have burred terminals (both ends), like an example from Westgarth Gardens, Suffolk (West 1985, fig 58, C7) and one has a single burred terminal, suggesting that they are rivets. These would have had any number of uses, including securing the individual components of a composite bone comb. SF26.

Burial B12 (adult, 15-18 years, sex unknown)

Three undiagnostic fragments of copper alloy. One piece measuring no more than 17mm x 4mm, has parallel sides and a curved profile; a similar example from Portway, Andover (Cook and Dacre 1985, fig 61, 3) has been identified as a loop, possibly for suspension.

Two very small undiagnostic amorphous sheet fragments that do not appear to join. Measurements: 6 x 5mm, 5 x 3mm. SF34.

Burial B13 (adult, sex unknown)

Incomplete double-sided composite bone comb, extremely fragmented and calcined (white/blue grey in colour), comprising 24 pieces, including fragments of tooth-plate, end-plate and side/connecting-plates; there are no teeth. The tooth-plate fragments measure no more than 11 x 9mm and all retain vestiges of the base of the teeth; measurements indicate that both sides of the comb had the same gauge, five teeth per centimetre, and this is paralleled by the spacing of the notches cut into the outer edge of the side-plate. Corrosion deposits on two fragments indicate that the individual pieces of the comb would originally have been secured with iron rivets. The presence of a small corner fragment from an end-plate (9 x 6mm) reveals that the comb would have been furnished with squared terminals. The fragments of side-plate measure no more than 14 x 8mm. Three small pieces join together to form a fragment measuring 24 x 8mm and the curvature of the pieces indicates that it is manufactured from a rib (Karen Deighton pers comm). The side-plate is simply decorated with two marginally placed, faintly incised longitudinal parallel grooves, rather like an example from West Stow (cf West 1985, fig 253, 3); in profile it appears to taper slightly and the longitudinal edges are chamfered and marked with short equidistant incisions, created during the cutting of the teeth. SF21.

Burial B14 (adult, sex unknown)

Copper alloy quoit brooch, complete (Fig 6.7). Plain broad-banded annular brooch with flat section and V-shaped pin slot in the inner circumference ('notch and stops' fastening). The pin–notch displays similarities to Agers Type D3, where the V-shaped slot is reinforced with a cast ridge which encloses the notch (Ager 1985, 2). The iron pin survives as a corroded mass over the central hole, together with the remains of one or two glass beads distorted by the heat of the pyre. The remains of the pin are evident on the X-ray, which shows that it is attached to the brooch by a circular perforation on the opposing side to the slot; the pin survives to a length of 31mm and is 2mm in diameter.

6. Anglo-Saxon burial and settlement (AD450-650)

This example may be compared to a pair of similarly plain examples from Marston St Lawrence, Northamptonshire; both have cast copper alloy bands with iron pins (Ager 1985, fig 26, a-b). Ager has indicated that Type D3 brooches are distributed mainly in the southern and eastern midlands and have 6th-century associations (*ibid*, 16-17). Small brooches of this type were generally used in pairs to fasten clothing; research has indicated that they would have been part of female dress and were often worn in association with beads like these examples. Diameter: external 44mm, internal 20mm. SF18.

Melted fragment of opaque white glass, probably a globular bead. Measurements: 9mm, SF28.

Burial B16 (adult, probably female)

Small vesicular fragment of melted white/blue glass, probably part of a circular/globular bead, adhering to small fragment of human bone. No measurements. SF30.

The beads

The assemblage is dominated by glass beads, examples of which were recovered from five burials (B6, B9, B11, B14 and B16). High temperatures during the cremation process has resulted in poor bead survival, therefore the condition of those that have survived is generally poor and it is difficult to distinguish shape and colour, therefore few types can be recognised.

There appear to be *c.*15 individual beads; identifiable forms include cylindrical multi-coloured (polychrome) beads and monochrome annular and globular beads. Burial B6 produced the largest number of beads (seven), with five from burial B9 and single examples from burials B11, B14 and B16 (Table 6.2).

The most distinctive beads are two cylindrical polychrome beads from burial B6 (Fig 6.5). The main body of the bead is red and they are decorated with applied yellow and green trails; this type of bead has been termed a 'traffic light bead' by Brugmann in her study of Anglo-Saxon beads (2004, 34). Beads of this type are predominantly recovered from East Anglia and, like this particular burial group, they are often recovered in association with blue beads. Brugmann's analysis has indicated that a combination of both types of bead suggests a date between the mid 5th to mid 6th centuries AD. Other bead forms represented include annular beads in blue glass, and globular beads in white and blue glass. Two burials (B6 and B16) produced beads fused to small fragments of human bone. It has been suggested that for this to occur, the body remained on top of the pyre for some time before its collapse (McKinley 1994a, 83-84).

Rushton

There are two Anglo-Saxon small finds from the Roman settlement at Rushton: part of a pair of tweezers from the subsoil and a rod fragment from gully 9.

The tweezers (one arm missing) have been manufactured from a strip of sheet metal which has been folded in half widthways; the surviving arm is tapered and terminates in a flared blade, the end of which is turned in at right-angles. The arm is decorated with marginally placed opposing facets flanked by incised transverse grooves. Stylistically these

Burial	Shape	Colour	Comments
B6	Cylindrical	Red with yellow and green trails	Polychrome bead damaged and distorted by heat. Difficult to be sure of original decorative scheme
	Cylindrical	Red with yellow and green trails	Amorphous mass, brown in colour with flecks of yellow and green. Probably similar to SF9.
	?Globular x2	Blue	--
	Unidentified	Red and green	Amorphous vesicular fragment adhered to fragment of human bone. Poss. monochrome beads
	Annular	?Dark blue	Complete but broken, surfaces vitrified through extensive heat.
B9	Annular x2	Blue	Amorphous lump of melted glass comprising *c* 5 individual beads
	Unident x2	Red	--
	?Globular x1	White	--
B11	?Globular	?Brown/dark blue	--
B14	Globular	White glass	Opaque
B16	?Globular	White/blue	Vesicular fragment adhered to fragment of human bone

TABLE 6.2: GLASTON, CATALOGUE OF ANGLO-SAXON GLASS BEADS

tweezers may be paralleled by examples recovered from cremation burials at Spong Hill, Norfolk dated to the 5th/6th centuries AD (Hills 1977, fig 116, 1460, 1647) and Buckland Cemetery, Dover (Evison 1987, Burial 41, 5).

The iron rod fragment is incomplete, at just 16mm long. It has a circular section, diameter 2.5mm, and terminates in a simple coiled terminal. Although it is difficult to be certain as to the identification of the object, it does display similarities to a range of iron pins recovered from Anglo-Saxon graves at Portway, Andover (Cook and Dacre 1985, Grave 25, 4 and Grave 19, 4).

Human bone from the Anglo-Saxon cemetery
by Sarah Inskip

There are the remains of 14 individuals from 13 bone deposits: four juveniles, eight adults and two of unknown age. They have been examined following the guidelines outlined in Brickley and McKinley (2004) and the English Heritage document *Human Bones from Archaeological Sites: A Guideline for Producing Assessment Documents and Reports* (Mays, Brickley and Dodwell 2004).

The material was received washed and dried. The bone deposits were passed through 10mm, 5mm, 2mm and 1mm sieves. Each sieved fraction was then recorded and weighed. The material was sorted into elemental groups: skull, long bones, axial skeleton and unidentifiable. Upper limb refers to the clavicle, humerus, ulna and radius. Lower limb refers to femur, tibia and fibula.

All the cremated bone deposits examined contained human remains, and burial B11 contained the remains of two individuals. Burials B12 and B13 contained some animal bone fragments, the weight of which was not included in the totals (Table 6.3).

Fragmentation, completeness and elemental representation

The number of identifiable fragments is usually related to the general size of the fragments; larger fragments result in more identifiable elements. The majority of material from Glaston remained in the 10mm and 5mm sieves (Table 6.3), so it was possible to identify many skeletal elements; only burial B5, weighing 5g, contained no identifiable remains (Table 6.4). Burial B16 contained a large fragment of femur (120mm long), suggesting that bones were not further crushed after cremation (Fig 6.4, foreground). The larger size of the fragments meant that age estimation was possible in nine of the fourteen individuals.

Experimental studies and modern cremation data have demonstrated that complete cremated adults should weigh in the region of 1-3kg (McKinley 1997 and 2000, Steele and Mays 1993, 4). Juveniles should present around 500g of bone (Mays 1998). This considered, burials B12 and B16 may theoretically represent complete individuals (Table 6.3). However, most of the bone deposits appear to be incomplete. McKinley (2000) suggests that the majority of cremation burials are incomplete and it is certainly true of most Anglo-Saxon cremated deposits. At Snape (Steele and Mays 1993, 4) and Mucking (Mays 1992), Mays indicated that on average the deposits contained around 10% - 15% of that which would be expected. As cremated bone preserves extremely well in poor soil conditions, the common observation of underweight, undisturbed cremation burials is thought to reflect incomplete collection from the pyre. Unfortunately, the Glaston burial deposits were damaged by medieval ploughing, with pottery fragments and bone found scattered around the area (Carlyle pers comm). It is therefore not possible to comment further on the completeness of individuals.

Bone size/ Burial	Total (g)	>10 mm (g)	>5mm (g)	>2 mm (g)	>1mm (g)	<1 mm (g)
B4	816	426	248	121	5	14
B5	5	4	<1	<1	<1	<1
B6	311	100	130	80	<1	<1
B7	71	21	27	21	2	0
B8	<1	<1	<1	<1	<1	<1
B9	78	10	28	36	2	<1
B11*	297	30	123	139	8	6
B12	614	216	228	151	9	9
B13	58	14	25	19	<1	<1
B14	272	65	99	99	6	3
B16	995	648	242	72	10	23
B18	86	28	34	23	2	<1
B20	14	8	6	<1	<1	<1

B11*, Two individuals

TABLE 6.3: GLASTON, WEIGHT OF CREMATED BONE DEPOSITS BY BONE SIZE

6. Anglo-Saxon burial and settlement (AD450-650)

Burial	MNI	Age	Sex	Colour	Other
B4	1	Adult	?f	mostly white	Osteochondiritis patella
B5	?	?	?	cream	--
B6	1	Adult	?	cream	--
B7	1	Juvenile	?	cream /white	Porous skull?
B8	?	?	?	cream	--
B9	1	Juvenile	?	mostly cream	--
B11	2	Adult + Juvenile	?	mostly cream	--
B12	1	Adult	?	mostly white	--
B13	1	Adult	?	mostly white	--
B14	1	Adult	?	cream /white	--
B16	1	Adult	?f	mostly white	--
B18	1	Adult	?	cream /white	--
B20	1	Juvenile	?	mostly cream	--

MNI = minimum number of individuals

TABLE 6.4: GLASTON, SUMMARY OF CREMATED BONE DEPOSITS

The quantification of elemental groups found in each burial (Table 6.5) shows that although all elemental groups are represented, there is a clear abundance of long bones and skull. McKinley (2000) highlights that many distinguishing skull landmarks exist, making even very small fragments identifiable. Furthermore, skull vault fragments are easily identifiable due to the presence of diploe.

Long bones consist of denser cortical bone than those of the axial skeleton, which are either thin or have higher trabecular bone content. Trabecular bone tends to disintegrate, which probably results in elements such as vertebrae, tarsals and pelvis making up a high quantity of the smaller unidentifiable fragments. Accordingly, the inflated quantity of long bones is a normal occurrence in cremated material. This trend was also seen at Westhampnett (McKinley 1997) and in the juveniles from Snape (Steele and Mays 1993).

Pyre conditions

According to experiments carried out by Shipman *et al* (1984), the colour of bone can be used as an approximation of pyre conditions, including temperature and oxygen levels. The white to cream colouration of the Glaston material suggests high levels of oxygen and temperatures far in excess of 600°C. Further evidence of pyre temperature comes from the melted glass bead found adhering to bone originating from burial 6. Mays (2010, 322) indicates that Calvin Wells research on glass beads demonstrated that glass starts to melt at 850°C. In fact, individuals from Mucking (Mays 1992) had similarly melted beads and Mays (2010, 324) suggested that temperatures in excess of 900°C may have been achieved in the Mucking pyres.

The material from Glaston was highly uniform in colour with over 95% of bone presenting cream to white colouration (Table 6.4). There was <5% of grey material and this was usually endosteal surfaces of long bones and endocranial (inner) surfaces of skulls. Intense heat causes fragmentation of the periosteal and ectocranial (outer) surfaces which would subsequently increase exposure of the inner surfaces of bone. Steele and Mays (1993, 5) suggests that evidence of skeletal material cremated at lower temperatures can also be related to shattering and fragmentation during cremation and fragments falling into cooler areas. Lack of colour variation between elemental groups suggests that intensive and, or even firing was achieved across the pyre. The uniformity in fragmentation and little colour variation between the elemental groups and burials, suggests that a standard method of cremation was probably used at Glaston.

Confusion with the classification of white fragments as a low temperature indicator (Williams 1983, 18) in the Thurmaston report means comparison to nearby contemporary Thurmaston is difficult. Yet, in similarity to Glaston, melted beads and metal indicate temperatures in excess of 800°C were also achieved at Thurmaston. Williams (1983) suggests that around 78% of the cremations were undertaken at a 'fairly high' temperature or above. Unfortunately, a definition of what 'fairly high' meant, was not forthcoming from the author, but one has to bear in mind that the Thurmaston report was written some 27 years ago in retrospect of work carried out in the 1950s.

Demography

In the fourteen cremated deposits examined there was evidence for fifteen individuals. Burial B11 appeared to

Burial	Skull	Ribs	Vertebrae	Scapula	Upper body	Hands	Pelvis	Lower limb	Feet	Long bones	Articular surfaces	Unidenti	Total
B4	77	6	53	-	113	6	30	180	24	66	35	219	**809g**
B5	<1	-	-	-	-	-	-	3	-	-	-	-	**4g**
B6	13	1	2	2	26	1	5	77	-	73	-	109	**309g**
B7	27	2	-	-	5	-	-	7	-	6	-	25	**72g**
B8	-	-	-	-	-	-	-	-	-	-	-	1	**1g**
B9	17	-	-	-	5	-	-	7	-	11	2	32	**74g**
B11	54	5	1	-	-	-	-	-	3	66	-	168	**297g**
B12	84	3	17	1	64	2	48	98	4	111	29	257	**718g**
B13	16	-	-	-	-	-	3	-	1	14	-	24	**58g**
B14	74	1	1	2	12	-	2	12	-	43	-	125	**272g**
B16	130	23	62	10	155	3	34	257	25	107	16	176	**998g**
B18	7	-	-	-	8	1	-	20	-	17	1	30	**86g**
B20	8	-	-	-	-	-	-	-	-	-	-	6	**14g**

TABLE 6.5: GLASTON, QUANTIFICATION OF HUMAN BONE BY ELEMENT

contain mainly juvenile elements but some adult bone was identified. In total, there were eight adults and four juveniles. Burials B5, B8 and B19 could not be placed into an age category, as too little bone was recovered. Accordingly, adults made up 64% of the identifiable material and juveniles 36%.

It was possible to estimate age in twelve of the fifteen deposits (Table 6.6). Eight adults were identified; burial B16 could be aged more specifically to the middle age range (35-45 years) as a particularly worn molar was identified. Burial B4 is likely to be that of a young to middle-aged adult based on the fact that the epiphyses are all fused but the cranial sutures remain open. Four deposits contained juvenile remains: burials B7, B9, B11 and B12. The unerupted crown of a permanent canine indicates that burial B7 is that of a 4-5 year old individual. The spinous processes in burial B12 are fusing. This, accompanied by an unfused humeral head, suggests that burial B12 is that of a 15 year old. Further evidence from an open crypt in the maxilla and an unerupted third molar suggests a teenage individual. As such, burial B12 was aged between 15-18 years. Burial B9 had unfused long bones, the dimensions of which suggest an individual younger than 10 years but older than an infant.

At Snape, Suffolk, 20% of the remains were immature (Steele and Mays 1993) (Table 6.7). At Thurmaston just 12% of the material was deemed immature (Williams 1983). The number of juveniles recovered at Glaston has greater similarity to Mucking where 33% of individuals were aged as immature. Although Glaston is the only site to have no infants, they were rarely recovered at any of the other sites and this absence may reflect the small sample size at Glaston rather than a true absence.

Sex

There is very little evidence to enable the sex of individuals to be determined. This is partially due to the destructive nature of the cremation process and also the incompleteness of most of the burials.

Only two burials provided indicators of sex. A sharp supraorbital margin indicates a possible female individual in burial B16. A small mastoid in burial B4 also indicates a female individual. It would be unwise to suggest that these individuals were definitely female from the skeletal remains alone, particularly considering the low accuracy of sexing incomplete human skeletons (Kjellström 2004). It is worthy of note, however, that McKinley (1994, 68) has noted a female bias in the Anglo-Saxon cremation record. Sex estimation was not carried out on juveniles given that no macroscopic technique has, as of yet, proved accurate and reliable enough.

Pathology

There was very little evidence of pathology in the collection. Steele and Mays (1993, 7) suggest that pathological findings in cremated material is rare due to the fragmentation and distortion of bones during the cremation process. Only three of the burials: B4, B16 and B12, had sufficient remains to permit assessment of osteoarthritis; no evidence for this disease was evident in any of the joints that were available for analysis.

Three juvenile individuals (burials B7, B9 and B11) had evidence for porotic hyperostotis on the occipital and parietal bones of the skull. Steele and Mays (1993) identified a similar lesion on an infant from Snape and

6. ANGLO-SAXON BURIAL AND SETTLEMENT (AD450-650)

Burial	MNI	Epiphysis	Dentition	Other	Overall age
B4	1	F	-	AS Phase1-4	Young/middle Adult
B5	?	-	-	-	?
B6	1	No UF found	-	Thick robust bones, pronounced flexor attachments on phalanges	Adult
B7	1	UF	4-5 years	-	4-5 years
B8	?	-	-	-	?
B9	1	UF long bones	--	Shaft size indicates a younger child but not an infant	>10 years
B11	2	UF long bones	-	UF cranial sutures	Adult and Juvenile
B12	1	UF humeral head/ F thoracic spinous process	Unerupted molar tooth (m3?)	UF cranial sutures	15 – 18 years
B13	1	F	Adult	Vertebral rings F	Adult
B14	1	-	-	Evidence of suture fusion	Adult
B16	1	F	Adult	Worn molar	middle Adult
B18	1	-	-	-	Adult
B20	1	-	-	-	Juvenile

Key = MNI = minimum number of individuals, UF = unfused, F= Fused

TABLE 6.6: GLASTON, AGE ESTIMATIONS FROM THE EPIPHYSES, DENTITION AND OTHER SOURCES

Site	Infants (0-2 years)		Children (2 – 18 years)		Adults		Total MNI
Glaston (C)	0	0%	4	33%	8	67%	12
Snape (C)	1	5%	3	15%	16	80%	20
Thurmaston (C)	2	3%	5	9%	51	88%	58
Mucking (C)	32	8%	66	16%	308	76%	406
Empingham (I)	2	1%	52	34%	98	64%	152

C= cremation cemetery, I= Inhumation cemetery

TABLE 6.7: GLASTON, RELATIVE NUMBER OF PEOPLE PER AGE GROUP FOR CONTEMPORARY SITES

Williams (1983) on an adult from nearby Thurmaston. Porotic hyperostotis is normally seen in immature individuals (Lewis 2000, 45) but can persist into adulthood if the condition fails to heal. Furthermore, this type of lesion can be present as a result of other conditions. As it is not possible examine the complete skeletons, a diagnosis beyond porotic hyperostotis is not recommended. The only other sign of any pathology was noted on Burial B4, which has a patella fragment that appears to have a cortical defect.

Discussion

Williams suggests that cremation was the predominant burial rite in the Anglo-Saxon period (2002, 48). Commonality of the cremation practice varies depending on national location. Cremation is almost exclusive in East Anglia but near absent in the North and the South-West (Williams 2002, 55). Glaston fits in a region of mixed inhumation and cremation cemeteries, making the finding of a cremation cemetery normal for the region.

There are a number of Anglo-Saxon cemeteries in the region against which comparisons can be made for the Glaston cremations. A large metropolitan cremation cemetery was found at Thurmaston (Williams 1983), just a few miles north of Leicester and west of Glaston. Other less local sites will be used in order to assess how Glaston fits into the broader context of Anglo-Saxon England. Empingham, just a few miles north of Glaston has two large inhumation cemeteries (Timby 1996). Spong Hill (McKinley 1994b), the largest Anglo-Saxon cemetery, is a good comparison due to the sheer volume of data. Smaller cemeteries at Snape, Suffolk (Steele and Mays 1993) and Mucking, Essex (Mays 1992) can also be referenced.

The number of individuals in the cemetery at Glaston is small compared to Thurmaston and Spong Hill. This is unsurprising considering that Glaston itself has never been a large town and is not directly related to a Roman town, where larger settlements were often located (Liddle nd). This may suggest that the cemetery is related to a single Anglo-Saxon settlement, as is common in the Leicestershire region (*ibid*, 2).

In terms of demography, the numbers of adults and children were not dissimilar to other Anglo-Saxon sites. Ratios of adults to children vary in Anglo-Saxon settlements. Mays (1992) indicates that in populations without modern health care 40% or more of individuals between 0-15 years can be expected to die (Mays 1992, 8). At Glaston, albeit a small sample, levels of children are slightly higher than most Anglo-Saxon cremation cemeteries (33% could be classed as immature) yet no infant remains (below two years) were found. This 40% mark is rarely identified and the location of these missing individuals is debated. McKinley highlights that infant remains do survive cremation, but they are small and extremely fragile (1997, 64). This makes infants problematic to identify. Conversely, as identified by Mays (1992), a general under-representation of infants in most Anglo-Saxon cremation cemeteries may suggest burial elsewhere. Unfortunately, the small size of the Glaston material does not really permit further speculation. Considering this, there seems to be nothing unusual about the representation of age groups at Glaston and the cemetery fits in with what is expected from a apparently normal population (eg it is not a battle/monastic site) during the Anglo-Saxon period.

The remains at Glaston share much in common with nearby Thurmaston, despite being far fewer in number. The white/buff colour of the bones and evidence of melted beads suggest pyre temperatures reached at least 800°C and above, with ample oxygen. The sites also shared a common trend with regards to skeletal fragments, where the inner surfaces appeared to be exposed to lower temperatures. In a similar fashion, animal bones were also recovered from cremations in both cemeteries. It is very common for animal bone to be found in Anglo-Saxon cremations (Bond 1996, table 1) and this was indeed the case at Snape (Steele and Mays 1993), Mucking (Mays 1992) and Spong Hill (McKinley 1994). It is difficult to understand exactly why animals are found in Anglo-Saxon cremations and a number of reasons have been proffered. These include straightforward explanations of provisioning for the dead or accompanying a master to the grave. Further suggestions could incorporate notions of animals taking on a symbolic role and playing a role in the identity of the individual or group. Whatever the reason, it is unlikely that whole animals were placed in with burials B12 and B13, as insufficient quantities of animal bone were recovered. The representation of animals in Anglo-Saxon cremations is an area of research that requires more attention, and cremated animal bones as a research entity, need to be reported and analysed more thoroughly.

Radiocarbon dating

A sample of cremated human bone from burial B16 has returned a date in the early Anglo-Saxon period, between the late 6th and mid-7th centuries AD (570-655 Cal AD, 95% confidence, 1440+/-30 BP, Beta 293240; Table 6.8).

Lab no. Sample no.	Origin of sample	Sample details	13C/12C ratio	Conventional radiocarbon age BP	Cal AD *68% confidence* **95% confidence**
Beta-293240 GLAS08/41	Burial B16	Human bone	-21.7 0/00	1440+/- 30	*600-645* **570-655**

Radiocarbon dating laboratory: Beta Analytic, Florida, Miami, USA
Method of analysis: AMS-standard delivery
Material pre-treatment: Bone carbonate extraction (cremated human bone)
Calibration: INTCAL04 (*Radiocarbon*, 2004, **46/3**)

TABLE 6.8: GLASTON, RADIOCARBON DATE FOR BURIAL B16

7. Medieval and post-medieval field systems

Evidence relating to the medieval and post-medieval field systems was recovered at Normanton Road, Seaton, Thorpe by Water and Caldecott, Rutland and at Swinawe Barn near Corby, Northamptonshire, and a small number of finds came from furrows and boundary ditches.

A field boundary wall and furrows at Normanton Road

The site was located close to the northern end of the pipeline route, approximately 1.1km to the north-east of Edith Weston and to the north of Normanton Road, near Oak Farm, Rutland (NGR: SK 9385 0586; see Fig 1.2). The deserted medieval village of Normanton, depopulated by Sir Gilbert Heathcote in 1764 to found Normanton Park, lies *c*.0.8km to the north-west of the site. The ground sloped imperceptibly to the north and lay at *c*.110m aOD; the underlying geology was Boulder Clay overlying Lower Lincolnshire Limestone (BGS 1978).

The excavation investigated an area immediately to the east of a right-angled geophysical anomaly, possibly part of a ditched enclosure of prehistoric date, which was located within the easement of the pipeline corridor but outside of the excavation area (Butler 2007, fig 21). The aim of the excavation was to determine if features associated with the enclosure extended into the area for the pipe trench.

No prehistoric features were encountered, although at the northern end of the site there was an undated oval pit, 4, 1.9m long by 0.73m wide by 0.64m deep, with a fill of dark grey-rown silty clay (3).

Immediately to the east of the pit was a probable furrow, 7, *c*.2.0m wide by 0.22m deep. Its near north-south alignment corresponds with linear geophysical anomalies interpreted as furrows.

Towards the southern end of the site were the foundation courses of a drystone wall, 8, constructed from roughly dressed limestone blocks and limestone rubble. It was aligned north-west to south-east and was 0.7m wide; a length of 2.6m remained *in situ*. The wall is probably a former post-medieval field boundary, similar to existing field boundary walls in the surrounding area, which are constructed from locally sourced stone.

A boundary ditch and furrows at Seaton

Approximately 160m to the north of the Iron Age pits investigated at Seaton (NGR: SP 8884 9839), there was a strong, linear geophysical anomaly that was initially interpreted as a ditch, aligned east to west and parallel with furrows to the north and at right angles to furrows to the south (Butler 2007, fig 39). Excavation confirmed that this feature was also a furrow, 3.5m wide by 0.22m deep. Approximately 20m to the south and on roughly the same alignment there was a small, undated ditch, 9, 1.85m wide by 0.71m deep, with a terminal at its eastern end. The ditch is probably the remains of a post-medieval or modern field boundary, and it appeared to have been deliberately backfilled.

A ditch and furrows near Thorpe by Water

The terminal of a probable post-medieval ditch was encountered to the south of Thorpe Road, approximately 0.6km to the west of Thorpe by Water (NGR: SP 8864 9632; see Fig 4.4, Site 2). The site lay on a south-east-facing slope overlooking the River Welland, at *c*.55m aOD. There are no known cropmarks in the vicinity to indicate the extent of the feature or any settlement to which it may belong. The ditch, 5, which extended 2m into the excavation, was up to 0.6m wide and 0.10m deep, with a fill of with brown-grey silty clay (4), which contained an abraded sherd of glazed medieval or post-medieval pottery.

Medieval or post-medieval furrows, spaced 7-8m apart, are evident on the geophysical survey plot on both sides of Thorpe Road (Butler 2007, fig 42): to the south they are aligned north-west to south-east, to the north, north-north-west to south-south-east.

A stone drain and furrows at Caldecott

Medieval/post-medieval plough furrows, spaced 8m apart, crossed the site of the Iron Age settlement on a north-west to south-east alignment (see Fig 4.5).

Overlying an Iron Age cobbled surface at the southern end of the site, there was a 2m-length of stone-lined conduit or drain, 67. It was made from two rows of worked ironstone blocks spaced 0.4m apart, with the dressed faces lining the channel. The conduit extended beyond the site to the north-west, while its south-eastern end appeared to open out into a shallow linear depression worn into the cobbled surface. A horseshoe recovered from the channel probably dates to the 16th or 17th centuries.

Boundary ditches and furrows at Swinawe Barn, Corby

A series of furrows, spaced 3-4m apart, extended the length of the excavated site on a north to south alignment, truncating the Iron Age remains (see Fig 4.9). The narrow spacing between the furrows would indicate that they are post-medieval in date. An abrupt curve to the south may suggest the presence of a now vanished obstacle in the field. A sherd of Roman pottery was recovered from one of the furrows.

Running parallel to the furrows down the eastern side of the site was a large ditch, 28/104 (Fig 7.1). It cut the eastern edge of one of the furrows, indicating that it dates to the later medieval or post-medieval period. To the north it was 3.8m wide by 2.1m deep with an extended sequence of fills, some of which appeared to be deliberate dumping. To the south the ditch was reduced to 1.4m wide by 1.0m deep.

At the southern end of the site ditch 28/1004 was cut by ditch 31, which was 1.3m wide by 0.40m deep, with a fill of grey-brown clay (30), overlain by mid brown-grey clay (29). It is probably the remains of a post-medieval or modern field boundary.

Furrows at other sites

At the southern end of the Roman site at Gretton there was a medieval/post-medieval furrow, 16 (see Fig 5.3). A similar wide shallow feature, 12, 15m to the north, containing several sherds of abraded Iron Age pottery, was initially interpreted as a ditch, but at 3.0m wide and only 0.07m deep it is more likely to be another furrow, containing residual pottery.

To the south of the Roman ditches at Violet Lane (see Fig 5.6) there were two medieval/post-medieval furrows aligned north-north-west to south-south-east, and the entire site was crossed by numerous 19th-century ceramic land drains.

At Willows Nursery the Iron Age remains (see Fig 4.16) were partly obscured by twelve post-medieval furrows, aligned east to west and spaced c.5m apart (not illustrated), and several modern land drains.

Finds of medieval and post-medieval date:

Medieval and post-medieval finds
by Tora Hylton

Glaston

Part of a cast copper alloy rumbler bell and an iron nail were recovered from the topsoil. The lower half of the bell is decorated with a 'sunburst' motif, a common design in the mid 18th and 19th centuries. The base of the bell preserves the remains of a worn makers mark (SC); the initials are unknown.

Cransley

Part of a medieval copper alloy folding clasp for securing straps was recovered from the subsoil. Just the squared frame survives; it has slightly convex sides with a small ridge at each corner and the outside edge is recessed and

FIG 7.1: SWINAWE BARN, MEDIEVAL/POST-MEDIEVAL DITCH 104, LOOKING NORTH (SCALE 2M)

would have held the folding end. The corroded remains of an iron pin adhere to the narrowed offset bar. Folding clasps were in use from the 13th to 15th centuries (Egan and Pritchard 1991, fig 77, 559).

Caldecott

A horseshoe was recovered from the fill of a stone conduit, 64. It is complete but displays signs of wear; corrosion deposits obscure the shape of the nail holes and both terminals are furnished with folded calkins. Stylistically the shoe displays similarities to Clarke's Type 4 horseshoe (1995, figs 86-89) which dates to the late medieval period. Outside London this shoe type continued in use until the 16th or early 17th centuries (Egan 2005, 179).

Nearby, an everted rim fragment and part of the curved body wall of an iron vessel was recovered from the surface of a pebble layer, 78. The form parallels tripod vessels in copper alloy (handled skillet/cauldron) which date to the medieval period. Available dimensions suggest that the vessel would have measured in excess of 260mm in diameter.

Swinawe Barn, Corby

A copper alloy brooch and a bone tool was recovered from medieval plough soil over an Iron Age roundhouse gully. The brooch has a plain annular frame with circular section; a constriction indicates where the pin (now missing) would have been positioned. A similar example dating to AD1350-1400 has been recovered in London (Egan and Pritchard 1991, fig 160, 1307).

The bone tool is double-ended with spatulate and pointed ends; both terminals display signs of wear. Typologically it displays similarities to pin-beaters used with vertical two-beam looms, but is rather a small example of its type as it measures just 71mm in length. Brown suggests that this type would have been used for tapestry weaving rather than cloth (1990, 227).

Three iron nails were recovered from a medieval ditch; two have T-shaped heads (both are incomplete) and measure up to 40mm long. Nails with T-shaped heads would have been used in timber where they would have sat flush with the surface.

Post-medieval floor tiles
by Pat Chapman

From Gretton Road there is one complete post-medieval floor tile and three sherds of probable floor tile, all from the topsoil. The complete floor tile is 223mm square and 45mm thick (8⅞x1¾ inches) with one surface worn smooth and white lime mortar on the sides and underneath. One of the sherds is 23mm thick, also with a worn surface. Three of the four tiles are made from very hard reddish-orange clay with a dark red surface. The other sherd is made from a pale orange with frequent small sub-rounded gravel and mortar along one edge.

8. Discussion

Project objectives

The fieldwork carried out along the course of the pipeline, comprising a mixture of geophysical survey, area excavation and watching brief, has added numerous new sites to the archaeological record and has enhanced knowledge of a few sites previously known from aerial photography.

From the evidence gathered, it has been possible to address many of the issues raised in the research objectives (see section 1.3), while accepting the limitations imposed by the constraints of the pipeline easement and the pipeline construction corridor. The sections below summarise the main findings by period, while this introduction considers the broader issues.

The settlements examined can be only partially understood as in no instance has a complete site plan been obtained, but in some instances it is still possible to set the archaeology within defined groups. For the Iron Age enclosure and roundhouses at Swinawe Barn, near Corby, there is sufficient evidence to set this enclosure within a well known group of domestic farmsteads of rectangular form, characteristically containing a principal house and other ancillary structures. Similarly, the ditches of the Roman settlement at White Hill Lodge produced building material including *tessarae* and tufa, indicating that the excavated ditch systems formed enclosures relating to a domestic centre of some status, perhaps a small villa with a bath suite. At Great Cransley there was an extensive domestic settlement, with the finds indicating the presence of pottery kilns, while a well located in the watching brief produced fragments of rotary querns, otherwise scarce at all sites.

The recovery of pottery was variable. For the Iron Age only Swinawe Barn produced a substantial assemblage that was worth fully quantifying, describing and illustrating. Even with the Roman sites the pottery assemblages were typically small, with only Thorpe Malsor and Great Cransley producing substantial contemporary groups from pit or ditch fills that were worthy of full analysis and illustration.

The bone assemblages were generally poor, in many instances due to poor preservation conditions. For the Iron Age, it was again only Swinawe Barn that produced sufficient quantity to define an economy based on cattle husbandry, with some older cattle and sheep implying the retention of animals for traction, breeding stock, and wool production. For the Roman sites, Thorpe Malsor and Great Cransley produced sufficiently large assemblages to define the emphasis on cattle for meat production, while at White Hill Lodge, the possible villa estate, the status of the site was further emphasised by a diverse bone assemblage denoting access to a more varied diet.

Despite an extensive programme of soil sampling, good deposits of charred plant remains were scarce. At the Iron Age sites, yet again it was Swinawe Barn where soils from the ring ditch of the principal roundhouse produced a wide range of cereal grains, nut shell, fruit stones and weed seeds. For the Roman period a single pit at Thorpe Malsor was the only outstanding deposit, containing cereal grains, chaff and weed seeds all indicative of charred waste from cereal processing.

For the Anglo-Saxon period the only evidence of substance was the recovery of part of a cremation cemetery, although a nearby watching brief may have enhanced understanding by locating a sunken-featured building 300m to the south that was perhaps part of the accompanying settlement.

While the restrictions of a pipeline corridor impose limits on the understanding of individual sites, a major positive aspect of a pipeline is that it transects a diversity of topography and geology, extending from valley bottom across the slopes and onto higher ground. Parts of this landscape have rarely been subject to other developments that are liable to enable any large scale fieldwork. So the pipeline from Empingham, Rutland to Hannington, Northamptonshire has broken much new ground in an archaeological sense, and the much of value of the present work lies in how it will inform future research in these little studied areas.

The late Bronze Age/early Iron Age pit alignment near Seaton

Domestic settlements of the late Bronze Age/early Iron Age are elusive in the archaeological record and are significantly under-represented. By far the most numerous sites within this period are pit alignments. These poorly understood boundary monuments are fairly widespread; in Northamptonshire alone, over 130 pit alignments have been identified from aerial photographs or investigated by excavation (Kidd 2004). In recent years, pit alignments have been investigated at Raunds (McAree 2005) and Upton, Northamptonshire (Carlyle 2010; Mason 2011), and Oakham, Rutland (Mellor 2007).

Pit alignments generally date to the late Bronze Age/ early Iron Age in origin, although there is evidence that some examples were perhaps constructed or at least maintained until as late as the middle/late Iron Age, such as Tallington, Lincolnshire (Simpson 1966) and Langford Downs, Oxfordshire (Williams 1946-7). Unfortunately, there was no material or environmental evidence to provide a date for the Seaton pit alignment.

The length of pit alignment investigated at Seaton, Rutland adds to the increasingly detailed pattern of pit alignments in the region. The excavated length comprised twenty-one pits over a length of 57m on a north-north-east to south-south-west alignment. Geophysical survey (Butler 2007) has shown that the alignment continues to the south of Seaton Road for at least a further 130m, but the ends have not been located.

There was a high degree of regularity in the shape, size, depth and spacing of the pits; any variation that was evident was largely due to truncation by ploughing. They were spaced approximately 1.5m apart and were typically shallow and roughly circular in plan, with steep sides and flat bases. The pits generally contained a homogeneous fill, and appear to have silted up due to natural weathering; as there was no evidence for deliberate in-filling or recutting.

The regularity of the pits is a characteristic that has been noted at many examples, including Gretton, Briar Hill, Aldwincle, Ringstead (Jackson 1974; 1977; and 1978), Pitsford (Hallam et al 2003) and Harlestone Quarry (Chapman et al 2015)HH near Northampton, and further afield at Tusmore, Oxfordshire (Mudd 2007), St Ives, Cambridgeshire (Pollard 1996), and Gayhurst Quarry, Buckinghamshire (Chapman 2007). Aerial photographs and the excavation of other pit alignments in the region and across the country show that regular spacing of the pits is a common feature (Hollowell 1971, Pollard 1996).

As only a short length of the alignment was exposed within the easement, it is not possible to comment on the method of construction in detail. However, the plan of the excavated and surveyed length of the Seaton alignment (Fig 3.1) does show a large scale pattern of abrupt but slight changes in alignment at intervals of perhaps 50-70m. There is a clear change in alignment to the south of Seaton Road, perhaps another in the length hidden beneath the road, and a further change in alignment occurred within the excavated area and was marked by the presence of an offset pit (see Fig 3.2, pit 21). Similar subtle changes in alignment have been seen at other pit alignments, including Gayhurst Quarry, Buckinghamshire (Chapman 2007, 181, fig 36).

On a smaller scale, slight displacements in the line of the pits have been noted at Aldwincle, Briar Hill, Gretton and Pitsford, Northamptonshire. At Gretton (Jackson 1974) this occurred at intervals of every five or six pits and was taken to indicate the work of separate digging teams, as has been suggested for Tallington, Lincolnshire (Simpson 1966, Pollard 1996) and Harlestone Quarry, Northampton (Chapman et al, 2015)HH.

The regularity in the form and spacing of the pits that form the alignments suggests that they were a deliberate monumental statement, not simply quarry pits to extract material to construct a bank or a series of mounds. Indeed, there is no clear evidence to suggest that the monuments had any other component features. However, excavations at a twin pit alignment at St Ives (Pollard 1996) produced evidence of hedgerow tree species and distinctive right-angled wood remains, as found in managed and laid hedgerows, so it is possible that pit alignments may have been associated with pre-existing land divisions, or were reinforced as a landscape boundary with hedgerows or brushwood fences. A bank constructed from soil excavated from the pits would have been negligible in size, which further reinforces the view that it was the pits that were the important component of the monument and not any other associated structure.

Pit alignments, due to their very nature, have often been interpreted as symbolic landscape divisions and not as physical barriers to the movement of people or livestock. However, extensive excavations at Wollaston, Northamptonshire, revealed a network of single and double pit alignments that appeared to mark out blocks of open grassland that would have been used for pasture (Meadows 1995).

The uniformity in the form of pit alignments over a relatively wide geographical area suggests that the possible presence of a hedgerow or fence may have been a secondary consideration, and it was the pits that were the primary concern of the people who invested their time and labour in digging them. The purpose and meaning of these common landscape features remains elusive, but they probably demarcated local territorial divisions and/or land-use boundaries. Indeed, they date to a period when there is evidence in the middle Nene Valley and elsewhere for the gradual expansion of settlement from the lighter, well-drained soils of the terrace gravels onto the heavier, higher ground overlying the boulder clay (Parry 2006), and the attendant social pressures that this must have engendered.

The Iron Age landscape

The identification and study of cropmarks shown on aerial photographs, combined with the increasing number of archaeological investigations over the last two decades, has gradually contributed to an increased understanding of the pattern of middle to late Iron Age settlement and land use in the region. This understanding is far from comprehensive and the pattern is far from complete, but certain trends can be discerned.

When interpreting such trends, the generally recognised problems associated with the dating of Iron Age settlements has to be borne in mind. Obtaining precise dates is rarely possible. Pottery is the primary means of dating features, and it can provide only a broad indication of date, but the majority of assemblages from Iron Age sites tend to be small, poorly preserved and largely comprise undiagnostic, undecorated body sherds. In addition, pottery forms tend to be long-lived and fabrics show little variation over time (Kidd 2004). Radiocarbon dating is of use, but it is unfortunate that the middle Iron Age spans a plateau on the radiocarbon calibration curve, so that radiocarbon dates within the 4th to 1st centuries BC typically have two possible date ranges for any given sample.

There are also limits on the interpretation of archaeological sites in general on linear schemes, such as the construction of pipelines and roads, where survey and excavation areas are constrained by the width of the easement or corridor. With such excavations, discrete features such as pits and postholes can become divorced from the settlement to which they belong, and the extent of enclosures and ditch systems can only occasionally be determined when rectified cropmarks have been mapped. The dating of settlements on such schemes is also open to doubt as only thin strips through a site are excavated and only the investigated features can be dated with any accuracy; other parts of the settlement beyond the easement or corridor may differ in date by many centuries.

With only small parts of such sites available for investigation, interpretation of their type and function can only be stated in general terms. On the current project, environmental sampling has been unable to add much to this general interpretation as the occurrence and preservation of ecofacts was generally poor at all of the sites examined.

There is an inevitable bias in the distribution of settlements in favour of areas of modern development or mineral extraction where there has been attendant archaeological investigation. Historically, this has tended to indicate that middle Iron Age sites were located on the gravel terraces or adjacent limestone geologies bordering the major rivers, such as the Nene, the Witham and the Trent, or in their tributary river valleys. It was assumed that the lack of known sites on higher ground was because the soils, generally formed over Boulder Clay, are heavier and were not suited to early arable agriculture; as a consequence, the higher ground may have been used for pasture or have remained wooded until later in the Iron Age, when population pressures led to their eventual clearance. This picture has been considerably modified in recent years with new discoveries being made on higher ground, often on Boulder Clay.

In Rutland, there is little excavated evidence for middle Iron Age settlement, although this may be a reflection of less intensive development in the county compared with elsewhere. One of the few sites where middle Iron Age activity has been identified is Site 4, Empingham West, which was excavated during the construction of Rutland Water (Cooper 2000). Here, several early Iron Age pits and three roundhouses of the middle to late Iron Age lay on the lower slopes of the Gwash valley. It is possible, therefore, that a number of the cropmarks that have been interpreted as being of Iron Age date, of which there are many in the county, were first established in the middle Iron Age, if not earlier.

In Northamptonshire, the number of known settlements dating to this period is far greater. The majority of these are located along the Nene and Ise valleys and their tributaries where the underlying geology, mainly gravel, limestone and Northampton Sands, have created lighter soils that were suited to the mixed agricultural economies of the period. Settlements have been investigated at Wilby Way, Wellingborough (Thomas and Enright 2003), Wollaston (Meadows 1995) and Weekley (Jackson and Dix 1986-7), and an extensive area of multiple open settlements, comprising the remains of at least 100 roundhouses, has been excavated on higher ground at the Daventry International Rail Terminal (DIRFT), near Crick and Kilsby, adjacent to Roman Watling Street and modern M1 motorway (Masefied *et al* 2015 and Hughes and Woodward 2015).

The results of the current project have reinforced the existing bias in the distribution of middle Iron Age sites in the region, with the investigation of a previously undiscovered middle-late Iron Age settlement at Swinawe Barn, near Corby, Northamptonshire. The site was located on Boulder Clay, on a gentle, north-east facing slope to the north of Harpers Brook, a tributary of the River Nene. The settlement was a small enclosed farmstead, comprising a relatively large ditched enclosure. The enclosure extended beyond the pipeline easement so its full extent is unknown, but it may have enclosed an area of about 0.5ha. Within the enclosure were the remains of two roundhouses, a smaller roundhouse that may have been used as a workshop, and a number of pits and postholes. Some of the pits had profiles characteristic of storage pits and at least one of these predated one of the roundhouses.

The pottery from the site, including quantities of middle Iron Age scored ware, was generally well-preserved and was largely recovered from one of the roundhouse ditches, with smaller quantities from the enclosure ditches and the other two roundhouse ditches. Some of the pottery may have dated to the 3rd to 2nd centuries BC, but the radiocarbon date (40 Cal BC-80 Cal AD, 95% confidence, 1980+/-30 BP, Beta-293241) and the rest of the pottery would be consistent with a late Iron Age date, the 1st century BC and the opening decades of the 1st century AD. A pit containing Roman pottery and several sherds of Roman pottery from the general area suggest that there was settlement nearby in the Roman period.

Tentative evidence for middle Iron Age activity was also found near Seaton, Rutland, where there was a cluster of late Iron Age pits, broadly dating to the late 1st century BC to the early decades of the 1st century AD. To the north of this cluster was a scatter of four isolated, unassociated pits, one of which contained a sherd of pottery dating to the 3rd-2nd century BC.

In the late Iron Age there is a marked increase in the density of settlement in the region, with more settlements being established on the upland 'clay' areas (Clay 2002; Kidd 2004). The general character of many of the settlements was essentially conservative, with many of the new centres of occupation differing little in appearance from the established middle Iron Age settlements, many of which continued to be occupied until as late as the 1st century AD. However, there does appear to be a trend at this time towards a greater diversity in settlement type, possibly reflecting the settlement requirements of a more varied agricultural economy, enhanced by greater levels of trade with other regions and socio-political changes in the century or so before the Roman conquest.

The increasing utilisation of marginal land, associated with an increase in the rate of land clearance, is likely to have been brought about by a rise in population in the later Iron Age. This may have been compounded by population migration associated with political unrest in the south-eastern part of the country. A study of the distribution of Iron Age coins and coin hoards in Rutland and Northamptonshire, which date from the early to middle 1st century BC, show that the area lay within the tribal territories of the Corieltauvi in the north and the Catuvellauni in the south. It is known that the Catuvellauni were actively expanding their territory at this time and it may have had an effect on local settlement patterns.

Three late Iron Age sites were investigated in the Welland Valley as part of the current project, near Seaton, Thorpe by Water and Caldecott, and in Northamptonshire settlements were investigated near Thorpe Malsor and at Willows Nursery, near Broughton.

At Seaton the site comprised a cluster of intercutting pits and four small gullies dating to the late 1st century BC to the early 1st century AD. As mentioned above, there was some evidence for middle Iron Age activity in the same area. Small assemblages of pottery and animal bone were recovered from the pits, suggesting that they lay close to areas of habitation, but the nature of the settlement remains unknown due to the limited extent of the geophysical survey and the absence of cropmarks. There was some evidence to suggest that the pits cut the terminals of two ditches that extended to the east of the site, but the remains were severely truncated and in the absence of other evidence it is not possible to confirm their identification. Pieces of slag recovered from three of the pits indicate that iron working was being carried out at the site.

The Iron Age ditch near Thorpe by Water was situated to the north of Thorpe Road, approximately 0.6km to the west of the village. The remains, which comprised the junction between two ditches, are not easy to characterise as only short lengths of the ditches were available for investigation, and their date is somewhat tentative, given that it relies solely on a single sherd of Iron Age pottery. However, it can be seen on the geophysical survey plot that the earlier of the two ditches may form part of a more extensive landscape feature. It shows the ditch extended for a distance of c.90m from north-north-east to south-south-west, and then turning sharply to the south-west, immediately to the south of the excavation area, and continuing for a further 40m. The sherd of pottery from the ditch was relatively 'fresh', suggesting that it had entered the ditch within a relatively short period after the ditch had been dug. The later ditch, which cut the earlier ditch at right-angles, is of uncertain date; the only pottery to be recovered from this ditch was an abraded sherd of Roman greyware that was collected from the stripped surface, suggesting that it may be intrusive.

In the field on the opposite side of Thorpe Road the remains of a cremation burial were unearthed by a mechanical digger during construction works. There were no associated grave goods to date the cremation, but it lay beneath a 1.0m thick layer of alluvium, suggesting that it is probably prehistoric or Roman in date.

Near Caldecott, close to the northern edge of the floodplain of the River Welland, a substantial sub-rectangular enclosure was identified by geophysical survey (Butler and Mudd 2006). Only its eastern corner lay within the surveyed area, but it was at least 40m long by 27m wide. The route of the pipeline was redirected slightly to avoid the enclosure, but Iron Age remains associated with the enclosure were investigated in the area immediately to its west.

The remains comprised a reasonably large ditch that extended from the corner of the enclosure to the west-south-west, possibly to form an annexe between the enclosure and a small stream that may have flowed past the site to the south. The position and alignment of the enclosure in relation to the silted up stream bed (palaeochannel) suggests that they are contemporary. The geophysical survey plot indicates a possible entrance to the enclosure on its south-west side, immediately to the east of the excavation area. It seems likely that an extensive area of cobbles and pebbles bordering the northern edge of the palaeochannel formed a track leading out of the annexe towards the enclosure entrance; rut marks created by the wheels of carts were noted in the surface of the metalled area.

Within the annexe were several smaller ditches and gullies, forming possible internal partitions, and a pit. There was no clear evidence for structures within this area, although a small quantity of late Iron Age pottery, animal bone, burnt cobbles and hearth waste was recovered from these features, suggesting habitation on or near the site. The pottery, mostly grog-tempered scored ware, broadly dates the annexe to the 2nd to 1st centuries BC; the enclosure may be of a similar date or earlier. Several Roman sherds were recovered from the surface of one of the ditches and the cobbled surface, indicating some activity in the area in the Roman period.

To the north of the enclosure and annexe were a series of small, parallel ditches that appear to have had an agricultural function; it is possible that the ditches were preceded by timber fences as they cut several large postholes.

In Northamptonshire, to the north-east of the village of Thorpe Malsor, part of a late Iron Age settlement was located on a relatively steep, north-east facing slope overlooking a small stream. The site comprised two large, adjoining ditches that are clearly shown on the geophysical survey plot, although the junction between the two ditches lay at the extreme western edge of the survey area, beyond the excavation area, so it was not possible to determine if they formed the north-west corner of an enclosure or were separate elements of a more complex ditch system.

The nature of the settlement remains near Thorpe Malsor is unknown, but the scale of the ditches suggests that relatively large areas were being enclosed, either to define areas of habitation or to create livestock corrals. Soil samples taken from the ditch were almost sterile, containing only occasional flecks of charcoal, and offer almost no clue as to the practices being carried out at the settlement, but small amounts of late Iron Age pottery and animal bone were recovered from deposits in both ditches, suggesting habitation nearby.

The Iron Age settlement at Willows Nursery, which lay approximately 1km to the south-west of Broughton, was situated on Boulder Clay on a low, almost imperceptible ridge of ground. The settlement, which dates to the 2nd to 1st centuries BC, with possible continuation into the early 1st century AD, comprised a system of ditches and gullies associated with an enclosure identified by geophysical survey to the east of the eventual route of the easement. The full extent of the enclosure could not be determined as its eastern corner lay beyond the surveyed area, but it was at least 40m long by 27m wide.

The area to the west of the enclosure that was investigated contained little evidence for domestic activity, although the small assemblage of pottery and animal bone recovered from the ditches does suggest habitation nearby. It is more likely that this part of the settlement was used for agricultural activities or specific domestic activities that were best carried out away from dwellings, as is indicated by the remains of the possible hearth/oven and the dark, charcoal rich deposits in the gully of the small, square enclosed area.

The Roman rural landscape

The route of the pipeline passes through a landscape that would have been densely settled in the Roman period. This landscape would have comprised a patchwork of fields, open pasture and woodland, scattered with many rural settlements, both in the valleys and on the hill-tops. From the 2nd century AD, villas became an increasingly notable feature of this landscape, particularly in the valleys of the Rivers Nene and Ise; often they were built on the sites of farming settlements that can be dated back to the Iron Age. Industrial sites, particularly those concerned with iron and pottery production, were also a component of this landscape, with concentrations around Kettering, Corby and the Lower Nene valley.

Further afield, the *civitas* capital of the *Corieltavi* at *Ratae Corieltavorum* (Leicester) lay to the west, and to the east, on Ermine Street, the main Roman road to the north, were the small towns of *Durobrivae* (Water Newton) and Great Casterton. To the south and south-east, in the Nene valley, were the Roman towns at Duston and Irchester, and further down the valley there were small Roman towns at Titchmarsh and Ashton. The town at Titchmarsh lay on the route of the major road from Roman Leicester to the south-east, which joined Ermine Street near *Durovigutum* (Godmanchester); the route of this road crosses the pipeline at Corby, at the junction between the A426 and A6003.

Due to the constraints outlined above, it has proved problematic to characterise the settlements and attempt to reconstruct their developmental history. Although the dating evidence for the parts of the Roman settlements that were available for investigation is more precise than that for the Iron Age sites, largely due to the more detailed chronology provided by Roman pottery and other classes of finds, and the abundance of material, their morphology largely remains a matter for conjecture. This places severe limitations on the interpretation of the settlements in terms of their social, agricultural and economic role in the local and regional Roman landscape.

One aspect of the pattern of settlement that was evident in the results of the current project was the apparent lack of settlement continuity between the late Iron Age and Roman periods. The Iron Age settlements generally contained little evidence for subsequent Roman occupation, other than the occurrence of occasional abraded sherds of Roman pottery in the upper fills of ditches or an occasional isolated pit, such as at Caldecott and Swinawe Barn. In general, the Iron Age settlements appeared to have been abandoned in the 1st century AD and, if occupation was maintained in the vicinity in the

Roman period, it was established at a new site nearby, as was seen at Thorpe Malsor. This is consistent with the findings from other sites in the area, like Wootton Hill (Jackson 1990), Earls Barton (Chapman and Atkins 2004) and Wollaston (Meadows 1996), where there was evidence for a substantial reorganisation of rural settlement in the 1st century AD, with a shift from small enclosed settlements towards agglomerated settlements comprising complexes of rectilinear enclosures associated with tracks or droveways. This transition appears to have been a long-term trend and was probably well under way before the Roman conquest, suggesting that the causes of change were probably associated with social and economic factors that were already manifest in the late Iron Age.

The investigations carried out as part of the current project have enhanced this picture of a predominately rural landscape between the valleys of the Rivers Nene and Welland in the Roman period. In Rutland, a settlement dating to the Roman period was investigated at Glaston and Roman cremations and a droveway were encountered near Gretton. In Northamptonshire, the remains of Roman settlements were investigated on the clay-capped hill-tops to the west of the River Ise near Thorpe Malsor, White Hill Lodge and Great Cransley, and at Rushton the remains were associated with a villa. To the north of Rushton the remains of a probable Roman field system were located to the west of Violet Lane.

The Roman settlement remains at Glaston predominately lay *c*.0.4km to the south-west of the modern village, on the gentle south-facing slope to the south of the A47, Uppingham Road. Here, cropmarks and geophysical survey (Butler and Mudd 2006) show a grid-like pattern of ditches extending over an area of *c*8 hectares, forming two or more large rectangular enclosures. Interpretation of the site is difficult as the route of the pipeline largely avoided the Roman enclosures so that only three small ditches were encountered within the easement, and the geophysical survey results appear to be at variance with the cropmarks, so it is not possible to make any meaningful statement about the settlement based on its morphology or the excavated evidence. The settlement appears to date to the late Roman period as the pottery recovered from the ditches on both sides of Uppingham Road dates to the 4th century, and one of those to the south contained late Roman and early Anglo-Saxon pottery.

At Gretton Road, the Roman remains comprised part of a track and three cremation burials placed in small pits, situated next to a small stream that was probably once fed by a spring on the slopes above. The Roman features appear to respect the course of the stream, suggesting that the stream was flowing in the Roman period. The track, which appeared to lead towards a possible sub-rectangular enclosure to the south of the easement, was formed by two parallel ditches that were aligned north-west to south-east and spaced 5m apart; a small quantity of 2nd- to 4th-century Roman pottery was recovered from the fill of the ditches. Two of the cremation burials lay close to the track, one on either side, and the third lay *c* 8m to the north of the stream; Roman pottery and a large number of nails were recovered from the burial deposits. The burials probably form part of a small cremation cemetery associated with a nearby farmstead; the pottery from one of the cremations indicates a 2nd-century date, which is consistent with Roman burial practices at this time.

In Northamptonshire, the remains of Roman settlement were more numerous and substantial. The Roman settlement at Rushton, which was situated on the north bank of the River Ise to the north-east of the village, probably formed part of the estate of the Roman villa currently being investigated by the Ise Archaeological Research Society. The remains of the villa's bathhouse are situated in the adjacent field to the west, and it was here that an early 4th-century decorated lead tank bearing a 'Chi Rho' symbol, was found in an associated ditch (Looker 2000). The discovery of this tank, which was probably used as a font in baptismal ceremonies, suggests that Christian rituals were being carried out at the villa.

The settlement remains identified by the geophysical survey and investigated by the current excavation may include features associated with a pre-villa farmstead; several sherds of abraded Iron Age pottery from the site suggest that the villa did have a late Iron Age predecessor. The ditches and gullies investigated within the easement were a little later in date and were probably established in the late 1st or early 2nd century AD; they may have formed small paddocks or stock pens by the side of a track at the edge of the settlement. There are no published detailed accounts of the excavations of the bathhouse, so it has not been possible to relate this part of the settlement with the excavations on the bathhouse. A pair of tweezers and part of a pin recovered from the site suggests that the area may have been settled or at least temporarily occupied in the early Anglo-Saxon period.

At Thorpe Malsor, the Roman settlement was situated at the edge of a plateau of high ground, approximately 50m to the south of the Iron Age settlement. The site comprised a T-shaped arrangement of two large ditches and a cluster of large pits; it is clear that the settlement is far more extensive, but there are no cropmarks or geophysical survey results to indicate the overall extent or morphology of the settlement.

The settlement appears to have been established in the first half of the 2nd century AD and to have been reorganised later in that century with the cutting of the two large enclosure or boundary ditches; these were subsequently recut in the 3rd century. The original purpose of the large pits clustered near the access through one of the main ditches is unknown, but they were subsequently used for the disposal of domestic rubbish, including cereal processing waste and cess. The evidence of the animal bone from this settlement, and the other Roman settlements investigated as part of this project, suggests that the rearing of cattle played an important, if not principal component of their economy. This preference for the keeping of cattle, as opposed to sheep, may be due to the more favourable conditions for cattle on the heavy clay soils.

A little over a kilometre to the south, on an adjacent hill-top, were the remains of the Roman settlement at White Hill Lodge. The geophysical survey showed a grid-like pattern of linear ditches that appear to be part of a larger complex of features that predominantly lie to the east of the easement, but the absence of information from cropmarks and the limited survey area hinder the interpretation of the site. Several large enclosure or boundary ditches and smaller partition ditches were investigated, and there may have been a track or droveway to the north.

There was a large quantity of ironstone rubble in the upper fills of the larger ditches, as was the case at Thorpe Malsor, and it is possible that this material came from a nearby Roman building. If there had been a Roman building in the vicinity, the dressed stone and better quality rubble may have been taken for buildings or walls elsewhere, and the smaller rubble dumped in the hollows left in the top of the largely silted-up ditches. The recovery of a moderate amount of *tesserae* from the topsoil during the watching brief and the recovery of Roman tile from the ditches raises the likelihood of there having been a Roman building at White Hill Lodge. The dumping of rubble in the ditches of late Roman settlements was noted at Milton Ham, near Northampton, where a Roman building was suspected to lie near an agricultural enclosure (Carlyle 2010). The possibility of there having been a villa nearby is further supported by the animal bone evidence, which indicates that a wide range of species, including wild species such as eel and pigeon, were being consumed at the settlement.

The remains of the Roman settlement near Great Cransley, located near the top of a south-east facing slope overlooking a small tributary valley, consisted of a complex of at least four possible enclosures situated either side of a broad track. However, the cropmarks were too indistinct and the survey area was too narrow to determine the full extent and pattern of the settlement. The pottery assemblage from the site indicates a 1st to 2nd century date for the settlement. A stone-lined Roman well within one of the enclosures had fallen out of use and been back-filled with domestic rubbish, including hearth waste, broken pottery, fragments of querns, animal bone and a horse's head. The presence of the horse's head may indicate a 'ritual' closing of the well, as has been suggested for a number of other sites (Fulford 2001), but this interpretation can not be validated in this case.

Approximately 2km to the south of Rushton, evidence for Roman arable agriculture, consisting of the remains of a probable field system, was identified on a steep, south-facing slope overlooking Slade Brook, to the west of Violet Lane. The site comprised three small, parallel ditches that roughly followed the contours of the slope.

The early Anglo-Saxon cremation cemetery at Glaston

The discovery of the early Anglo-Saxon cremation cemetery at Glaston, Rutland, adds to the increasing number of such cemeteries that have been investigated in the East Midlands region. Nationally, over 240 cemeteries containing cremation burials had been identified by the end of the 20th century (Lucy 2000), with the majority located in East Anglia and the eastern counties of England, between the Humber and the Great Ouse. They occur as individual or small groups of two or three cremation burials, or in larger numbers in cemeteries that may contain many hundreds, if not thousands of burials. Most occur in 'mixed' cemeteries that also contain inhumation burials; indeed, of the total number of cemeteries containing cremation burials, 175 are of the 'mixed' variety (*ibid*, 140).

Early Anglo-Saxon cemeteries, in general, are not well understood as many were discovered by quarry workers in the 19th and 20th centuries, and as a consequence they are poorly recorded (the skeletal remains were rarely retained) and the urns and accompanying grave goods have become dispersed or lost. Other, more recent excavations may have been recorded to modern standards, but only parts of the cemeteries have been investigated.

Perhaps the largest and most well-known cemeteries are those at Spong Hill, Norfolk (Hills and Penn 1981), and Loveden Hill (Fennell 1957) and Cleatham (Leahy 2007), Lincolnshire, which contained at least 2250, 1450 and 1200 cremation burials respectively. In the valleys of the Great Ouse and Cam, mixed cemeteries containing *c* 130 cremations have been investigated at Girton and Little Wilbraham, Cambridgeshire. At Sandy, Bedfordshire, there are records of urns, most of which date to the late 5th to early 6th centuries AD, having been unearthed from as early the first half of the 18th century (Kennett 1973). Closer to Glaston, small cremation cemeteries have been discovered at Thurmaston, near Leicester (Williams 1983), and Kettering, Northamptonshire (Markham 1964), and at North Luffenham, Rutland, three early Anglo-Saxon cremation urns, along with a small number of inhumation burials, were discovered in 1855 (VCH 1908). A small Anglo-Saxon cemetery, containing ten inhumation burials radiocarbon dated to the mid 6th to mid 7th centuries, was excavated in Oundle in Northamptonshire 25km to the south-east (Maull and Masters 2005).

The combined evidence of the pottery and the radiocarbon date from one of the cremation burials at Glaston suggests that the cemetery probably dates from the late 5th to early/mid 7th century AD. One of the urns, containing the remains of a young child, can be dated to the mid 5th century, but its worn appearance hints at the likelihood that it may have been buried at a slightly later date. This date range is consistent with other early Anglo-Saxon cremation burials in the region.

At this time the Anglo-Saxon settlers in this part of the East Midlands region, including the community at Glaston, were pagan. Study of their material culture suggests that they entered the Rutland area from the east and south-east, through Norfolk, Cambridgeshire and Northamptonshire (Stafford 1985). Their social and political structures were built around loose federations of tribal groups and it was not until the second half of the 7th century that they were converted to Christianity, a move that corresponded with the rise of the Anglo-Saxon kingdoms and the centralisation of political power, in this case under the rule of the Mercian kings.

The cremation cemetery at Glaston was only partly excavated and it is likely that other cremation burials remain to be discovered nearby, particularly in the area to the east, in the grounds of Bisbrooke Hall. If the cemetery does extend into this area, it likely to be reasonably well-preserved as the earthworks of medieval ridge and furrow are still clearly visible here, indicating that the land has not been subjected to modern ploughing. Given the current number of cremation burials so far recovered, and their distribution, the burial ground can probably be categorized as a 'small' cremation cemetery, perhaps containing no more than 20-30 cremation burials. Early Anglo-Saxon inhumations have also been found in a sand pit approximately 450m to the east (Thurlow Leeds and Barber 1950), close to the junction between Uppingham Road and Wing Road; the cemetery contained at least eleven graves, from which were recovered a number of bronze brooches and other items of jewellery, pottery vessels and a shield boss. The evidence from the two cemeteries indicates the presence of a well-established settlement at Glaston in the 6th and 7th centuries AD.

Given that only a part of the cemetery was available for investigation, it has not been possible to identify any grouping or any other pattern in the distribution of the cremation burials. However, the cremation burials are reasonably well-spaced, suggesting that their locations may have been marked on the surface, possibly with a timber post or other marker. Similarly, the small sample size and the lack of information on the sex and age of the individuals preclude any attempt to find correlations between the individuals and the style and decoration of urns or type of grave goods.

The recovery of a small quantity of pottery from a Bronze Age jar, found in association with one of the disturbed Anglo-Saxon cremation burials and a bone comb, suggests that the fragments of vessel may have been placed with the human remains as a type of talisman. This act may have been carried out to link the deceased with the land through possession of artefacts associated with past inhabitants of the region. The presence of the Bronze Age pottery also raises the likelihood of there being one or more barrows in the vicinity, as early Anglo-Saxon cemeteries were often established on or near sacred sites such as barrow cemeteries. A circular cropmark c 200m to the south of the cemetery, just below the crest of the slope, may be a barrow and if it is, others may lie nearby.

Medieval and post-medieval field systems

The remains of pre-Enclosure furrows of former ridge and furrow field systems were noted at the majority of the sites investigated. In most cases they were widely spaced, at 8-9m between centres, which suggests they date from the medieval period. However, the open field system of ridge and furrow, prevalent in much of the Midland region, could have been maintained into the post-medieval period, until Enclosure in the 18th and early 19th centuries (Rackham 1986, 167-180). The very regular, narrowly spaced furrows at Willows Nursery were probably established in the post-medieval period.

A substantial boundary ditch investigated at Swinawe Barn may mark the edge of an estate or woodland. In the medieval period the area was a deer park and the feature may relate to this, but due to the lack of dateable finds this is not certain.

Another boundary feature, in this case the foundation courses of a drystone wall, was recorded at Normanton Road. Drystone walls surrounding fields are common in the Normanton area and the alignment of the stone foundations, from north-west to south-east, accorded with the alignment of the surrounding field boundaries.

The well-built stone conduit at Caldecott, which probably dates to the 16th or 17th centuries, is unlikely to be an isolated feature and may have been a drain leading away from a nearby barn or dwelling situated to the west of the easement.

Bibliography

Ager, B M, 1985 The smaller variants of the Anglo-Saxon quoit brooch, *Anglo-Saxon Studies in Archaeology and History*, **4**, 1-58

Amorosi, T, 1989 *A postcranial guide to domestic neo-natal and juvenile mammals*, British Archaeology Reports, International Series, **533**

Aufderhiede, A C, and Rodriguez-Martin, C, 1998 *The Cambridge Encyclopaedia of Human Paleopathology*, Cambridge, Cambridge University Press

Avery, M, Sutton, J E, and Banks, J W, 1967 Rainsborough, Northants, England: Excavations 1961-5, *Proceedings of the Prehistoric Society*, **33**, 207-306

Biddle, M, (ed) 1990 *Object and economy in Medieval Winchester; Artefacts from Medieval Winchester*, Winchester Studies, **7.2**, Oxford

Blinkhorn, P, 2000 The Early Anglo-Saxon Pottery, in N J Cooper 2000, 98-104

Bogaard, A, 2005 Garden agriculture and the nature of early farming in Europe and the Near East, *World Archaeology*, **37(2)**, 177-196

Bond, J M, 1996 Burnt Offerings: Animal Bone in Anglo-Saxon Cremations, *World Archaeology*, **28**, 76-88

Booth, P, 1995 The Anglo-Saxon pottery, in A Boyle *et al*, 1995, 101-3

Boyle, A, Dodd, A, Miles, D, and Mudd, A, 1995 *Two Oxfordshire Anglo-Saxon cemeteries: Berinsfield and Didcot*, Oxford Archaeological Unit, Thames Valley Landscapes Monog, **8**

Brain, C, 1981 *The Hunters or the Hunted? An Introduction to African Cave Taphonomy*, Chicago, University of Chicago Press

Brickley, M, and McKinley, J, 2004 *Guidelines to the Standards for Recording Human Remains*, Institute for Archaeologists Paper, **7**

Briscoe, T, 1985 The use of brooches and other jewelry as dies on pagan Anglo-Saxon pottery, *Medieval Archaeology*, **29**, 136-42

Brothwell, D R, and Higgs, E S, (eds) 1969 *Science and Archaeology*, London, Thames and Hudson

Brown, D, 1990 Weaving tools, in M Biddle 1990, 225-232

Brugmann, B, 2004 *Glass beads from Early Anglo-Saxon graves*, Oxbow Books

Buikstra, J, and Ubelaker, D, 1994 *Standards for data collection from human skeletal remains*, Proceedings of a Seminar at the Field Museum of Natural History, Fayetteville, Arkansas Archaeological Survey Research Series, **44**

Butler, A, and Mudd, A, 2006 *AWS Empingham to Hannington Pipeline: Archaeological Geophysical and Metal Detecting Surveys, Phase 1*, Northamptonshire Archaeology report, **06/189**

Butler, A, 2007 *AWS Empingham to Hannington Pipeline, Wing Water Treatment Works Extension, Rutland; Geophysical Survey*, Northamptonshire Archaeology report, **07/141**

Butler, A, Fisher, I, and Mudd, A, 2008 *AWS Empingham to Hannington Pipeline Welland Temporary Lagoon Site, Rutland, Archaeological Geophysical Survey*, Northamptonshire Archaeology report, **08/66**

Carlyle, S, 2010 A pit alignment near Upton, Northampton, *Northamptonshire Archaeology*, **36**, 75-87

Carlyle, S, 2010a *Neolithic cremations and a Romano-British enclosure at Milton Ham, Northampton*, Northamptonshire Archaeology report, **10/109**

Carlyle, S, Clarke, J, and Chapman, A, (ed) 2011 *Archaeological investigations along the route of the Empingham to Hannington (Wing Extension) pipeline, Rutland and Northamptonshire, January 2008 to July 2009*, Northamptonshire Archaeology report, **11/107**

CBA 2000 *South Midlands Archaeology*, Council for British Archaeology, **30**

Chapman, A, and Atkins, R, 2004 Iron Age and Roman settlement at Mallard Close, Earls Barton, Northamptonshire, *Northamptonshire Archaeology*, **32**, 23-56

Chapman, A, 2001 Excavation of an Iron Age Settlement and Middle Saxon Cemetery at Great Houghton, Northampton, *Northamptonshire Archaeology*, **29**, 1-41

Chapman, A, 2007 A Bronze Age barrow cemetery and later boundaries, pit alignments and enclosures at Gayhurst Quarry, Newport Pagnell, Buckinghamshire, *Records of Buckinghamshire*, **47.2**, 81-211

Chapman, A, 2010a The Iron Age pottery, in E Taylor 2010, 24-30

Chapman, A, 2010b Querns, in S Carlyle 2010, 26-27

Chapman, A, forthcoming *A middle Iron Age settlement with copper alloy casting, at Coton Park, Rugby, Warwickshire*, MOLA Northampton report

Chapman, A, Foard, A, and Clarke, J, 2015 *Excavation of a Bronze Age and early Iron Age landscape at Harlestone Quarry, Northamptonshire, 2007-2014*, MOLA Northampton report, **15/111**

Chapman, J, and Smith, S, 1988 Finds from a Roman well in Staines, *The London Archaeologist*, **6(1)**, 3-6

Clarke, J, 1995 *The Medieval Horse and its Equipment c 1150-c 1450*, Medieval Finds from excavations in London, **5**

Clarke, J, 2007a *AWS Empingham to Hannington Pipeline, trial trenching*, Northamptonshire Archaeology report, **07/196**

Clarke, J, 2007b *AWS Empingham to Hannington Pipeline, archaeological strip and record works; test pit results*, Northamptonshire Archaeology report, **07/184**

Clarke, J, and Carlyle, S, 2010 *Archaeological investigations along the route of the Empingham to Hannington (Wing Extension) pipeline, Rutland and Northamptonshire: Assessment report and updated project design*, Northamptonshire Archaeology report, **10/72**

Clay, P, 2002 *The Prehistory of the East Midlands Claylands*, Leicester Archaeology Monog, **9**

Cook, A M, and Dacre, M W, 1985 *Excavations at Portway, Andover 1973-1975: Anglo-Saxon Cemetery, Bronze Age Barrow and Linear Ditch*, OUCA Monog, **4**

Cool, H E M, 1990 Roman Metal Hair Pins from Southern Britain, *Archaeol J,* **147**, 148-182

Cooper, N J, 2000 *The Archaeology of Rutland Water*, Leicestershire Archaeology Monog, **6**

Cooper, N J, 2006 *The Archaeology of the East Midlands: an archaeological resource assessment and research agenda*, Leicester Archaeology Monog, **13**

Crummy, N, 1983 *Colchester Archaeological Report 2: The Roman small finds from excavations in Colchester 1971-9,* Colchester Archaeological Trust

Cunliffe, B, 1976 Danebury, Hampshire. Second interim report on the excavations 1971-5, *Antiquaries Journal*, **56**, 198-216

Dannell, G B, 1973 The potter 'Indixivixus, in A P Detsicas (ed), 1973, 139-42

Dannell, G B, Hartley, B R, Wild, J P, and Perrin, J R, 1993 Excavations on a Romano-British pottery production site at Park Farm, Stanground, Peterborough, 1965-7, *Journal of Roman Pottery Studies*, **6**, 51-93

Deighton, K, 2010 The animal bone, in J Clarke and S Carlyle 2010, 60

Detsicas, A P, (ed) 1973 *Current Research in Romano-British Pottery*, Council for British Archaeology Research Report, **10**

Driesch, A, von den 1976 *A guide to the measurement of animal bones from archaeological sites*, Cambridge, Massachusetts, Harvard University Press

Egan, G E, 2005 *Material Culture in London in an age of transition: Tudor and Stuart period finds c1450-1700 from excavations at riverside sites in Southwark*, MoLAS Monog, **19**

Egan, G, and Pritchard, F, 1991 *Dress Accessories c 1150 - c 1450*, Medieval Finds from Excavations in London, **3**

EH 1991 *Management of Archaeological Projects 2*, English Heritage

EH 2002 *Environmental Archaeology: A Guide to Theory and Practice for Methods, from sampling to post-excavation,* English Heritage

EH 2006 *Management of Research Projects in the Historic Environment (MoRPHE),* English Heritage

Evison, V I, 1987 *Dover: The Buckland Anglo-Saxon Cemetery*, Historic Buildings and Monuments Commission for England, **3**

Fazekas, I, and Kosa, F, 1978 *Forensic Foetal Osteology*, Budapest, Akademiai Kaido

Fennell, K R, 1957 Excavation of an Anglo-Saxon Cemetery at Hough-on-the-Hill, Lincolnshire, *Journal of the RAF Cranwell*

Ferris, B, Bevan, A, and Cuttler, R, 2000 *The excavation of a Romano-British shrine at Orton's Pasture, Rocester, Staffordshire,* British Archaeological Reports, British Series, **314**

Fitzpatrick, A P, (ed) 1997 *Archaeological Excavations on the Route of the A27 Westhampnett Bypass, West Sussex, 1992, Vol. 2*, Wessex Archaeological report, **12**

Fulford, M, 2001 Links with the past: pervasive 'ritual' behaviour in Roman Britain, *Britannia,* **32**, 199-218

Grant, A, 1982 The use of toothwear as a guide to the age of domestic ungulates, in B Wilson *et al* 1982, 91-108

Hallam, T, Lloyd, R, and Yates, A, 2003 *Pitsford Quarry, Archaeological recording: Bottom Sheep Dale Field*, Northamptonshire Archaeology report, **3421**

Hambleton, E, 1999 *Animal Husbandry Regimes in Iron Age Britain*, British Archaeological Report, British Series, **282**

Hills, C, and Penn, K, 1981 *The Anglo-Saxon cemetery at Spong Hill, North Elmham, Part II: Catalogue of Cremations*, East Anglian Archaeology, **11**

Hirst, S M, 1985 *An Anglo-Saxon inhumation cemetery at Sewerby, East Yorkshire,* York University Archaeological Publications, **4**

Hollowell, R, 1971 *Aerial photography and field work in the Upper Nene Valley*, ed A E Brown, Bulletin of the Northamptonshire Federation of Archaeological Societies, **6**

Hughes, G, and Woodward, A, 2015 *The Iron Age and Romano-British Settlement at Crick Covert Farm: Excavations 1997-1998 (DIRFT Volume I)*, Archaeopress Archaeology

IfA 2008a *Standard and guidance for archaeological excavation,* Institute for Archaeologists

IfA 2008b *Standard and guidance for archaeological watching briefs,* Institute for Archaeologists

IfA 2008c *Code of Conduct*, Institute for Archaeologists

Jackson, D, 1974 Two new pit alignments and a hoard of currency bars from Northamptonshire, *Northamptonshire Archaeology*, **9**, 13-45

Jackson, D, 1977 Further excavations at Aldwincle, Northamptonshire, 1969-71, *Northamptonshire Archaeology*, **12**, 9-54

Jackson, D, 1978 A Late Bronze-Early Iron Age vessel from a pit alignment at Ringstead, Northamptonshire, *Northamptonshire Archaeology*, **13**, 168

Jackson, D, 1990 An Iron Age enclosure at Wootton Hill Farm, Northampton, *Northamptonshire Archaeology*, **22**, 3-21

Jackson, D, 2010 *Dennis Jackson: A Northamptonshire Archaeologist*, Northamptonshire Archaeological Society

Jackson, D, 2010 A proposed chronology of Iron Age ceramic assemblages, in D Jackson 2010, 147-160

Jackson, D, and Dix, B, 1986-7 Late Iron Age and Roman settlement at Weekley, Northants, *Northamptonshire Archaeology*, **21**, 41-94

Jeanty, P, 1983 Foetal limb biometry, *Radiology*, **147**, 601-602

Jupp, P C, and Gittings, C, 1999 *Death in England*, Manchester, University Press

Kennett, D H, 1973 Seventh-century cemeteries in the Ouse valley, *Bedfordshire Archaeology Journal*, **8**, 99-108

Kidd, A, 2004 Northamptonshire in the 1st millennium BC, in M Tingle 2004, 44-62

King, N, 1994 The pottery; pottery kilns 1 (MK44, F74) and 11 (MK357), in R J Zeepvat et al 1994, 79-82

Kjellström, A, 2004 Evaluations of *sex* assessment using weighted traits on *incomplete* skeletal *remains*, *International Journal of Osteoarchaeology*, **14**, 360-373

Lauwerier, R, 1988 *Animals in Roman Times in the Dutch Eastern River Area,* Amersfoort, ROB Nederlandse Oudheden, **12**

Leahy, K, 2007 *'Interrupting the Pots'. The excavation of Cleatham Anglo-Saxon cemetery,* Council for British Archaeology Research Report, **155**

Lewis, M E, 2000 Non-adult palaeopathology: current status and future potential, in S A Mays and M Cox (eds), 2000, 39-57

Liddle, P, no date *An archaeological resource assessment of Anglo-Saxon Leicestershire and Rutland,* East Midlands Archaeological Research Framework

Looker, J, 2000 The Rushton bath house, *South Midlands Archaeology*, **30**, 40

Lucy, S, 2000 *The Anglo-Saxon Way of Death,* Sutton

Lucy, S, and Reynolds, A, (eds) 2002 *Burial in Early Medieval England and Wales*, Society of Medieval Archaeology Monog, **17**

Lunt, E, 2006 *Empingham to Hannington Pipeline, Environmental Statement; Volume 1, Main Document*, Mott MacDonald report, **225738/01/A**

Lyman, R L, 1994 *Vertebrate Taphonomy*, Cambridge, Cambridge University Press

Mackreth, D F, 1994 The brooches, in R T Williams and R J Zeepvat 1994, 285-303

McAree, D, 2005 A pit alignment at Warth Park, Raunds, Northamptonshire, *Northamptonshire Archaeology*, **33**, 9-18

McKinley, J, 1994a Bone fragment size in British cremation burials and its implications for pyre technology and ritual, *Journal of Archaeological Science*, **21**, 339-42

McKinley, J, 1994b *The Anglo-Saxon Cemetery at Spong Hill, North Elmham Part VIII: The Cremations*, East Anglian Archaeology, **69**

McKinley, J, 1997 The cremated human bone from burial and cremation-related contexts, in A P Fitzpatrick (ed) 1997, 55-72

McKinley, J, 2000 The analysis of cremated bone, in S Mays and M Cox (eds), 439-454

Maltby, J M, 1994 The animal bones from a Romano-British well at Oakridge II, Basingstoke, *Proceedings of the Hampshire Field Club and Archaeological Society*, **49**, 47-77

Manning, W H, 1985 *Catalogue of the Romano-British Iron tools, fittings and weapons in the British Museum*

Markham, C A, 1964 Anglo-Saxon cemetery at Kettering, *Northamptonshire Natural History Society and Field Club Journal*, **25**

Masefield, R, (ed), Chapman, A, Ellis, P, Hart, J, King, R, and Mudd, A, 2015 *Origins, Development and Abandonment of an Iron Age Village: Further Archaeological Investigations for the Daventry International Rail Freight Terminal, Crick & Kilsby, Northamptonshire 1993-2013 (DIRFT Volume II)*, Archaeopress Archaeology

Mason, P, 2011 *Archaeological evaluation at Upton Park, Weedon Road, Northampton*, Northamptonshire Archaeology report, **11/72**

Maull, A, and Masters, P, 2005 A Roman farmstead and Anglo-Saxon cemetery at Glapthorn Road, Oundle, *Northamptonshire Archaeol,* **33**, 47-78

Mays, S A, 1992 *Anglo-Saxon human remains from Mucking, Essex*, Ancient Monuments Laboratory report, **18/92**

Mays, S A, 1993 Infanticide in Roman Britain, *Antiquity*, **67**, 883-888

Mays, S A, 2010 *The Archaeology of Human Bones*, London, Routledge

Mays, S A, 2011 Perinatal infant death at the Roman villa site at Hambleden, Buckinghamshire, England, *Journal of Archaeological Science* (early view), 1-8

Mays, S, Brickley, M, and Dodwell, N, 2002 *Human bones from archaeological sites. Guidelines for producing assessment documents and analytical reports*, BABAO/English Heritage

Mays, S A, and Cox, M, 2000 Sex Determination in skeletal remains, in S A Mays and M Cox (eds) 2000, 117-130

Mays, S A, and Cox, M, (eds) 2000 *Human Osteology in Archaeology and Forensic Science*, London, GMM Press

Meadows, I, 1995 Wollaston, *South Midlands Archaeology*, **25**, 41-45

Meadows, I, 1996 Wollaston, *Current Archaeology*, **150**, 212-15

Mellor, V, 2007 Prehistoric multiple linear ditches and pit alignments on the route of the Oakham Bypass, Rutland, *Transactions of the Leicestershire Archaeological and Historical Society*, **81**, 1-34

Mudd, A, 2004 Iron Age and Roman enclosures near Higham Ferrers: the archaeology of the A6 Rushden and Higham Ferrers bypass, *Northamptonshire Archaeology*, **32**, 57-94

Mudd, A, 2007 *Iron Age and Roman Settlement on the Northamptonshire Uplands: Archaeological work* on the *A43 Towcester to M40 Road Improvement scheme in Northamptonshire and Oxfordshire*, Northamptonshire Archaeology Monog, **1**

Murphy, E M, (ed) 2010 *Deviant burial in the archaeological record*, Oxford, Oxbow

Myres, J N L, 1977 *A Corpus of Anglo-Saxon Pottery of the Pagan Period*, 2 vols, Cambridge

NA 2006 *Archaeological Fieldwork Manual*, Northamptonshire Archaeology

Needham, S, and Spence, T, (eds) 1996 *Refuse and disposal at area 16 East Runnymede*, Runnymede Bridge Research Excavations, **2**

Parry, S, 2006 *Raunds Area Survey; An Archaeological Study of the Landscape of Raunds, Northamptonshire 1985-94*, Oxbow/English Heritage monog

Payne, S, 1985 Morphological distinctions between the mandibular teeth of young sheep and goats, *Journal of Archaeological Science*, **12**, 139-147

Perrin, J R, 1999 Roman Pottery from Excavations at and near the Roman Small Town of Durobrivae, Water Newton, Cambridgeshire, 1956-58, *Journal of Roman Pottery Studies*, **8**

Perrin, R, 2010 Roman pottery, in J Clarke and S Carlyle 2010, 23-30

Pollard, J, 1996 Iron Age Riverside Pit Alignments at St Ives, Cambridgeshire, *Proceedings of the Prehistoric Society*, **62**, 93-115

Price, J, and Cottam, S, 1998 *Romano-British Glass Vessels: A handbook*, Council for British Archaeology, Practical handbook in Archaeology, **14**

Prummel, W, and Frisch, H, 1986 A guide for the distinction of species, sex and body side in bones of sheep and goat, *Journal of Archaeological Science*, **13**, 567-577

Rackham, O, 1986 *History of the British Countryside*, London

Richards, J D, 1987 *The Significance of the Form and Decoration of Anglo-Saxon Cremation Urns*, British Archaeological Report, British Series, **166**

Rogers, G B, 1974 *Poteries Sigillees de la Gaule Centrale*, Gallia Supplement, **28**

Rogers, J, and Waldron, T, 1995 *A Field Guide to Joint Disease in Archaeology*, Chichester, Wiley

Scheuer, L, and Black, S, 2000 *Developmental Juvenile Osteology*, London, Academic Press

Serjeantson, D, 1996 The animal bones, in S Needham and T Spence (eds) 1996, 123-34

Shaffrey, R, 2006 *Grinding and Milling: A study of Romano-British rotary querns and millstones made from Old Red Sandstone*, British Archaeological Report, British Series, **409**

Shaw, M, 1979 Romano-British pottery kilns on Camp Hill, Northampton, *Northamptonshire Archaeology*, **14**, 17-30

Shipman, P, Foster, G, and Schoeninger, M, 1984 Burnt bones and teeth: an experimental study of colour, morphology, crystal structure and shrinkage, *Journal of Archaeological Science*, **11**, 307-325

Silver, I A, 1969 The ageing of domestic animals, in D R Brothwell and E S Higgs 1969, 101-126

Simpson, W G, 1966 Romano-British settlement in the Welland Valley, in A C Thomas 1966, 15-26

Stace, C, 1997 *New Flora of the British Isles* (2nd edition), Cambridge University Press

Stafford, P, 1985 *The East Midlands in the early Middle Ages*, Leicester University Press

Steele, J, and Mays, S, 1993 *Cremated Anglo-Saxon human bone from Snape, Suffolk (excavated 1862-3, 1972, 1985-92)*, Ancient Monuments Laboratory report, **102/93**

Symonds, R P, 2003 Romano-British Amphorae, *Journal of Roman Pottery Studies*, **10**, 50-9

Taylor, A, 2010 Aspects of deviant burial in Roman Britain, in E M Murphy (ed) 2010, 45-67

Taylor, E, 2010 *An Iron Age settlement at Tattenhoe Park, Bletchley, Milton Keynes, Buckinghamshire*, Northamptonshire Archaeology report, **10/134**

Thomas, A, and Enright, D, 2003 Excavation of an Iron Age settlement at Wilby Way, Great Doddington, *Northamptonshire Archaeology*, **31**, 15-70

Thomas, A C, (ed) 1966 *Rural Settlement in Roman Britain*, Council for British Archaeology Research Report, **7**

Thurlow Leeds, E, and Barber, J L, 1950 An Anglian cemetery at Glaston, Rutland, *Antiquaries Journal*, **30**, 185-9

Timby, J, 1993 Sancton I Anglo-Saxon Cemetery: excavations carried out between 1976 and 1980, *Archaeol J*, **150**, 243-365

Timby, J, 1996 *The Anglo-Saxon Cemetery at Empingham II, Rutland*, Oxbow Monog, **70**

Timby, J, 2004 The pottery from Site 3, in A Mudd 2004, 72-80

Tingle, M, (ed) 2004 *The Archaeology of Northamptonshire*, Northamptonshire Archaeological Society

Trotter, M, and Hixon, B B, 1974 Sequential changes in weight, density and percentage ash weight of human skeletons from an early foetal period through to old age, *Anatomical Record*, **179**, 1-18

Ubelaker, D, 1978 *Human skeletal remains*, Washington, Taraxacum

Upson-Smith, T, 2007 *AWS Empingham to Hannington Pipeline, Wing Water Treatment Works Extension, Rutland; Archaeological Evaluation*, Northamptonshire Archaeology report, **07/170**

VCH 1908 *Victoria County History: Rutland*, **1**

Waldron, T, Taylor, G M, and Rudling, D, 1999 Sexing of Romano-British baby burials from the Beddingham and Bignor villas, *Sussex Archaeological Collection*, **137**, 71-79

Watkinson, D, and Neal, V, 1998 *First Aid for Finds*, UKIC

Watts, M, 2002 *The Archaeology of Mills and Milling*, Tempus

Wessex Archaeology, 2004 *South Cliff Farm, South Carlton, Lincolnshire,* Wessex Archaeology report, **52568.11**

West, S, 1985 *West Stow: The Anglo-Saxon Village Volume 2: Figures and Plates*

Westgarth, A, 2006a *Desk-based assessment for a proposed pipeline between Empingham and Hannington: Leicestershire and Rutland section*, Northamptonshire Archaeology report, **06/9**

Westgarth, A, 2006b *Desk-based assessment for a proposed pipeline between Empingham and Hannington: Northamptonshire section*, Northamptonshire Archaeology report, **06/10**

Williams, A, 1946-7 Excavations at Langford Downs near Lechlade, Oxfordshire in 1943, *Oxoniensia,* **11** and **12**, 44-64

Williams, H, 2002 The Remains of Pagan 'Saxondom'? Studying Anglo-Saxon cremation practices, in S Lucy and A Reynolds (eds) 2002, 47-71

Williams, P W, 1983 *An Anglo-Saxon Cemetery at Thurmaston, Leicestershire*, Leicestershire Museums, Art Galleries and Records Service report, **8**

Williams, R J, and Zeepvat, R J, 1994 *Bancroft: A late Bronze Age/Iron Age settlement, Roman Villa and Temple Mausoleum*, Buckinghamshire Archaeological Society Monog, **7**

Wilson, B, 1996 *Spatial patterning among animal bones in settlement archaeology,* London, British Archaeological Report, British Series, **251**

Wilson, B, Grigson, C, and Payne, S, (eds) 1982 *Ageing and sexing animal bones from archaeological sites*, British Archaeological Reports, British Series, **109**, Oxford

Woods, P J, 1972 *Brixworth Excavations: Excavations at Brixworth, Northants, 1965-70. The Romano-British Villa. Part 1, The Romano-British Coarse Pottery and Decorated Samian Ware,* reprint from Journal of Northampton Museum and Art Gallery, **8** (1970)

Woods, P J, and Hastings, B C, 1984 *Rushden: The Early Fine Wares*, Northamptonshire County Council

Zeepvat, R J, Roberts, J S, and King, N A, 1994 *Caldecotte, Milton Keynes, Excavation and Fieldwork 1966-91,* Buckinghamshire Archaeological Society Monog, **9**

Maps

BGS 1976 *Kettering, Solid and Drift Geology*, British Geological Survey (England and Wales), Sheet 171, 1:50,000

BGS 1978 *Stamford, Solid and Drift Geology*, British Geological Survey (England and Wales), Sheet 157, 1:50,000